THE HISTORY OF CHRISTIAN MISSIONS
IN GUANGXI, CHINA

Studies in Chinese Christianity

G. Wright Doyle and Carol Lee Hamrin,
Series Editors
A Project of the Global China Center
www.globalchinacenter.org

THE HISTORY OF CHRISTIAN MISSIONS IN GUANGXI, CHINA

ARTHUR LIN

PICKWICK *Publications* · Eugene, Oregon

THE HISTORY OF CHRISTIAN MISSIONS IN GUANGXI, CHINA

Pickwick Publications
An Imprint of Wipf and Stock Publishers
199 W. 8th Ave., Suite 3
Eugene, OR 97401

www.wipfandstock.com

PAPERBACK ISBN: 978-1-5326-7769-4
HARDCOVER ISBN: 978-1-5326-7770-0
EBOOK ISBN: 978-1-5326-7771-7

Cataloguing-in-Publication data:

Names: Lin, Arthur, author.

Title: The history of Christian missions in Guangxi, China / Arthur Lin.

Description: Eugene, OR: Pickwick Publications 2020. | Studies in Chinese Christianity. | Includes bibliographical references.

Identifiers: ISBN 978-1-5326-7769-4 (paperback). | ISBN 978-1-5326-7770-0 (hardcover). | ISBN 978-1-5326-7771-7 (ebook).

Subjects: LCSH: Christianity—China. | Missions—China—History. | China—Church history—19th century. | China—Church history—20th century.

Classification: BV3415.2 L54 2020 (print). | BV3415.2 (ebook).

Manufactured in the U.S.A.   01/28/20

Contents

Figures and Tables

FIGURES

TABLES

Preface

THE HISTORY OF CHRISTIAN missions in Guangxi is one of people in a historical context unfamiliar to modern readers. In order to get acquainted with these individuals and the period in which they lived, I have used numerous quotations throughout this book. This has the advantage of allowing those of previous generations to speak for themselves; however, frequently interjecting quotations has a tendency to interrupt the flow. For one, the rules of English grammar and word usage have changed over the past century and a half, and unfortunately, such differences are likely to distract some readers. (So don't be surprised when you see words like "succor," "fastnesses," and "tramp" [to walk or trek], or when words like "City" are capitalized in the middle of a sentence.) Second, many of the quotations are from British writers, so you'll see spellings like evangelise, colour, unridable, and tyres that differ from the rest of the book, which uses American spelling. Third, the Romanized spelling of Chinese place names was not standardized before the 1950s. That means that the spelling of places will be different throughout. (As an example, "Guangxi" could be written Kwangsi, Kwang Si, Kwang-si, Kuangsi, Quang-si, Koung-si, Kouang-Si, Kwong Sai, Kouangsi, and even others.) A fourth problem is that many quotations are from sources that were not carefully edited. They come from newsletters, biographies, autobiographies, reports, surveys, and letters. Occasionally words were misspelled; sometimes the writers got their facts or dates wrong. While these differences and errors are not extensive, I hope that the reader will take the quotations as they are and not "miss the forest for the trees." To smooth out some of the rough spots, I have added brackets with my own definitions or standardized place names. Also, while some Catholics prefer the term "missioner," I have chosen to use "missionary" throughout this book unless "missioner" is found in quotations.

I have sought to make the history of Christian missions in Guangxi as accurate and untarnished as I can. However, I want to remind the reader that writing about history risks over- or underinflating the actual history. The instances of events in the following pages are based on the records and resources available to me. They are a sampling and most likely not the only occurrences of such events. For example, a few boat wrecks are mentioned in the following pages. Other boat wrecks likely occurred but no record survived, or the missionaries did not consider them worthy of recording, or I did not have access to the resource. It is also impossible to know the number of *safe* boat trips that took place over the many *decades* which this book covers. I believe it is important to keep these limitations in mind so as to minimize a skewed perspective of this history.

For corrections or feedback, or for additional resources you may have about Christian missions in Guangxi, please contact me at arthurlinbooks@ protonmail.com.

Finally, the theologies, methodologies, and strategies of the missionaries and their societies herein are presented as is. They do not necessarily reflect my own.

Arthur Lin
January 2020

Abbreviations

CMA   (The) Christian and Missionary Alliance

CMS   (The) Church Missionary Society

FMSA   (The) Foreign Mission Society of America

SBC   (The) Southern Baptist Convention

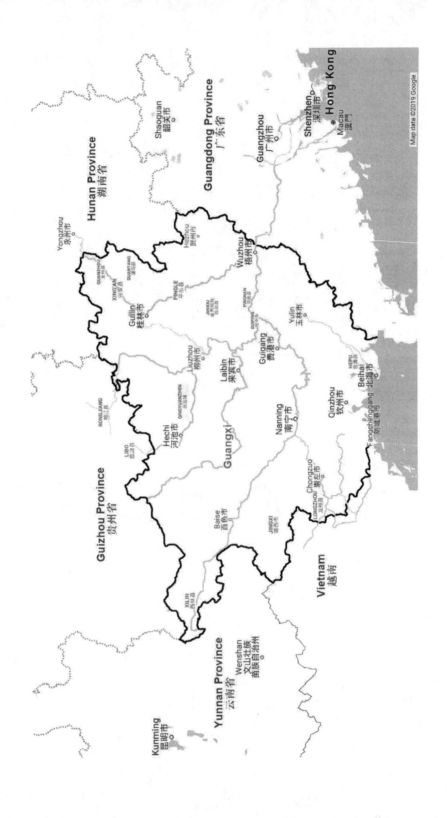

1

Guangxi—the Land and Its People

"Notoriously turbulent," "intensely anti-foreign," "confused and disordered," "insurrection-ridden"[1]—these were a few ways that China's Guangxi Zhuang Autonomous Region[2] was described in the past. Guangxi was full of "overwhelming obstacles and dangers" and characterized by "chronic unrest."[3] It was jokingly said to produce two things: mountains and thieves.[4] Spiritually, it had the reputation of being the "most difficult and most disheartening mission in all China."[5] And yet it was into such a place that missionaries were boldly willing to step in order to take the gospel of Jesus Christ.

Guangxi's past is indeed tumultuous. Part of the land of what is today Guangxi came under the jurisdiction of China in the Qin dynasty (221–207 BC). China's first emperor, Qin Shi Huang, deployed a large army to the south and conquered much territory in today's southern China. A portion of today's Guangxi became the province of Guilin. Later, during the Han dynasty in 111 BC, a large force was sent to suppress a rebellion in Guangxi.

1. Latourette, *History of Christian Missions*, 273, 240; James, *Notable American Women*, 685; Tozer, *Let My People Go*, Kindle Location 457.

2. China has five autonomous regions, each giving a small degree of autonomy to the minorities that reside there. The other four are Tibet (Tibetans), Inner Mongolia (Mongolians), Ningxia (the Hui, a Muslim group), and Xinjiang (the Uighurs, another Muslim group).

3. Oldfield, *Pioneering in Kwangsi*, 7; Broomhall, *Chinese Empire*, 273.

4. Jaffray, "Thou Crownest the Year," 641.

5. Cuenot, *Kwangsi*, 199–200. Similarly, James E. Walsh remarked, "Kwangsi is well known to be one of the most unpromising places for missionary endeavor." FMSA, *Maryknoll Mission Letters, China*, 279.

"From that day to this," said Marshall Broomhall of the China Inland Mission, "Kwangsi [Guangxi] has been in the balance, oscillating between successful and abortive rebellions."[6]

The most famous uprising in China, the Taiping Rebellion (1850–1864), originated in Guangxi. Its leader, Hong Xiuquan, was from a rural Hakka family in Guangdong. After failing the civil service exams for the fourth time, he experienced visions which he interpreted in light of some Christian tracts he had received. He came to believe that he was the son of God and younger brother of Jesus Christ. The early name of the movement was the "Worship God Society."[7] It would not have succeeded had it not been for the militia bands of Guangxi, which existed to maintain law and order at the local levels. In 1850, after gathering a number of armed men in Guangxi, they took control of Liuzhou, one of Guangxi's key cities.[8] The following year, Hong Xiuquan proclaimed himself the Heavenly King and appointed Guangxi native Yang Xiuqing his commander-in-chief. Their rebel army left Guangxi in 1852, continued through Wuhan, and went on to Nanjing, ultimately conquering some six hundred walled cities along the way. They were finally defeated in Nanjing in 1864 but left nearly twenty million dead as a result of the revolt and flooding along the Yangtze River.[9]

Shortly after the Taiping army left Guangxi, Wu Lingyun caused another insurrection as he led small rebellions against the Qing Dynasty[10] forces in Guangxi. By 1853 he had established several bases around Guangxi and controlled a large area of Qing territory. In 1861, he proclaimed the Kingdom of Yanling which challenged the Qing imperial rule. Two years later, Wu Lingyun died in a battle with Guangxi provincial troops. His son took over the movement, massacred those disloyal to his father, and set up a base in western Guangxi.[11] A splinter movement, the Black Flags, broke away from the rebellion and relocated to Vietnam. Afterward, Wu Lingyun's kingdom came to an end.[12]

While Wu Lingyun was resisting Qing troops, another rebellion was taking place. Members of the Heaven and Earth Society launched the Hong Soldiers' Rebellion[13] in Guangdong. They were driven out by the Qing army

---

6. Broomhall, *Chinese Empire*, 274.

7. *bai Shangdi hui* (拜上帝会).

8. Oldfield, *Pioneering in Kwangsi*.

9. Morton & Lewis, *China*; *Encyclopedia Britannica*, s.v. "Taiping Rebellion."

10. This was China's last dynasty and lasted from 1644 to 1912.

11. In Guishun.

12. Davis, *Imperial Bandits*; Wakeman, *Great Enterprise*.

13. *hongbin qiyi* (红兵起义).

and relocated to Guangxi in 1855 where they established a kingdom called Dacheng ("Great Accomplishment") located in modern-day Guiping. Qing forces finally subdued them six years later in 1861.[14]

Guangxi remained turbulent in the twentieth century. The period from 1916 to 1928 in China is known as the "warlord era." In 1920, Guangxi was engaged in an armed battle with its neighbor to the east, Guangdong. A warlord from Guangxi[15] controlled both regions but Cantonese leaders started to rebel. The Cantonese united with Sun Yat-sen and drove Guangxi's forces back. The following year, Guangxi forces mounted a counterattack in Guangdong, but the Cantonese successfully resisted. In June 1921, the prominent city of Wuzhou in Guangxi fell to the Cantonese. They went on to capture Guilin and all major centers in Guangxi by the end of the year. The two provinces remained in a state of turmoil from 1923 to 1925 until three of Guangxi's leaders united and allied themselves with the Nationalist government in Guangzhou. The two provinces were officially unified in March, 1926. In late 1929 and in the summer of 1930, however, an army from Guangxi again sought to retake control of Guangdong but was soundly defeated.[16]

From 1930 to 1931, a conflict between an army in Hunan and Guangxi rebels took place which brought disorder in northeast Guangxi. During that time, Guilin was besieged for three weeks when at least seventy bombs were dropped on the city.[17]

From the 1920s until "Liberation" in 1949, the Communists ("Reds") menaced various parts of Guangxi.[18] These "cruel and wily"[19] zealots fought against capitalism and private ownership of land, terrorizing landlords and leading intellectuals. They passed through territory pillaging, looting, killing, destroying, and intimidating local civilians in their revolutionary efforts. On occasion, they stole from churches and mission hospitals. Christian and Missionary Alliance (CMA) missionary William Newbern, writing of the suffering and destruction caused by Communists in western Guangxi in 1930 and 1931, went so far as to say that the Reds were instruments of Satan.[20] Many distraught and ragged refugees from other parts of China

14. Lu, *Politics and Identity.*

15. Lu Rongting (陆荣廷).

16. Wiest, *Maryknoll in China.*

17. Holden, "Bishop's Letter" (September 1930).

18. Holden, "Bishop's Letter" (March 1931); Stevens, "Bishop's Foreword" (April 1950).

19. Oldfield, *With You Alway*, 190.

20. Newbern, "The Regions Beyond."

found their way to mission stations and mission hospitals in Guangxi during this period. They told stories of cruelty, the murder of their loved ones, and even of being left to die in burning villages.[21]

From 1937 to 1945, Guangxi suffered heavily from the air raids and invasion of the Japanese.[22] The prominent cities of Nanning, Wuzhou, Guilin, Longzhou, and Liuzhou were all captured at various times by the ruthless Japanese. In 1949, the Communists defeated the Kuomintang (Nationalists) in Guangxi, and Guangxi became a province of the People's Republic of China.[23] Other calamitous events of the fifties and sixties such as the Great Leap Forward and the Cultural Revolution brought distress to many of Guangxi's people, but they were country-wide rather than Guangxi-specific.

Much of Guangxi's history is integrally linked with its geography and demographic makeup. Regarding its size, missionaries compared it to regions in their own frame of reference—Southern Baptists to Oklahoma,[24] the Christian and Missionary Alliance (CMA) to Ohio plus Pennsylvania, and the British to a combined England and Scotland.[25] Accurate demographic data was not available, but between the late nineteenth and early twentieth centuries, Guangxi was estimated to number between eight and fifteen million people.[26] Of these, 78 percent were engaged in agriculture.[27] The principal cities were Wuzhou, Guilin, and Nanning.[28]

Many described Guangxi's weather and climate as "exceedingly hot with a humidity in the atmosphere that is most oppressive."[29] It was "never visited by the winter's foot"[30] and its summer was one of "baking heat."[31] Others used words and phrases such as "steamy," "broiling," and having

21. Newbern, "The Regions Beyond."

22. Woerner wrote, "Of all the weapons of modern warfare in China, perhaps none is so effective in striking terror to the hearts of the Chinese as the airplane." Woerner, "An Angel Guard," 781.

23. Falkenheim & Kuo, "Guangxi."

24. Another Southern Baptist said that Guangxi and Guangdong are larger than Louisiana, Mississippi, and Alabama combined. Lackey, *Laborers Together*, 28.

25. Ray, *Southern Baptists in China*; Snead, *Missionary Atlas* (1936); Taylor, *China's Spiritual Needs*.

26. Cuenot in *Kwangsi* (author's preface, xii) said that in the Official Postal Guide of 1920, Guangxi had 12,258,355 residents.

27. Oldfield, *Pioneering in Kwangsi*.

28. Cuenot, *Kwangsi*, author's preface, xii.

29. Oldfield, *Pioneering in Kwangsi*, 12.

30. Staunton, *Miscellaneous Notices*, 333.

31. Child, "Encouragement at Kueilin," 95.

"continual heat and humidity night and day."[32] CMS bishop Percy Stevens wrote, "My wrist sticks to the desk as I write!"[33] Pioneer CMA missionary Walter Oldfield spoke of an accompanying problem: "All bedding and wearing apparel must be sunned frequently to prevent mould and mildew. Where this precaution is not taken, leather goods, such as suitcases, grips, saddles, and shoes are apt to grow whiskers [mold]."[34]

In addition to heat and humidity, famine was not a rare occurrence. Drought and flood were common causes, but famine could also be instigated by war. In 1903, a severe famine occurred along the West River.[35] In Guilin in 1924, famine conditions arose inside the city walls when it was under siege; four missionaries were located in Guilin and trapped inside during the crisis. Of a flood that covered three-fourths of Wuzhou in 1915, Walter Oldfield wrote, "It is pitiable to see the gardeners, whose land has been submerged, as they paddle about in boat in the shallower waters pulling up their vegetables and garden produce."[36] In Guiping during a famine, it was said that even the flesh of executed criminals was being sold in the market.[37]

Several types of wild animals made their home in Guangxi. Tigers prowled and infested certain locations.[38] Wild boar, leopards, civet cats, and poisonous lizards were also common.[39] In addition to these, many missionaries experienced the destructive effects of the "white ants" which ate through their houses, books, and furniture.[40] They were referring, of course, to termites.

Disease was also no stranger. Common ones included malaria,[41] tuberculosis,[42] typhoid, cholera,[43] dysentery,[44] and even the bubonic

---

32. Gray, "Kweilin Parish," 12; Lambert, *China's Christian Millions*; Cuenot, *Kwangsi*, author's preface xii.

33. Stevens, "Bishop's Foreword" (July 1934), 3.

34. Oldfield, *Pioneering in Kwangsi*, 12–13.

35. Broomhall, *Chinese Empire.*

36. Oldfield, "Disastrous Floods," 378.

37. CMS, *Church Missionary Gleaner.*

38. Guiping and others. Fulton, *Inasmuch*; Couling, *Encyclopedia Sinica.*

39. Oldfield, *Pioneering in Kwangsi*; Macdonald, *Roderick Macdonald, M.D.*, 109.

40. Farmer, *Ada Beeson Farmer*; Fulton, *Inasmuch.*

41. Malaria claimed the life of Miss Dora Campbell (CMA). Edith Dyer (CMA) contracted it but recovered. Oldfield, *With You Alway*, 62.

42. It was termed "consumption" and was "frightfully common." Clift, *Very Far East*, 62.

43. Macdonald, *Roderick Macdonald, M.D.*

44. "Victims of dysentery and malaria, diseases so common in the east." Cuenot, *Kwangsi*, 238.

plague.[45] There were occasional cases of leprosy.[46] Tetanus ended the lives of many babies.[47] Smallpox claimed the life of CMA missionary Miss Dyer as well as the three-year-old daughter of CMA missionaries Mr. and Mrs. Landis, Gertrude, "a beautiful, healthy child with golden curls and big blue eyes."[48] Ms. Watkins of the Church Missionary Society was bitten by "an almost certainly rabid"[49] dog and taken to Shanghai for treatment. At least one case of malignant malaria broke out in Guilin in 1929.[50] The eye disease trachoma was also "rife" and "wrecked the sight of hundreds in Kwangsi."[51] In addition to these, missionaries and Chinese alike were frequently bedridden or died of "fever," itself considered a disease in the nineteenth and early twentieth century.[52]

Guangxi did have one feature that captivated many missionaries—natural beauty. The awe-inspiring scenery of the karst, mountainous landscape,[53] especially around Guilin, was a cause for marvel and wonder. J. T. Williams wrote, "To say that the scenery is beautiful is putting it mildly. It is simply grand."[54] Mrs. Oldfield, said, "I was enraptured as I beheld it for myself."[55] Other missionaries spoke similarly describing parts of Guangxi as "magnificent," "extremely picturesque," and "unsurpassed."[56]

45. Fulton, *Inasmuch*; Oldfield, *Pioneering in Kwangsi*; Cuenot, *Kwangsi*; Macdonald, *Roderick Macdonald, M.D.*

46. Latourette quoted, "Just how common leprosy is in China is unknown, for no reliable statistics have been compiled, but the disease is frequently found in the South, especially in . . . Kwangsi [Guangxi]." Latourette, *History of Christian Missions in China*, 457. However, in Guilin, leprosy was said to have been "decidedly rare." Child, "Snapshots from Kweilin," 81.

47. Bacon, "Inasmuch."

48. Oldfield, *With You Alway*, 49; CMA, "The Passing of Miss Edith Dyer," (March 17, 1917); Oldfield, *Pioneering in Kwangsi*. A smallpox epidemic also broke out in Beihai's Hepu County (then "Linchow") in 1918, killing over one thousand. Oldfield, "Smallpox Epidemic." Mrs. Oldfield remarked, "Smallpox, a terrible disease very prevalent in South China, was wholly uncontrolled during my earlier years." Oldfield, *With You Alway*, 48.

49. Holden, "The Bishop's Letter" (April 1933), 4.

50. Bacon, "Report of the Kweilin Hospital."

51. Bacon, "Five Years' Work," 43, "Out-Patients," 18.

52. "In the 19th Century the term fever was used to classify a group of diseases, much as the term 'cancer' is used today." "A 19th-Century View of Fever."

53. A landscape shaped by the erosion of limestone. "Karst."

54. Williams, "A Trip to Kwei Lin," 13.

55. Oldfield, *With You Alway*, 82.

56. Farmer, *Ada Beeson Farmer*, 56; Oldfield, *Pioneering in Kwangsi*, 17; Cuenot, *Kwangsi*, xii.

On the negative side, Guangxi's mountains were ideal hideaways for bandits, commonly called "robber bands" by the missionaries.[57] The bands were often composed of soldiers who grew tired of little or delayed payment and entered the lucrative business of banditry. In fact, it was not uncommon for the head of a group of bandits to have been a high officer in the Chinese army.[58] CMA missionary Robert Jaffray remarked, "I have never seen such wicked men in my life. . . . I could never have believed that men and women . . . could sink to such utter depths of depravity."[59]

Until the late 1920s, travel around mountainous Guangxi was arduous and time-consuming. Marshall Broomhall of the China Inland Mission noted an "absence of easy means of communication apart from the rivers."[60] Up until the 1920s and 30s, there were still no railways and "of proper roads, [Guangxi] is sadly deficient."[61] The roads were only three to four feet[62] wide and consisted of all sorts of odd-shaped slabs sticking up at various angles. A CMS missionary wrote in 1916 that wheeled vehicles such as carts and bicycles could not travel these roads. Even walking was so uncomfortable that people took narrow paths beside the road that had been beaten down from frequent use.[63]

To travel around Guangxi, missionaries had three main forms of transportation: boat, foot, and sedan chair carried by coolies. Riverboat travel was the easiest way to travel around the province, but it was long. It took twenty days to get from Guangzhou to Guilin, eighteen from Guangzhou to Guiping,[64] fifteen from Wuzhou to Guilin, six from Liuzhou to Qingyuan,[65] and four from Guilin to Quanzhou.[66] When the water level was high, steamships, which appeared after the traditional riverboats, could make the trips much faster, such as a "swift" four-day trip from Nanning to Wuzhou. When the water was low, the same journey by native boat could take up to two weeks.[67]

57. Oldfield, *Pioneering in Kwangsi*.

58. Tozer, *Let My People Go*.

59. Tozer, *Let My People Go*, Kindle Locations 491–493.

60. Broomhall, *Chinese Empire*, 273.

61. Broomhall, *Chinese Empire*, 281.

62. 1 to 1.2 meters.

63. CMS, "Questions and Answers."

64. Fulton, *Inasmuch*; Shortt, "Oddments." Guizhou to Guiping was a distance of four hundred miles.

65. Oldfield, *Pioneering in Kwangsi*.

66. Holden, "The Bishop's Letter" (November 1928).

67. Clift, *Very Far East*.

Not only was boat travel long, it was also risky and dangerous. Wrecks, river pirates, and bandits along long sections of river between towns endangered passengers. Between Guilin and Wuzhou on the Cassia River[68] were three hundred and sixty-five rapids.[69] Mr. and Mrs. Byrde of the Church Missionary Society crashed twice on this river, once with their nine-week-old daughter.[70] On the West River between Wuzhou and Nanning, Mrs. Clift of the Emmanuel Medical Mission smashed into the bank twice.[71] CMA missionaries Rev. and Mrs. Newbern also had a particularly nightmarish experience on this river. While traveling from Wuzhou to Nanning with their two children, the pilot of the boat apparently turned the wheel over to another while he smoked an opium pipe. Before long, the boat struck a boulder. The boatmen, instead of assisting, boarded a small lifeboat and escaped while the passengers pleaded for help. Nearby villagers heard the commotion and the cries of the passengers and rushed to the scene. Instead of rescuing the passengers, however, they made off with as many of their belongings as they could carry. Some did help, but first demanded large sums of money. During the incident, two large steamers came within fifty feet of the wreck but cruised right on by. The Newberns lost everything except the clothes they were wearing. They later learned that a superstition fueled the behavior of the locals: the rapids must be "fed" a boat each year, and if anyone interfered with the business of the dragon who was behind it all, his or her family would suffer the following year.[72]

While Rev. and Mrs. Newbern and their two kids made it out alive, a least a couple of missionaries did not, the most famous being medical missionary Roderick Macdonald of the Wesleyan Methodist Mission Society (see chapter 3). The river was so full of perils that "the Alliance missionaries always make it a rule to remember in prayer those on the rivers travelling."[73] Walter Oldfield said of the Cassia River, "[It] will always be remembered by many missionaries as the place where they were robbed, or kidnapped, while trying to reach their inland homes on the upper reaches of this beautiful, yet dangerous stream."[74]

---

68. A combination of today's Guijiang (桂江) and Lijiang (漓江).

69. Some sources say 360.

70. CMS, *Church Missionary Gleaner*.

71. Clift, *Very Far East*, 111.

72. Oldfield, "Tragedy on the West River"; Newbern, "Our Foreign Mail Bag."

73. Clift, *Very Far East*, 115.

74. Oldfield, *Pioneering in Kwangsi*, 22. Non-missionaries also died on the river. An Englishman named Philips who was in charge of the Asiatic Petroleum Company in Nanning was murdered going from Longzhou to Chongzuo. Cuenot, *Kwangsi*.

Guangxi, at the turn of the twentieth century, included seventy walled cities.[75] The large city walls provided a line of defense against the bandits and armies in surrounding areas. At night, the city gates were customarily closed and entry or exit to the city was not permitted; those who arrived late had to sleep outside the city. Walled cities made invasion more difficult, but they still were vulnerable to siege by larger armies. The largest walled cities at the time included Wuzhou, Guilin, Nanning, and Liuzhou. Wuzhou was the large port city inside the Guangxi on the West River from Guangzhou. It had been the capital before AD 1665 and was the "key" to Guangxi from the east.[76] A British consulate was located in Wuzhou.[77] To Catholics, it was the "city of no conversions."[78]

Guilin, most renowned for its natural beauty, could be reached by boat from Wuzhou. It served as the capital from AD 1665 until 1907 when Nanning took its place. Guilin's people were said to have been friendly, but British medical missionary Dr. Clift and his wife noted while in Guilin, "We seem so far away from the civilized world."[79]

Nanning, the present capital of Guangxi, was called the city of "Southern Rest" or "Southern Tranquility," a direct translation of its Chinese name.[80] In the late 1800s, Nanning was "notoriously anti-foreign,"[81] but only a decade later "most friendly,"[82] at least to Mrs. Clift. She also added that Nanning had the reputation of being "the most immoral port in China."[83] In the early twentieth century, Nanning was still largely undeveloped. When preparing to take a trip from to Wuzhou, Mrs. Clift, who had relocated from Guilin to Nanning, remarked, "I am looking forward to it [going to Wuzhou], for I have not been in 'civilized parts' for so long!"[84]

Liuzhou was, "from a commercial standpoint, one of the most important cities in the province."[85] It was the center for lumber trade, and due to

---

75. There were ninety-one in 1912. Oldfield, "In Memoriam"; Banister, "Appeal for Kweilin."

76. Broomhall, *Chinese Empire*, 279.

77. It was opened July 31, 1903. Macdonald, *Roderick Macdonald, M.D.*, 214.

78. Cuenot, *Kwangsi*, 216. This was before the large presence of Maryknoll missionaries (see chapter 2).

79. Clift, *Very Far East*, 61.

80. Broomhall, *Chinese Empire*; Clift, *Very Far East*.

81. Clift, *Very Far East*, 10.

82. Clift, *Very Far East*, 10.

83. Clift, *Very Far East*, 10.

84. Clift, *Very Far East*, 190.

85. Oldfield, *Pioneering in Kwangsi*, 132.

the low price of coffins, was said to be "the place to die!"[86] Liuzhou could be reached by river from Wuzhou.

The people of Guangxi primarily made a living farming. They plowed, sowed, and harvested day after day, year after year. They customarily ate two meals a day, one around 10 a.m. and the other around 4 p.m. CMS missionary Louis Byrde called their lives "humdrum."[87] A strong social custom prevented men and women from interacting in public. They did not eat together and even husband and wife could not be seen walking together down the street.[88]

Mandarin and Cantonese were the two main languages. The Mandarin section in the north included the cities of Guilin, Liuzhou, and Baise; the Cantonese section in the south included Wuzhou and Yulin.[89] Other languages spoken in Guangxi included Hakka and the languages of the "aborigines."

While the political and geographical conditions did not lend themselves to an easy transmission of the gospel, one would hope that primitive conditions and the spiritual climate would. However, neither was this the case. The reality was that Guangxi was "bitterly opposed to the preaching of Christianity within its borders."[90] Walter Oldfield wrote, "Missionaries who attempted to enter Kwangsi [Guangxi] met with . . . open hostility. They were threatened, stoned, attacked by mobs, and repeatedly had to make a hurried retreat in order to escape mob violence."[91] American Presbyterian Donald MacGillivray wrote, "The fact is well-known to those acquainted with the Empire that this province [Guangxi] was second only to Hunan in the term of its successful resistance to missionary occupation."[92] In 1899, a placard posted on a wall in Wuzhou read,

> Foreign devils should escape early if they would avoid death, and not daily preach Christianity to deceive the people, for the sight of a foreigner's face provokes Chinese hatred, and this is intensified upon hearing them speak. The Chinese anger has reached the point of driving them out now.[93]

86. Oldfield, *Pioneering in Kwangsi*, 132.

87. Byrde, "Traveling by Land," 68.

88. Oldfield, *With You Alway*.

89. The dividing line can roughly be seen by drawing a line connecting and extending beyond Guigang Shi and Pingle in Guilin Shi.

90. Tozer, *Let My People Go*, Kindle Location 246.

91. Oldfield, *Pioneering in Kwangsi*, 57.

92. MacGillivray, *Century of Protestant Missions*, 362.

93. Macdonald, *Roderick Macdonald, M.D.*, 135.

In 1908, Dr. Macdonald described Wuzhou's people:

> We had planted ourselves down in the midst of a people out-
> wardly civil and nonaggressive for the most part, owing to the
> strict proclamations of the mandarin officials as to the treatment
> of foreigners. But in their hearts there smouldered that secret
> antipathy and resentment which only needed unwise action on
> our part to fan it into flame.[94]

Spiritually, the people were described as "poor slaves of error and
superstition."[95] A gripping fear of devils and demons was ever-present. In one
location,[96] belief in a "chicken devil" prevailed. The heads of chickens were
placed on poles with mouths opened to neutralize the chicken devil's powers.
During the Yuan dynasty, people refused to quarry the stone on the mountains for fear of the spirits.[97] When a son fell ill, it was believed that a demon
was making off with his soul; an elaborate ritualistic process usually ensued to
remedy this situation.[98] At night, people rarely slept without a light on for fear
of the dark and demons.[99] Even in the mission hospitals, the nurses were fear-
ful of night duty "because of the old heathen ideas of devils walking about."[100]
In a town seventeen miles north of Guilin, there were no straight streets in the
town. This was not a result of geography but of city planning—they believed
that the devil would lose his way on the curvy, winding streets.[101]

Mrs. Clift commented on the people's response to a season of heavy
rain:

> They have been to the idols to ask how many days the rain will
> continue. The idol is supposed to answer by a pen suspended by
> a string from the roof. This pen, as it sways to and fro, writes the
> answer in the sand on the floor. The answer this time was, "More
> than twenty days." So they firmly believe that the rain will not
> depart for three weeks![102]

Many forsook medical care due to superstitious folklore. In one location, the people believed that the missionary made medicine out of the eyes

94. Macdonald, *Roderick Macdonald, M.D.*, 111.

95. Cuenot, *Kwangsi*, 123.

96. Longzhou (龙州).

97. Oldfield, *Pioneering in Kwangsi*.

98. Clift, *Very Far East*.

99. Byrde, "Little Mei Mei."

100. Bacon, "C.M.S. Medical Mission in Kweilin," 7.

101. Cannell, "Spirit Streams."

102. Clift, *Very Far East*, 33.

of children and breasts of women.[103] In Guilin, Dr. Clift saw a meager eighty patients in his first two weeks. His wife remarked, "You would know how good that is, if you had any idea how frightened these people are at first of foreign medicine and foreign doctors. . . . wonderful considering how timid and superstitious these people are."[104]

The local people blamed missionaries for any mishap and were hesitant to associate with them. During a famine in 1893, locals in Pingnan faulted the recently-built chapel. They determined that if rain did not come by the fifth day, they would destroy the chapel. The Christians banded together to pray and rain came on the fourth day, so the chapel was spared.[105] In another case, a missionary hired some local workers to clear a piece of land. When a tree from the land fell on a nearby granary, the blame went to the missionary.[106] Ms. Waterson shared her experience as a midwife:

> Country people are very superstitious and when we go out to do midwifery on the district we have to be very careful to use whatever basin the family sets apart for the baby's use. I once, because I could find no other, used the family face basin to give a baby its first bath, and created a great fuss amongst the relatives and friends and nearly brought down the wrath of the ancestors on my head. Fortunately, the baby was a boy so the family did not grudge the money for a new one.[107]

Dr. Charlotte Bacon recounted a story from the CMS hospital in Guilin: "The first two [births in the new building] being boys was a very good omen, as the heathen still think it a positive misfortune to have a girl, and in spite of all teaching the Christians cannot as yet in their hearts be made to think otherwise."[108]

Many people were terrified of dead bodies. Once, when Mr. and Mrs. Fee's daughter, Margaret, neared death while traveling by boat, they were made to get off the boat. They walked to the nearest town, were refused entry, and had to bury their little daughter outside the city.[109] Dr. Charlotte Bacon also observed this reality in the hospital:

---

103. Cuenot, *Kwangsi.*

104. Clift, *Very Far East*, 22, 24.

105. McCloy, "Sketch."

106. Bacon, "Farewell to Kweilin."

107. Waterson, "Joy at Hingan," 10.

108. Bacon, "Kweilin Medical Notes," 51.

109. Oldfield, *Pioneering in Kwangsi*. She was buried in Guiping. Oldfield, *With You Alway.*

One encouraging feature was that we were able to allow six people to die in hospital without causing an immediate evacuation of all the other patients—we have still a long way to travel before the awful fear of death will sufficiently lessen to make it anything but a very serious thing for such an event to take place among us.[110]

Ada Farmer said that this "awful bane of superstition" was a contributing factor in Guangxi's lack of development.[111] Mrs. Oldfield claimed that it resulted in a prevalence of demon possession.[112] Mrs. Clift speculated on its experiential side:

Life must be burdensome when one has to constantly propitiate the "Kitchen god" for fear the rice is spoilt, the "Fire god" for fear he burns the house down, the god who protects the bed, who if he is not worshipped will make the children cry and toss restlessly in their sleep, and a thousand and one spirits and demons, all supposed to be waiting to work one harm.[113]

Not only were such false beliefs "burdensome," they were also costly. Dr. Macdonald's wife shared a telling experience of one of her husband's patients:

One very superstitious heathen neighbour came to the doctor in great distress and grief. Some years before, her husband, an opium-smoker, had died, and she assured the doctor that she had well paid a necromancer, a "fung-shui" Sin Shang[114] [a male Feng Shui practitioner], to find a suitable hill-site on which to place his tomb. But now her only two grandchildren had died, and she discovered, on consulting a witch, that her husband's spirit was not happy in Hades; his tomb had been wrongly placed; and to show his vexation, he had fetched away both his grandchildren. In vain the doctor tried to convince her that the little children had died from lack of proper nourishment and care in dysentery. Another necromancer's aid was obtained, the grave was opened, and the coffin buried in a more propitious site. All this cost a considerable sum of money. In course of time she came again—was she not right? Her husband's spirit was at

110. Bacon, "1930 in the Kweilin Hospital," 33.

111. Farmer, *Ada Beeson Farmer*, 58. The CMA's *Atlas* (1924) said lawlessness was perhaps the main reason.

112. Oldfield, *With You Alway*.

113. Clift, *Very Far East*, 93.

114. *xiansheng* (先生).

rest once more; and as an invincible argument she carried in her arms a tiny grandson! She begged for some medicine that would make it well and strong. It was a puny, sickly child, and we did our best for it; but with all the love and care we fain would lavish on these people, their superstition baffles us at every turn. In times of sickness and of sorrow it is strongest, and the love that every human heart possesses in some degree is crushed beneath its power. In spite of the love she bore her grandchild, to prove whether the child was human, or the spirit of one of the departed grandchildren returned to earth, she allowed it to be exposed all through the cold night under the bamboos near the house. In the morning, when I visited the scene, a little crowd stood round the tiny bundle, not even the sad young mother daring to touch it. Taking it in my arms and chafing its tiny limbs in the hope of saving it, a faint flicker of life was perceptible. Seeing this, the poor mother held out her arms, silently, and took it to her bosom. Alas! what can these ignorant young mothers do with the inexorable mother-in-law? The grandmother insisted that once more exposure must be tried! Infanticide! No, this is not what they, nor we, call infanticide. That dreadful name is only used when there is the intent and purpose to destroy life; but how many little ones who would otherwise be welcome in the homes of China are chased by superstitious relatives in pain and suffering from the earth![115]

In addition to superstition, social problems abounded. They included drug use, wife beating, infanticide, gambling, and bound feet.[116] One of the most prominent ones was opium use. Baise, in western Guangxi, was one of the main centers of the opium trade.[117] Broomhall wrote, "Opium-smoking and its consequent evils are widely disseminated through the province."[118] Walter Oldfield added, "Opium smoking is exceedingly common. . . . Kwangsi [Guangxi] is the highway over which each year millions of dollars' worth of the drug passes from Yunnan and Kweichow [Guizhou]. . . . Of the total provincial revenue of some $22 million a year, $10 million comes from opium and gambling."[119] A missionary from Hunan once journeyed to Guangxi and wrote,

115. Macdonald, *Roderick Macdonald, M.D.*, 152–54.

116. Clift, *Very Far East*; Farmer, *Ada Beeson Farmer*; Launay, *Histoire*; Graves, *Forty Years in China*.

117. Jaffray, "The City of Po-She"; Newbern, "Communism Returns to Poseh."

118. Broomhall, *Chinese Empire*, 286.

119. Oldfield, *Pioneering in Kwangsi*, 14.

I have often heard of the prevalence of opium smoking and gambling in Kwangsi, but it was not till I had made this journey that I came to realise the grim reality of it. As we passed through certain towns, whole streets were literally given up to gambling dens. Men and boys were crowded round the tables, either gambling or watching others gamble. Most of the inns in these parts were equipped with opium-smoking apparatus, and often the best room was set apart for addicts. Often we saw small huts or booths by the roadside. These too were specially prepared to cater for this debasing vice.[120]

Another prevalent societal ill was slavery, often coupled with human trafficking.[121] Chinese law permitted slavery, and nearly all but the poorest families owned at least one slave girl. Women and girls were regularly sold into slavery out of desperation, especially during times of famine or other crises. During one famine in southern Guangxi, a report came from Beihai's Hepu that eight out of ten wives were being sold by their husbands to buy food. During the famine months of 1903, more than two hundred slave girls passed through Wuzhou daily. They were sold for as little as forty to fifty cents each.[122] Louis Byrde relayed the bartering of a slave:

A crowd on the river bank attracts attention. In the centre two men are holding a pole across their shoulders and to this a scale is attached. What are they weighing? Look closer—it is one of the girls we saw this morning. Her head is bent down with a sense of shame, for she is now being sold as a pig is sold. But resisting would be useless, so she submits. Listen! The man weighing shouts "55 lbs."

"No" shouts an old woman, "56, Look the scale is not level."

"All right, 56 lbs. Be quick there's a lot more."

"What will you give?" says the old woman, addressing another.

"Sixpence a pound."

---

120. Tindall, "In Journeyings Often," 803.

121. Byrde, "Two Pressing Financial Needs."

122. Macdonald, *Roderick Macdonald, M.D.*, 196. It is difficult to give a precise modern equivalent. The Kwangsi Hunan Newsletter (CMS) sometimes mentions a ten-to-one dollar-to-pound ratio. That would equal one dollar to two shillings (and fifty cents for one shilling). According to MeasuringWorth.com and the Bank of England's inflation calculator, a shilling in 1904 equaled between five and six pounds (six to eight US dollars) in 2017. To put it in a historical perspective, around the time, twenty cents could hire a coolie for a day. Bank of England, "Inflation Calculator"; Byrde, "A Short Overland Journey."

"What? Sixpence? Why, look, she is plump, and eleven years old."

"No, Sixpence."

"See, she has on good clothes, and bracelets all thrown in. Give Sevenpence?"

"What's the good of bracelets and such trash to me—I only want her."

In the end sixpence halfpenny a pound is agreed upon. So she changes hands for £1:10:4 [one pound, ten shillings, and four pence].[123]

Mrs. Ada Farmer bemoaned the plight of the girls in early twentieth-century Guangxi:

The little girls all have bound feet and the youngest, who is five years old, was engaged the other day to some one she perhaps will never see till the day she is taken to his mother's house to be his slave, and the servant of his mother.[124]

DEVELOPMENT IN GUANGXI

CMA missionary Walter Oldfield remarked that Guangxi was "formerly known as one of the most backward of the provinces of China."[125] Even of its most developed city, Wuzhou, Mrs. Oldfield said, "At the time of my first arrival [1903] sanitation was quite unknown; it was a very filthy city with open drains and narrow alleys. . . . so narrow one cannot hold an umbrella."[126] Despite the primitive conditions in which the first missionaries encountered, advancements did come, and in some cases, rapidly. In the early 1900s, electric lighting came into existence, policemen first appeared in the streets, and steamships made river travel much faster.[127] In Guilin in 1911, John Bacon claimed that he was the first to ride a bicycle there.[128]

Reports from the early 1920s still painted a dismal picture. Policemen were only located in two or three main cities in 1921 and the following year,

---

123. Byrde, "Two Pressing Financial Needs," 7. According to the Bank of England, one pound in 1904 would equal 116 pounds in 2017. Bank of England, "Inflation Calculator."

124. Farmer, *Ada Beeson Farmer*, 145.

125. Oldfield, *Pioneering in Kwangsi*, 23.

126. Oldfield, *With You Alway*, 43.

127. Clift, *Very Far East*.

128. Bacon, "Kweilin's First Bicycle."

Guangxi was reported to have one of "the poorest postal facilities of any province in China."[129] In 1924, Howard Bailey described Guilin:

> Kweilin is not a place of trams, railways and well-paved streets, and telephones and seven-storied buildings. Alas! here, men and women live amongst the pigs and chickens. Their houses are built of mud and wood. The narrow streets are atrociously paved with slabs of stone which have, in the course of ages, become sadly uneven, so that as you walk along you cannot take your eyes off the ground for long. Close around you are evidences of deep poverty and dirt, and the people love to have it so.[130]

Two years later, Wuzhou was still a jumble of narrow alleys prone to flooding with only one bicycle in the entire city.

Real advancement came in 1928 thanks to the warlord-turned-governor Huang Shaohong[131] who had taken up office a couple of years prior. As a result of his administration, Wuzhou began to see paved roads, cement sidewalks, new three- and four-story buildings, and a number of motorized vehicles.[132] Two thousand miles of motorways connected Guangxi's cities[133] and good roads around cities like Longzhou allowed missionaries to travel for miles around by bicycle.[134] The security situation was strong and CMS Bishop Stevens said there was no present danger to any of their stations or missionaries in Guangxi.[135] In Guilin, bicycles became increasingly common, government schools sprang up, and idol worship and superstitious practices were forbidden by law.[136] Quanzhou, in the far northeast, gained a large road, a boulevard with sidewalks, and underground sewers.[137] In 1929 and into the early thirties, electric lighting became commonplace and the unsanitary killing of pigs on the streets was outlawed. Nanning and Wuzhou organized fire squads to battle the devastating effects of fire which could wipe out large sections of wooden stores and houses.[138] In Nanning

129. Oldfield, "The Bible through Chinese Eyes"; China Continuation Committee, *Christian Occupation*, 115.

130. Bailey, "The Green One," 530–31.

131. 黄绍竑.

132. CMA, "General Wong."

133. Oldfield in *Pioneering in Kwangsi* spoke of a motorway connecting Nanning and Baise, making it passable by bus or car. Before that, one had to take a small boat.

134. CMA, "General Wong."

135. Holden, "The Bishop's Letter" (August 1928).

136. Cannell, "Kweilin."

137. Tindall, "In Journeyings Often."

138. The CMS wrote of a fire engine and squad in Guilin in 1910. CMS, "A Chinese Fire-Engine," 76.

and other cities, local and long distance telephones were installed.[139] At that time about half the counties could be reached by motorized vehicle.[140] CMA missionary Rev. James Poole bought a secondhand motorcycle from Hong Kong. It allowed him to cut down the travel time of his evangelistic trips by some fourteen days, leaving ten full days to preach and sell books. The missionaries welcomed the changes and advancements in technology. Rev. Poole remarked, "In these days when the harvest is plenteous and the laborers are so few, anything that can be done to make the best use of the few laborers we have is worth while."[141]

In 1921, Father Dietz wrote in Wuzhou, "So far as I have been able to observe, war is the only national sport of this county, much as baseball [is] in America."[142] However, in the late 1920s, sports participation accelerated. In 1931, an athletic festival was held in Guilin and many shops sold sports equipment.[143] Wheelbarrows, which aided in agricultural and industrial development, also came into use following the introduction of motorized vehicles. In 1931, two Christians in a church in Guilin owned flashlights, which aroused great interest in the other parishioners.[144] Two years later, Nanning and Liuzhou had surpassed Guilin in modernizing. Nanning and Liuzhou both had wide roads and the missionaries were able to buy bread.[145] Guilin caught up quickly, however, in 1933 when a large road was constructed through the heart of the city.[146] The following year a missionary who returned to Guilin after a season away remarked, "Kweilin has much improved—I hardly recognised it."[147]

In 1935, new medical regulations were instituted and a large public hospital was under construction in Guilin. One change was that prescriptions needed to come from a doctor approved by the local government. Public health bureaus were opened in Nanning and other large cities. Some four thousand miles of road connected Guangxi at that time. Security was strong, and Guangxi had been free of bandits for three years. Two cinemas also opened that year. J. R. Wilson wrote of Guilin, "The walls were the walls of Kweilin, but inside what a change! It seemed as if a bit of Shanghai had

---

139. Woerner, "Present Evangelistic Opportunities."

140. Woerner, "Present Evangelistic Opportunities."

141. Poole, "Motor Cycle Trip," 633.

142. Dietz, in FMSA, *Maryknoll Mission Letters, China*, 287.

143. Gray, "An Athletic Festival at Kweilin"; Wilson, "Schoolboys."

144. Gray, "With the Faithful."

145. Gray, "A Tale of Two Cities."

146. Bacon, "Pulling Down and Putting Up."

147. Goodman, "Returning to Kweilin," 7.

been suddenly planted down inside the old walls. Such fine wide streets, new style buildings, magnificent shops, and bicycles and motor cars buzzing about."[148] In Wuzhou and Nanning, they even started to make ice, leading to the opening of the first ice cream parlors.[149]

In 1937 and following, other developments came, some as a result of wartime needs in the war with Japan. Guangxi gained a new form of transportation, the railroad, as Chinese troops retreated southward from the Japanese taking railroad tracks with them.[150] By 1938, Guilin was said to be "one of the most modernised cities of inland China."[151] The following year, the first CMS missionary departed the Guangxi-Hunan diocese by airplane.[152] Even the small walled city of Jingxi with its seven thousand inhabitants in far western Guangxi was connected by road and saw its first automobile, creating much excitement.[153] In 1940, Dr. Charlotte Bacon returned after a long furlough "to find Kweilin a modernised city: roads, motors, bicycles, telephones and hospitals."[154] But it was long before lights, trains, and ice cream when the pioneer missionaries first set foot in Guangxi.

148. Wilson, "Kwangsi Life," 10.

149. Oldfield, *Pioneering in Kwangsi*.

150. Snead, *Missionary Atlas* (1950).

151. Leach, "A Visit to Kweilin Parish," 6–7.

152. Stevens, "Bishop's Foreword" (September, 1939).

153. Kowles, "Our Foreign Mail Bag" (November 12, 1939), 697.

154. Bacon, "Back in Kweilin," 6.

2

The Early Years
Catholic Missions

INTO UNDEVELOPED, SUPERSTITIOUS, AND mountainous Guangxi, the Catholics arrived first. They did so in the sixteenth century. In 1577,[1] Pope Gregory XIII created the (enormous) diocese[2] of Macao which included China, Japan, and the Far Eastern Islands. Missionaries were sent to the region soon after. In 1583, an Italian Jesuit named Michele Ruggieri[3] made an exploratory trip to China and spent a number of weeks[4] in Guangxi.[5] According to one source, Ruggieri was overly-insistent and violated protocol in setting up a meeting with a royal official in Guilin.[6] This led to his expulsion and permanent banishment from Guilin. He wrote two Chinese poems about his visit to Guangxi[7] and Hunan.[8]

---

1. Other sources say 1575 or 1576.

2. "The territorial jurisdiction of a bishop." *Merriam-Webster Dictionary*, s.v. "Diocese," https://www.merriam-webster.com/dictionary/diocese.

3. Also seen as Ruggeri and Ruggerius.

4. It's uncertain exactly how long he stayed.

5. Chan, "Michele Ruggieri"; Latourette, *History of Christian Missions in China*, 94; Brockey, *Journey to the East*.

6. Liu, "True."

7. "寓广西白水围" (simplified Chinese) in Chan, "Michele Ruggieri," 175. After significant research on the location where Ruggieri stayed, Chan concluded that it was about thirty kilometers south of Quanzhou near the Hunan border. Chan, "Michele Ruggieri."

8. Chan, "Michele Ruggieri."

A decade before the Ming Dynasty ended (1644), the Jesuits were active in Guangxi. They took advantage of the country's instability and expanded their work. They linked scattered Jesuits and moved into new areas where they found Chinese allies.[9] A Franciscan named Francesco d'Escalone also arrived in Wuzhou at this time.[10]

When the Manchus[11] finally toppled the Ming Dynasty in Beijing, remnants of the Ming went south. They maintained strongholds in parts of Guangdong and Guangxi. The Jesuits, many of whom sought to reach the Ming dynastic court, accompanied the fleeing Ming to southern China. Two of those were the Austrian Andrew Xavier Koffler[12] and his Polish co-laborer, Michel Boym. The Ming viceroy of Guangxi at the time, Thomas Qu Shisi,[13] was a professing Christian.[14] He and another Christian, Luke Jiaolian,[15] helped to defeat Manchu forces at a battle in Guilin. The victory prompted the emperor of the Southern Ming, Yong Li, to relocate to Guilin. While there, the three ladies closest to him were baptized by the Jesuits. The empress dowager, his mother, and his wife took the baptismal names Helen, Mary,[16] and Anne, respectively. Anne bore a son and a question arose regarding his baptism. Father Koffler laid down three conditions for his baptism: he must be raised a Christian, he could only have one wife, and he could not have concubines. This deterred their decision until the child fell deathly ill. They then submitted him for baptism and Father Koffler baptized him in Nanning. He took the baptismal name Constantine.

When Manchu invaders were advancing south, the empress dowager wrote to Pope Innocent X in Rome asking for a pardon of sins and a plenary indulgence. She also prayed for peace and unity within the Ming empire. In 1651, the Manchus captured Father Koffler and executed him on December 12.[17] Several years later, Father Boym, his co-laborer, was

---

9. Brockey, *Journey to the East.*

10. Montanar, "Kwang-Si."

11. The minority from northern China who founded the last dynasty, the Qing (1644–1912).

12. He was born in 1603 and also known as Andrew Wolfgang Koffler. Cordier, "Martyrs in China."

13. 瞿式耜. The *Ave Maria* used the name "Thomas Kiu Cheu-Seu." The Sisters Marianites of Holy Cross, *Ave Maria*, 409.

14. Latourette, *History of Christian Missions in China.*

15. 焦璉. Yan, *Guangxi.*

16. Or Marie. Yan, *Guangxi.*

17. Cordier, "Martyrs in China."

returning to Guangxi from Italy but died of exhaustion on the border of today's Vietnam.[18]

In 1659, Pope Alexander VII created two vicariates apostolic[19] in China, one of which included the province of Guangxi.[20] Near the end of that century, several new priests arrived. Spanish Augustinians established themselves in Guilin and Wuzhou and Franciscans in Wuzhou.[21] French and Spanish Catholics used Changsha in today's Hunan[22] as a "stepping stone" into northern Guangxi, despite the 300-kilometer distance between the two.[23]

Between 1712 and 1714, two Catholics, de Tartre and Cardoso, assisted missionary work by creating maps of several of China's provinces including

18. Couling, *Encyclopedia Sinica*; Charbonnier, *Christians in China*.

19. "A Roman Catholic missionary district over which a vicar apostolic exercises jurisdiction." *Merriam-Webster Dictionary*, s.v. "Vicariate Apostolic," https://www.merriam-webster.com/dictionary/vicariate apostolic. The 1913 Catholic Encyclopedia explains: "During the last few centuries it has been the practice of the Holy See to govern either through prefects Apostolic, or through vicars Apostolic (q. v), many of the territories where no dioceses with resident bishops exist. These territories are called respectively prefectures Apostolic and vicariates Apostolic. This had been done by the Holy See when, owing to local circumstances, such as the character and customs of the people, the hostility of the civil powers and the like, it was doubtful whether an episcopal see could be permanently established. The establishing of a mere prefecture Apostolic in a place supposes that the Church has attained there only a small development. A fuller development leads to the foundation of a vicariate Apostolic, i.e., the intermediate stage between a prefecture and a diocese. A prefect Apostolic is of lower rank than a vicar; his powers are more limited, nor has he, as a rule, the episcopal character, as is ordinarily the case with a vicar Apostolic. The duties of a prefect Apostolic consist in directing the work of the mission entrusted to his care; his powers are in general those necessarily connected with the ordinary administration of such an office, as, for instance, the assigning of missionaries, the making of regulations for the good management of the affairs of his mission, and the like. Moreover, he has extraordinary faculties for several cases reserved otherwise to the Apostolic See, such as, for instance, absolutions from censures, dispensations from matrimonial impediments. He has also the faculty of consecrating chalices, patens, and portable altars, and some prefects Apostolic have the power to administer Confirmation. The prefects Apostolic we have described so far have independent territories and are subject only to the Holy See. Sometimes, when a vicariate or a diocese extends over a very large territory, in which the Catholic population is unequally distributed, the Holy See places a portion of such territory in charge of a prefect Apostolic; in which case the faculties of the prefect are more limited, and in the exercise of his office he depends on the vicar Apostolic or the bishop, whose consent he needs for the exercise of many of his functions, and to whose supervision his administration is subject." Papi, "Prefect Apostolic."

20. Cordier, "China."

21. Montanar, "Kwang-Si."

22. Called "Huguang" at the time.

23. Brockey, *Journey to the East*.

Guangxi. The maps were helpful in planning routes since they allowed missionaries to decrease travel time and avoid geographical barriers. In 1722, two Catholic churches were reportedly located in Guangxi.[24] The Yongzheng Emperor,[25] who sought to ban Catholicism from China, expelled all the missionaries in 1724. For the next 130 years, Guangxi remained without a missionary.[26] However, the church did not die and the English traveler and Orientalist Sir George Staunton wrote in 1822, "In Quang-si [Guangxi] there are some Christians, on the borders of Tonquin [Tonkin]"[27] (see figure 2).

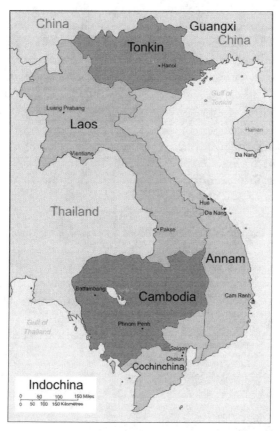

Figure 2: Map of French Indochina showing Annam and Tonkin.
(Credit: Bearsmalaysia, "French_Indochina_subdivisions.svg," Wikimedia Commons, CC BY-SA 3.0.)

24. Latourette, *History of Christian Missions in China.*
25. 雍正皇帝.
26. Montanar, "Kwang-Si."
27. Staunton, *Miscellaneous Notices*, 82.

In 1848, the missions of Guangxi and Guangdong were entrusted to the Paris Foreign Mission Society by the Sacred Congregation of Propaganda, the body responsible for carrying out Roman Catholic missionary work.[28] Before that, both Guangxi and Guangdong had been under the jurisdiction of Macao.[29] According to Joseph Cuenot, no descendants of Catholics who had been baptized under the Jesuits in previous centuries remained at that time.[30] Catholic merchants could be found, but they were not native to Guangxi.

In 1850, the French set up a base in Guigang.[31] It was also around that time that the Taiping Rebellion began in Guangxi, a movement which later resulted in fierce opposition to Christianity and the Catholic foreign missionaries in Guangxi.

In 1856,[32] Guangdong and Guangxi were detached from Macao and made into a single prefecture apostolic[33] of Rome.[34] Also that year, Catholics further divided Guangdong and Guangxi into separate missions due to their size.[35] By 1858, the work had advanced to the degree that Catholic priests were being appointed from the Chinese and ministering to their own people.[36]

One of the most significant events affecting Catholic missions in Guangxi was the martyrdom of one of its French priests, Auguste Chapdelaine. In 1854, Chapdelaine was sent to Guangxi to find Catholic families who had emigrated from Guizhou. In 1856, having been in Guangxi for a little over two years, false accusations were brought against him. It was claimed that he wanted to overturn the (Manchu) Qing Dynasty. He was also accused of causing discord among families and inciting the people to rebel against the authorities.[37] Local Christians urged Chapdelaine to leave Guangxi immediately. He responded that if he left, they would only suffer more. Chapdelaine was arrested and treated brutally. He was beaten twice with three hundred blows, his limbs were dislocated[38] twice from torture,

---

28. Benigni, "Sacred Congregation of Propaganda."

29. Cuenot, *Kwangsi.*

30. Cuenot, *Kwangsi.*

31. Broomhall, *Chinese Empire.*

32. Latourette in *History of Christian Missions in China* said 1858.

33. See footnote 19 on page 22.

34. Cordier, "The Church in China."

35. Cuenot, *Kwangsi.* Apparently this was an informal division as it was formally divided in 1875.

36. Latourette, *History of Christian Missions in China.*

37. Cuenot, *Kwangsi.*

38. Called *mei jen chong* in Cuenot, *Kwangsi.*

and he was finally placed in a death cage. In the cage, he was suspended from his neck so as to cause strangulation. After convulsing, his cage dropped to the ground where he was presumed dead. However, he was later beheaded and his head hung up to serve as a warning to others against becoming Christians.[39] His death, which took place in Baise's Xilin County (western Guangxi), embittered France. While other motives were likely present, they used it as a pretext to join Britain who was at war with China in the Second Opium War (1856–1860).[40]

The victory of the Western powers in the Second Opium War resulted in special privileges for Catholics in Guangxi.[41] Twenty-eight missionaries received passports for inland travel and the French government obtained the right to build a railway from Beihai to Nanning.[42] Missionary advancement under such circumstances, however, backfired as seen in the anti-foreign outbreaks that occurred in later years. In 1866, several missionaries tried to enter Guangxi but were unable to stay. Quite a few did arrive between 1868 and 1871 when Father Mihière was appointed superior to the Guangxi mission. One of them, Father Foucard, worked as a wood-cutter to "avoid arousing the suspicions of the mandarins."[43]

From 1875 to 1899, Catholic work in Guangxi was said to be both "twenty-five years of trial" yet also "one of success."[44] In 1875, the mission of Guangxi separated from Guangdong and became a prefecture apostolic.[45] The following year, the Sino-British Treaty of Yantai opened Beihai (which belonged to Guangdong at the time) as a treaty port. French missionaries arrived soon after and established schools, churches, and other institutions in Beihai and other southern cities.[46] In 1878, eleven groups of Catholics numbered 250 to 350 Christians in Guangxi. From 1883 to 1885, China and France were once again in conflict in what is known as the Sino-French War. The cause was that France had controlled several provinces in today's

39. Cuenot, *Kwangsi*; Hattaway, *China's Christian Martyrs*.

40. Cordier, "Martyrs in China"; Pletcher, "Opium Wars"; Hattaway, *China's Christian Martyrs*. Yan in *Guangxi* said Chapdelaine wore Yi minority clothing and went to Xilin at the end of 1855. Many Yi and Han and some Zhuang became Catholic at that time. Local officials sent him back to Guizhou but he returned in December, 1856 when he was killed.

41. Cordier, "The Church in China."

42. Reinsch, *World Politics*.

43. Montanar, "Kwang-Si," first paragraph.

44. Cuenot, *Kwangsi*, 4–5.

45. Montanar, "Kwang-Si"; Cuenot, *Kwangsi*.

46. Yan, *Guangxi*. The other cities mentioned included Leizhou, Qinzhou, Fangcheng, Lingshan, and Hepu.

Vietnam and began moving northward. In 1884, a section of northern Vietnam called Annam was declared a French possession (again, see figure 2). They clashed with Chinese troops who controlled a large area in today's northern Vietnam, then known as Tonkin. After the Chinese were defeated, a peace treaty was signed (1885) granting France trade rights to Tonkin and the removal of Chinese troops.[47] This gave French Catholics easy access to Guangxi since they could now enter directly from Tonkin.[48] However, parts of the treaty were not honored. One clause permitted missionaries to buy, build, or rent property throughout China, but this was not upheld in Guangxi. The following year, despite privileges gained from the war, there were still fewer Catholics in Guangxi (and Gansu) than in any other province in China.[49] Worse, according to Jean-Paul Wiest, the conflict "caused the lurking hatred of missionaries and converts to erupt violently."[50] During the last two decades of the century, at least six missionaries left Guangxi and waited in Hong Kong for peace to return.[51]

The first decade of the twentieth century was considered to be "one of golden years for the Church . . . on account of the friendly relation between Church and state."[52] In 1907, 592 Catholic baptisms took place.[53] Between 1910 and 1920, few missionaries arrived as a result of antireligious laws and World War I (1914–1918). The latter significantly affected French missions to Guangxi as many had to return to France for wartime service.[54] While many of the priests left, the Sisters of St. Paul de Chartres stayed and continued to oversee schools in Nanning and Longzhou.[55]

In 1917, the superior of the Catholic Foreign Mission Society of America (Maryknoll), James A. Walsh, made an exploratory trip to the Far East in search of a mission field. He visited China and was given a portion of South China which included eastern Guangxi and western Guangdong. A small Maryknoll missionary band departed in September 1918 and took up residence in Guangdong. In 1920, Rome again divided up Guangxi

---

47. *Encyclopedia Britannica*, s.v. "Sino-French War."

48. Oldfield, *Pioneering in Kwangsi*.

49. Latourette, *History of Christian Missions in China*.

50. Wiest, *Catholic Mission*, 176.

51. Cuenot, *Kwangsi*.

52. Cuenot, *Kwangsi*, 199.

53. This compared to 90 in Tibet, 663 in Yunnan, and 2,037 in Guangdong. Latourette, *History*, 542.

54. Wiest, *Maryknoll in China*.

55. Cuenot, *Kwangsi*.

among Catholics; the eastern third[56] was given to Maryknoll and the other two-thirds remained with the French.[57] In 1920, at the invitation of Bishop Ducoeur, vicar apostolic of Guangxi with the Paris Society, Maryknoll missionaries took up residence in Wuzhou under the direction of Father James E. Walsh.[58] Walsh wrote of the city,

> Wuchow has the unique distinction of never having registered a convert to the Catholic Faith. Among the missioners of Kwang-tung [Guangdong], this has passed into a proverb, and whenever a man is discouraged at the slow rate of conversion in his mission, he will be told, "Oh, you are not so unfortunate. Think of the missioner of Wuchow, who is obliged to hire a pagan to serve his Mass!"[59]

The Maryknoll missionaries came at a trying time. In 1920 and 1921, during the middle of China's warlord era (1916–1928), two short wars[60] broke out between Guangxi and Guangdong, both of which possessed powerful warlords. As a result of the fighting, "officials, mandarins, the educated, and the business men came to the [Catholic] missions for protection against various kinds of lawlessness, and asked the fathers to be intermediaries between the different military factions."[61] From 1921 to 1925, Maryknoll had only two missionaries in Guangxi; their primary mission was said to have been in Pingnan.[62]

In 1936, after a history of over eighty years in Guangxi, the Paris Mission Society included thirty-one churches, fourteen missionaries, and a Catholic membership of 4,899.[63] A preparatory seminary was located in Nanning and convents (not *converts*) in Nanning, Guigang, and Lung Nui.[64] Maryknoll convents were located in Pingnan and Wuzhou and a catechist school in Pingnan.[65] Two years later, Guilin was made a prefecture

56. Nine prefectures in the east/southeast according to Cuenot in *Kwangsi*.

57. Latourette, *History of Christian Missions in China*; Cuenot, *Kwangsi*.

58. He was unrelated to James A. Walsh.

59. Walsh, in FMSA, *Maryknoll Mission Letters, China*, 275.

60. August 16–29, 1920, and May 20—July 15, 1921.

61. Cuenot, *Kwangsi*, 14.

62. Cuenot, *Kwangsi*; Snead, *Missionary Atlas* (1936).

63. Oldfield, *Pioneering in Kwangsi*.

64. About halfway between Pingle and Liuzhou.

65. Wiest, *Maryknoll in China*.

apostolic and ceded to Maryknoll.[66] Between 1939 and 1940, Maryknoll recorded over two thousand baptisms in Wuzhou and Guilin.[67]

Catholics exhibited various shifts in their missions over time. Early on, Jesuits worked in the cities seeking to Christianize Chinese society from the top down. However, the later ban on Christianity resulted in most missionaries leaving and Chinese Catholics hiding in remote countryside villages. When China reopened to the missionaries, they largely worked in villages with existing Chinese Catholics. In the early 1900s, some progressive Catholic thinkers insisted that the hope of the Church in China depended on reaching the educated in the cities. However, when Maryknollers arrived in China, most missionaries maintained that the hope of the Church was in the rural areas where over 80 percent of the population lived.[68]

It is noteworthy to mention French Catholic motives for missions, especially before the twentieth century. While they are to be commended for arriving first, it is also apparent, at least at times, that they came with mixed motives. Jean-Paul Wiest, former project coordinator of the Maryknoll China History Project, wrote, "Astute leaders of state and monarchs saw overseas missions as an effective means to further their national and colonial ambitions."[69] Rome launched a "civilizing mission" in 1838, an initiative with clear links to colonialism. The mission assumed the superiority of European culture and sought to civilize and Christianize people perceived as backward. In an article called "Catholic Mission Theory and Practice," Wiest summed up the French motives:

> [China] was seen as a backward, pagan country under the influence of evil. . . . To evangelize non-Christian China, the MEP[70] [Paris Mission Society] used French government support to establish their mission in the provinces of Guangdong and Guangxi. In addition, the Opium War of 1840–42[71] was seen as a crusade to open China to Christianity.[72]

While dual interests drove French Catholic missions at the highest level, the individual French missionaries who set foot on Guangxi soil exhibited a much greater emphasis on bringing salvation through the church[73]

66. Cuenot, *Kwangsi*.

67. Ryan, "American Contributions."

68. Wiest, *Maryknoll in China*.

69. Wiest, *Catholic Mission*, 173.

70. Missions Étrangères de Paris.

71. Most sources say the First Opium War began in 1839.

72. Wiest, *Catholic Mission*, 173–74.

73. *extra Ecclesiam nulla salus.*

and other spiritual aims. In addition, Maryknoll missionaries had a much clearer separation in politics. One of the few criticisms they had toward their French Catholic predecessors was their political ties with France.[74]

Year	Bishops	Missionaries	Seminaries	Schools / students	Churches	Christians
1889	1	11	1	21 / 211	16	1,249
1900	1	17	1	24 / 310	32	1,536
1908	1	27	2	34 / 379	?	4,212

Table 1. Figures for Roman Catholics in Guangxi, 1889–1908.
Compiled from Montanar, "Kwangi-si."
These numbers differ somewhat from those in other sources such as
Broomhall, Wolferstan, and Planchet.

74. Wiest, *Maryknoll in China.*

3

1866–1925

Enter the Protestants

MORE THAN A DECADE passed after Chapdelaine's martyrdom in 1856 before Protestant missionaries set foot in Guangxi. Probably the earliest to travel into Guangxi was the Southern Baptist medical missionary R. H. Graves who reached Guilin in August, 1866. He also made several trips to Wuzhou where a dispensary was established but later discontinued.[1]

It may also come as no surprise that Hudson Taylor's China Inland Mission (CIM) was also one of the first to arrive; they did so in 1877.[2] CIM missionaries George Clarke and Edward Fishe entered Guangxi by way of Guizhou Province to the north. M. G. Guinness wrote of their call,

> When the brethren looked away beyond the southern border of Kwei-chau [Guizhou] to vast Kwang-si [Guangxi] in all its darkness—larger even, and more populous than their own province, but without one single missionary[3]—what could they say except, "Here am I; send me?"[4]

Clarke and Fishe were unable to gather any helpful information about the best route or even whether the people of Guangxi would receive them. They had been told that the people were hostile to foreigners, that Roman

1. Graves, "Statistics."

2. Guinness, *Story of the CIM*; Clarke, *Among the Tribes*; Latourette, *History of Christian Missions in China*.

3. Protestant missionary, that is.

4. Guinness, *Story of the CIM*, 202.

Catholics had failed to make an entrance,[5] and that selling Christian literature was useless. Nevertheless, they went forth in faith. They arrived at the
border of Guangxi in mid-July of 1877, crossed a river into Guangxi, and
soon arrived at their first city. Mr. Clarke preached and sold books and was
surprised that the people were actually interested in buying them. When
the missionaries returned to their boat to resupply, the people crowded on
board and started pulling the books out of the boxes in order to be the first
to obtain them.[6]

Clarke and Fishe spent more than six weeks preaching the gospel and
selling books. They returned to Guiyang[7] to give an encouraging report of
their trip and the people's openness to the gospel. However, within a month
after returning, they both contracted fevers. George Clarke recovered, but
on September 6, 1877, just a few weeks after having returned from Guangxi,
Edward Fishe "fell asleep in Jesus."[8]

In June 1882 in London at the China Inland Mission's anniversary
conference, Rev. George Piercy of the Wesleyan Missionary Society appealed for workers for Guangxi.[9] That night, an announcement was made
before the conference attendees that a lady had made a large donation of
two hundred pounds[10] to set up a mission station in Guangxi. Two years
later, twenty-eight-year-old CIM missionary William Macgregor "went
forth with his heart filled with holy zeal for the glory of God in the salvation of men, and with a deeply cherished desire that, when he had acquired
the language, he might be appointed to labour in the province of Kwang-si
[Guangxi]."[11] In a letter to Benjamin Broomhall, general secretary of the
China Inland Mission at the time, the young Macgregor wrote,

> You will be glad to hear that after quite two years of prayer (I
> might say, more) the Lord is going to give me the desire of my
> heart, and send me to Kwang-si [Guangxi], to carry the light
> of the Gospel to that, at present, dark province. I used to pray
> specially for this province before offering myself for work in
> China, and afterwards I changed the "Lord, send someone to
> Kwang-si," to "Lord, send me to Kwang-si." This the Lord has

5. Which was not completely true.

6. Guinness, *Story of the CIM*.

7. The capital of Guizhou Province.

8. Guinness, *Story of the CIM*, 204.

9. Taylor, *China's Millions*, 1883.

10. This would equal 22,872 pounds in 2017 according to the Bank of England's
inflation calculator. Bank of England, "Inflation Calculator."

11. Cited in Taylor, *China's Millions*, 1883, 18.

now assured me He is going to do, thus answering both prayers. I really cannot tell you with what joy I look forward to the time when I shall be able to go. Since coming to China I have been told what kind of reception I may expect to get in Kwang-si, and have also learned that there are several reasons which, humanly speaking, make the opening of work in that province both difficult and dangerous. This may be so; but, Mr. Broomhall, I do believe the Lord is going to astonish His servants by the way in which He will open Kwang-si.[12]

Unfortunately, and to the bewilderment of many, Macgregor contracted smallpox and died in Anhui Province[13] before he could make it to Guangxi.[14] Miss Hughes, a member of his mission party, remarked, "It seems so mysterious to us that the Lord should so lay Kwang-si on his heart, and prepare such a devoted messenger, and then call him away."[15] The China Inland Mission did not give up, however, and in 1887, Hudson Taylor appealed to God's people to pray for laborers for Guangxi:

Kwang-si [Guangxi], also east of Yun-nan, and bordering on Tong-king [Tonkin], nearly equals England and Scotland in extent, and has five millions of people, but NO missionary! . . . Is it not time we cried mightily to the great Lord of the harvest, to succor [help] the lonely ones, and to send forth more labourers into His great harvest field? Help us, Christian friends, by your prayers![16]

Despite being one of the earliest to enter Guangxi and the passionate appeals of its founder, Hudson Taylor, the China Inland Mission was barely spoken of again in the history of missions to Guangxi. In 1893 Mary Geraldine Guinness of the CIM wrote,

In the face of much criticism and of many difficulties the CIM was privileged not only to open many of the earliest stations in the interior of China, but also to send the first women workers to nine of the inland provinces. These were . . . all of the nine unoccupied provinces except Kwangsi.[17]

---

12. Cited in Taylor, *China's Millions*, 1883, 22.
13. Anqing, Anhui (安徽安庆).
14. Taylor, *China's Millions*, 1883.
15. Taylor, *China's Millions*, 1883, 23.
16. Taylor, *China's Spiritual Needs*, 35.
17. Broomhall, *Jubilee Story*, 123.

In his thirty-year history of the China Inland Mission, Hudson Taylor wrote, "The second decade[18] [of the CIM] was one of widespread itineration and exploration of the more distant provinces, during which the first stations were opened in all the unoccupied provinces except one, Kwang-si [Guangxi]."[19]

By 1880, Protestant missionaries resided in every province of China except Henan, Hunan, and Guangxi. Which society would be the first to gain a long-term foothold in Guangxi? Several made the attempt, including the American Presbyterians. In the mid-1880s, they entered Guangxi from the east. Medical missionary Dr. Albert Fulton, his wife, and his sister Mary opened a medical clinic in Guiping. All seemed to be going well despite their small residence and meager facilities. They set out to build a hospital, and just as they were about to complete it in May of 1886, Mary wrote home,

> When you receive this, you can think of us in our clean, new hospital with its fine view of river, plain, and mountain, our wards full of patients, and the Gospel being proclaimed to those who have never before heard it.[20]

However, the very next letter read,

> You will be surprised to see this is written from Canton [Guangzhou] instead of from Kwai Ping [Guiping]. Still more surprised will you be to learn our new hospital, which was almost ready for occupancy, "went up in smoke," as did the house in which we had been living, together with all we had—household furnishings, medical books, instruments, medicines, etc.[21]

The American Presbyterians had been driven out of Guangxi. However, it was not simply that they were foreign missionaries. According to Mary Fulton, the local magistrate had taxed gambling so highly that regular gamblers had nothing better to do than wander about in the streets causing mischief. It was under such circumstances that these ruffians decided to "drive out the foreign devils."[22] They formed small mobs and attacked the hospital. Mary, Mrs. Fulton, and daughter Edith locked themselves inside, but the mob burned straw and smoked them out. Dr. Fulton was attacked on

18. 1875–1885.

19. Taylor, *Three Decades*, 5.

20. Fulton, *Inasmuch*, 34.

21. Fulton, *Inasmuch*, 34. Dr. Macdonald of the Wesleyan Methodist Mission journaled on May 8, "Heard of Fulton's house in Kwai Ping burnt, and loss of all." Macdonald, *Roderick Macdonald, M.D.*, 35.

22. Fulton, *Inasmuch*, 34.

his way to find the local magistrate. They all managed to avoid any physical harm and to safely make their way to the river. Mary sold her class ring to book passage for all of them back to safety in Guangzhou.

Their departure did not cause them to forget Guangxi, however, which was still in dire need of the gospel. Three months later they attempted to return. When local women threw sticks at Dr. Fulton, they realized they were still unwelcome. They continued to make repeated visits to Guangxi over the next few years. On a trip three years after the hospital was destroyed, Dr. Fulton baptized his first three converts in Guangxi. The following year, however, Mary did not sense the doors were open for missionary residence and wrote, "Kwong Sai [Guangxi] still appears hostile to the entrance of the Gospel."[23] The American Presbyterians were never able to establish a long-term presence in Guangxi but carried out a fruitful ministry in Guangzhou. Mary Fulton's service in China earned her later inclusion in a biographical dictionary of notable American women.[24]

In the late 1880s, Herbert Richmond Wells of the American Bible Society in China traveled at least twice into Guangxi distributing literature. On one trip in 1888, he departed from Guangzhou by boat and spent a month in Guilin where he sold three thousand Bible portions.[25]

Despite these early missionary trips, Guangxi still did not have a single resident Protestant missionary by 1895.[26] It was also one of only four provinces in China without a medical missionary.[27] However, in the mid-1890s, light began to gleam through the cracks of Guangxi's slowly opening doors.

THE CHRISTIAN AND MISSIONARY ALLIANCE (CMA)

The Christian and Missionary Alliance (CMA or "Alliance" for short) had the honor of having the first permanent resident missionary in Guangxi.[28] They also maintained the largest presence and established the most stations

---

23. Fulton, *Inasmuch*, 86.

24. James, *Notable American Women*. For more information on Mary Fulton, see Smylie, *Notable Presbyterian Women* and the article "'Lady' Physicians in the Field: Women Doctors and Presbyterian Foreign Mission Work, 1870–1960" in *The Journal of Presbyterian History* (1997–).

25. Ure, *Governors*; Wells, "Bible-Selling in Kwong Sai," "Mr. Wells' Report."

26. MacGillivray, *Century of Protestant Missions*; Oldfield, *Pioneering in Kwangsi*.

27. Graves, *Forty Years in China*.

28. MacGillivray, *Century of Protestant Missions*; Couling, *Encyclopedia Sinica*; Oldfield, *Pioneering in Kwangsi*. The CMA was originally called The International Missionary Alliance. Oldfield, *Pioneering in Kwangsi*.

in Guangxi until the middle of the twentieth century when all societies would be forced to leave.[29]

The origin of their work stemmed from two trips of CMA's founder, A. B. Simpson, who traveled to China in 1892 and 1894. At this time, only Guangxi and Hunan were closed to the gospel. Dr. Simpson learned of the plight of these areas and appealed for workers. After hearing of the needs, one couple, Mr. and Mrs. Reeves, applied and were sent out by the Alliance. Mr. Reeves traveled into Guangxi in 1893 with a colporteur of the National Bible Society of Scotland to sell books.[30] While there, he saw the "destitute condition of its eight millions of souls without the gospel."[31] At the same time, students at the Alliance Missionary Training Institute in Nyack, NY became burdened for Guangxi. A small band of five men from the school set sail for China the following year to join the work. Two of them traveled into Guangxi in 1895 with two Chinese colporteurs (Chinese Christians who sold and distributed Christian literature).[32] However, they found the weather unbearably hot, returned to Guangzhou, and left the colporteurs there to preach. Later, locals from the area where the colporteurs were left behind traveled to Guangdong to make a request for missionaries to come.[33] As a result of these early trips, CMA opened its first work among a Hakka community in the market town of Tung-tsun in 1895.[34] Over the next couple of years, the CMA itinerated in the eastern portion of Guangxi along the West River.

In 1896, CMA missionaries gained a permanent foothold in Wuzhou, the gateway city from Guangdong in the east.[35] The Alliance transferred their headquarters from Guangzhou to Wuzhou soon after. Over the next three years, work opened up in several new locations including Guiping, Nanning, and Guilin.[36] In 1900, a setback occurred during the Boxer

29. Walter Oldfield, once acting chairman of the Alliance's South China Mission, told their story in *Pioneering in Kwangsi* (1936).

30. Reeves, "Missionary Letters"; Oldfield, *Pioneering in Kwangsi*. In fact, piecing together the details of these early trips is not easy. Oldfield mentioned he traveled with a colporteur, but Reeves did not. Yan mentioned that the CMA explored Guangxi in 1892 but the earliest account of Reeve's journey in *The Alliance Weekly* was in 1893.

31. Farmer, *Ada Beeson Farmer*, 60.

32. John E. Fee and L. B. Quick. Oldfield, *Pioneering in Kwangsi*.

33. The reasons were not necessarily spiritual as foreign missionaries could also be associated with protection by foreign governments.

34. Quick, "An Incident in Quangsi"; Oldfield, *Pioneering in Kwangsi*. Tung-tsun was located somewhere between Guigang and Guiping on the West River.

35. CMA, "Good News from Quangsi"; Oldfield, *Pioneering in Kwangsi*; Broomhall, *Chinese Empire*.

36. In 1897, 1898, and 1898 respectively.

Rebellion when the Alliance missionaries had to leave. The Boxers killed numerous missionaries and Chinese Christians in other parts of China,[37] but, fortunately, Guangxi was spared, and the missionaries were able to return the following year. Work progressed consistently after the threat of the Boxers and within a decade, the CMA had established men's and women's Bible schools,[38] boys' and girls' schools, and a receiving house for new missionaries to learn Cantonese at their headquarters in Wuzhou. In 1913, the Alliance Press began printing and circulating Bible portions and tracts from Wuzhou.[39]

While many stations had opened and the societies had made considerable progress by this time, missionary work in other provinces dwarfed the work in Guangxi by comparison. Cochrane, in his 1913 *Survey of the Missionary Occupation of China*, said Guangxi was "one of the least thoroughly occupied of the provinces."[40] Latourette presented some numbers: "In 1911 Chekiang [Zhejiang] had one missionary to about every 38,000 of the population, but Yunnan had only one to every 326,000 and Kweichow [Guizhou] one to every 332,000. Kwangsi [Guangxi] and Kansu [Gansu] were almost without missionaries."[41] The Alliance pressed forward, however. They slowly advanced their work and set up a number of stations in

37. "Of the foreigners who were murdered, 135 protestant missionaries and approximately 51 of their children were murdered. Of these, 41 Swedish missionaries together with 15 children died. Of those in the Christian and Missionary Alliance, 21 missionaries and 14 children, of the Holiness Alliance 10 missionaries, of the Scandinavian Alliance Mongol Mission 5 missionaries and of the China Island Mission 2 missionaries." "The Boxer Rebellion."

38. The men's was set up in 1899 and the women's two years later. Snead, *Missionary Atlas* (1936).

39. Couling, *Encyclopedia Sinica*.

40. Cochrane, *Survey*, 5.

41. Latourette, *History of Christian Missions in China*, 606. In 1922, the China Continuation Committee wrote, "Kwangsi was one of the last provinces of China to be entered and occupied by Christian missionaries, and ever since an entrance has been gained, the province has been sadly neglected." China Continuation Committee, *Christian Occupation*, 151. They go on to list four reasons why Guangxi had been neglected. First was the *sparsity of the population* due to mountains, robbers, and poverty. Second was the *difficulty of access*, referring to the difficulties of traveling by small boat among the many robbers and pirates. Third was the *hostility of the people*, referring to their anti-foreign orientation, religious opposition, and racial prejudice. Fourth was the *loss of Christian workers* in Guangxi due to death, World War I, and financial limitations.

Guangxi, predominantly in the eastern half.[42] By 1925,[43] they had established seventy-seven stations and outstations throughout the province.[44]

SOUTHERN BAPTISTS

Following R. H. Graves' early trips, Southern Baptists made additional trips in 1886 or 87. In 1889, there were four Christians connected with their missions in the province. A work was opened in a district of Pingnan by a returned boatman who was converted in Guangzhou as he stood fast through persecution. In early 1891, fourteen Christians were located in Pingnan and they built their first church building (termed "chapel") the following year. A second station was established in Pingle. It was opened when a Christian from Shantou in Guangdong Province relocated to Pingle and began witnessing of his faith in Christ. A Chinese preacher and an ordained minister later followed up, baptized the inquirers, and established a church.[45] In 1893, the CMA mentioned these two stations and a chapel and remarked, "The Baptist brethren who have opened the way will be only too glad to welcome us and help us all they can."[46] In 1897, the Wuzhou station opened up and gained a foreign missionary.[47] The Yale historian Kenneth Scott Latourette commented on the Southern Baptist's effective outreach in the following years.[48]

In 1912, they expanded their work and opened a station in Guilin.[49] The following year, they organized the first Baptist church in Guilin with twelve members; by 1920, it had grown to over 400. Despite the growth, the intention was never to get people merely to come; Guilin served as a base for evangelizing surrounding areas. An American doctor and co-worker traveled around Guilin with the two-pronged approach of preaching and

42. In Kaiping (northwest of Wuzhou on the Cassia River), Guilin, Nanning, Teng County in Wuzhou, Yulin, Pingle (in Guilin Shi), Pingnan, Liuzhou, Longzhou County, Baise, Qingyuan (in Yizhou), and other places. Jaffray, "A General Resume."

43. Under the leadership of Robert Jaffray.

44. Tozer, *Let My People Go.*

45. McCloy, "Sketch." This occurred in Shek-tong village in Pingnan.

46. CMA, "Editorial," 5.

47. Love, *Seventy-Fourth Annual Report*; Broomhall, *Chinese Empire*; Lowe, *Gleanings*; Ray, *Southern Baptists in China.*

48. Latourette, *History of Christian Missions in China.* He specifically mentioned the years 1901–1914, but it is unclear why he limited their effective outreach to these years.

49. Lobenstine, *China Mission Year Book 1917.*

distributing tracts. By 1921, Guilin and surrounding areas had a church membership of 1,196.[50]

The Southern Baptists established a variety of institutions including boys' and girls' schools, training centers, and hospitals. In Wuzhou, the Stout Memorial Hospital became the largest Baptist hospital in China, having five stories and over two hundred beds. It even served as a bomb shelter during the Japanese air raids in the late 1930s and early 40s. They also established a Baptist hospital in Guilin. However, its meager size and facilities could not compare with Stout Memorial in Wuzhou, and J. T. Williams wrote of its beginnings, "The house Dr. Mewshaw has for a hospital would make a fairly good cow shed and he has two boards laid on saw horses for an operating table."[51]

While the hospitals met people's physical needs, they also served as centers of evangelism.[52] At the Stout Memorial Hospital in Wuzhou, a room on the first floor was designated the office of the hospital preacher. Preaching was conducted twice a day. When people gathered at the clinic before examinations, one preached and others watched to see who expressed interest.[53] Nurses were designated to preach to the coolies who waited outside the hospital after bringing patients. Packets of medicine were wrapped with tracts. A list of names of those interested in the gospel was kept so that they could be visited by the "Bible women." Margaret McRae Lackey remarked, "No one comes in contact with the Hospital or the doctors without hearing of the Great Physician."[54]

Outside the hospital, Southern Baptists conducted nightly preaching in the chapel. Literature was also widely distributed. One of their goals was to have a Christian calendar in every home in Guilin.[55] Curious inquirers could come and learn more about the gospel in a bookroom established for that purpose. Printed tracts explained the gospel and encouraged readers to visit the bookroom. C. J. Lowe, head of the Mandarin section of the South China mission for the Southern Baptists, stated the priority of their mission:

> Every phase of the work in this field centers around the evangelistic. We have made it our aim to emphasize at all times the spirit of man-to-man evangelism. We have tried to impress

50. Lackey, *Laborers Together.*
51. In Lowe, *Gleanings,* 15.
52. Lowe, *Gleanings.*
53. Lackey, *Laborers Together.*
54. Lackey, *Laborers together,* 59.
55. Lowe, *Gleanings.*

upon the constituency the responsibility they have in leading others into the marvelous light as it is in Jesus.[56]

Samuel Couling of the Royal Asiatic Society also commented on the Southern Baptist ethos: "Its work is considered along evangelistic, educational, medical, and literary lines, with the evangelistic work well in the lead."[57] Walter Oldfield (CMA) wrote later,

> The Southern Baptist Mission was among the first to enter the province, and throughout the years they have carried on an aggressive missionary campaign, their medical, educational, and evangelical agencies uniting in one great front to give the Gospel message to all they can reach.[58]

THE CHURCH MISSIONARY SOCIETY

A third mission society that gained an early presence[59] in Guangxi was the Church Missionary Society (CMS), an agency of the Church of England. They had already established a church, hospital, and leper ministry in Beihai by 1895,[60] but Beihai was still considered a part of Guangdong at the time. In 1899, they attempted to set up work in Guilin. The pioneer missionaries were the Reverend and Mrs. Louis Byrde.

Louis Byrde was a native of Bedfordshire, England and had studied math at Corpus Christi College in Cambridge. He was also one of the founders of the Student Volunteer Missionary Union (SVMU) in England and its acting chairman from 1893 to 1894. While serving as a chaplain in Hawaii for three years, he came into contact with many Chinese people.

In 1899, he and his wife Constance sailed from Wuzhou to Guilin to begin the CMS work there. They were unable to rent a house in the city, so they lived on a boat for four or five months providing basic medical services.[61] A local Muslim (a "Mohammedan") named Mr. Song sought

56. In Love, *Seventy-Sixth Annual Report*. The quote is found in the South China Mission's annual report in the third paragraph of the subsection called "The Mandarin-Speaking Section."

57. Couling, *Encyclopedia Sinica*, 522.

58. Oldfield, *Pioneering in Kwangsi*, 57–58.

59. However, if "Guangxi" refers to today's Guangxi, then the CMS came much earlier. Before the 1950s, Beihai was considered part of Guangdong.

60. CMA, "Outgoing Missionaries"; Keen, "Church Missionary Society Archive." The hospital was established in 1886.

61. MacGillivray, *Century of Protestant Missions*; Stock, *History of the CMS*.

them out due to his father's health problem. Mr. Song soon became Rev. Byrde's language teacher and helped him find a place to rent in the city. Rev. Byrde moved in with Mr. Cunningham of the CMA who had reached Guilin slightly before he had.[62] In 1900, the Byrdes left Guilin due to the Boxer Rebellion. A year later they returned and Mr. Song, their first convert, was baptized in 1902. The Byrdes experienced two boat wrecks on the river between Guilin and Wuzhou over the next two years, the second of which almost took their lives.

In 1903, Rev. Byrde began pioneering northeast into Hunan where he set up a second station in Hunan's Yongzhou, just twenty to thirty miles across the border. It was around that time that he conceived the idea of a newsletter. The first Kwangsi-Hunan Newsletter[63] began publication in 1904 and, with the exception of the years 1941 to 1945, stayed in print until 1951. Their motto was, "Go forward in intercession and self-sacrifice for the evangelization of the world and the salvation of souls."[64]

While Louis Byrde remained in Hunan, the CMS continued to send new workers to Guilin. There, they established a bookstore and reading room in 1904 where they distributed tracts, Scriptures, and other Christian publications. In 1909, they opened a "gospel hall" on a major thoroughfare in the city.[65] Also that year, Guangxi-Hunan changed status from mission to diocese,[66] and William Banister was consecrated its first bishop.[67] The following year, they organized a small high school for boys in Guilin. In 1911, their long-term prayer for a medical doctor was answered in the person of Dr. Charlotte Bailey (later Charlotte Bacon) who was said to have been the first person to ever practice western medicine in Guilin.[68] The Church Missionary Society went on to establish three churches in Guilin: St. John's,

---

62. Stevens, "Archdeacon Louis Byrde."

63. Which had various names including The Newsletter, C.M.S. Central China Field; The Newsletter of the C.M.S. Kwangsi Hunan Mission; The Newsletter of the Kwangsi Hunan Mission, C.M.S. & C.E.Z.M.S.; The Newsletter. C.M.S. Central China Mission; and the Kwangsi-Hunan Diocesan Newsletter.

64. CMS, Kwangsi Hunan Newsletter 1 (August 1904), 1. The motto was changed in 1907 to "Go forward! In intercession and Self-sacrifice for the Evangelization of the Whole Creation and the Salvation of all Men." CMS, The Newsletter. C.M.S. Central China Field 9 (February 1907), 1.

65. CMS, "News in Brief."

66. The territory under a bishop. Catholic, Anglican, Lutheran, and other denominations all have dioceses.

67. Latourette, History of Christian Missions in China.

68. Stevens, "Bishop's Foreword" (December 1946).

with its "imposing front on the principal street of the city,"[69] St. Peter's, and a third small church across the river.[70]

In 1916, the CMS joined forces with the Church of England Zenana Mission Society (CEZMS) which specifically sent female missionaries to serve women. From 1918 to 1920, the diocese as a whole fell on hard times.[71] Louis Byrde, then located at the headquarters in Hunan, died in 1918 of a gastric ulcer at the age of forty-seven.[72] Soon after, John Bacon, Dr. Bacon's husband, died of pneumonia in France while ministering to Chinese coolies.[73] The third blow came when Mr. Parker, also located at the headquarters in Hunan's Yongzhou, died of dysentery.[74] CMS missionary J. R. Wilson wrote in 1920, "It seems that whoever comes to Kweilin comes only to die soon."[75] The money given for Louis Byrde's memorial fund was to be applied toward the support of an evangelist in northeastern Guangxi between Guilin and Yongzhou.[76] Louis Byrde's wife Constance took over as honorary secretary of the newsletter in 1921, a position she held until 1941.

New workers replaced those who had died, however, and the CMS continued to establish stations and outstations around Guilin. While city work occupied much of their time, work in the countryside and neighboring areas was not neglected. By 1923, ten outstations had been opened around Guilin, some of which later became main stations.

THE ENGLISH WESLEYAN MISSION

The pioneer of the English Wesleyan Mission[77] was medical missionary Roderick Macdonald. Dr. Macdonald, a Scotsman born in England, was the son of a Wesleyan minister. At his appointment to Wuzhou in 1987, he was already an experienced China missionary, having served in Guangdong[78] since 1884. He arrived in Wuzhou only two days after it opened for trade in 1897. He commenced his mission work there by ascending the Pagoda Hill and singing the doxology at the ruins of a temple "where probably no

69. Wilson, "Kwangsi Life," 11.

70. Leach, "A Visit to Kweilin Parish."

71. CMS, "Editorial Notes."

72. Holden, "The Ven. Archdeacon Byrde."

73. CMS, "The Rev. J. L. Bacon."

74. Holden, "A Big Dose."

75. Wilson, "When Troubles Come," 237.

76. Holden, "Editorial Notes," "The Ven. Archdeacon Byrde."

77. Also known as the Wesleyan Methodist Missionary Society.

78. Foshan (佛山) and Shaoguan (韶关).

Christian hymn had ever previously been sung."[79] Dr. Macdonald, like Rev. and Mrs. Byrde, was unable to rent a house in town and lived on a boat with his wife and son for several months. The frequent storms on the river, however, caused the destruction of many of his medicine bottles. His son was unable to tolerate the boat life and was soon sent back to Guangzhou. After some months, Dr. Macdonald acquired a piece of land where he built a small wooden shanty for their residence and set up a dispensary for seeing patients.

Dr. Macdonald labored faithfully in Wuzhou for a decade where his wife said he "had no hobby but his work."[80] He left Wuzhou but once a year—not even for a vacation or during the Boxer Rebellion in 1900—to attend the annual Wesleyan synod in January in Guangzhou. Through his medical and evangelistic ministry, Dr. Macdonald established a church. When funds were available, he spent time building a hospital with Chinese laborers. In 1905, he bought a small island near Wuzhou for thirty dollars where he set up a leper colony.[81] He also sensed an unprecedented openness and opportunity that year in the newly emerging colleges in Guangxi. His hope was for a Wesleyan headmaster for each college starting in Wuzhou. Unfortunately, they did not come. Dr. Macdonald, too, had to turn down the opportunity to superintend English teaching at Wuzhou's largest college due to his other ministries and the construction of the hospital.

Unfortunately, Dr. Macdonald never witnessed the completion of the hospital. In 1906 he left Wuzhou to attend the synod of the Chinese Wesleyan Church. While returning, pirates attacked the British steamer, the *S. S. Sainam*, on which he was traveling. They shot the ship's captain and Dr. Macdonald hurried to provide assistance. In the process of helping the captain and seeking safety, Dr. Macdonald too was shot and killed.[82] One source claimed the pirates sent a letter to his wife apologizing; they stated that if they had known it was Dr. Macdonald, they would not have shot him.[83]

---

79. Macdonald, *Roderick Macdonald, M.D.*, 107.

80. Macdonald, *Roderick Macdonald, M.D.*, 132.

81. Macdonald, *Roderick Macdonald, M.D.*

82. CMS, "Roderick Macdonald, M.D."; Pritchard, *Methodists*; Tatchell, *Medical Missions in China*. The pirates attacked and shot the captain, but he escaped to the saloon with the other two Europeans on board, the chief engineer and Dr. Macdonald. Dr. Macdonald began to take off the captain's jacket when a stink-pot, a small round weapon filled with chemicals, was thrown into the saloon. The men promptly left and were confronted again by the pirates when Dr. Macdonald was shot twice, once in the head. "Top Ten Pirate Weapons"; Macdonald, *Roderick Macdonald, M.D.*, 261–65.

83. Findlay, *History*.

It was estimated that Dr. Macdonald treated more than one hundred thousand patients during his tenure in China. Ironically, he too had his share of physical afflictions and trials, having faced or suffered from jaundice, acute lower back pain, malaria, typhoid, hemorrhaging of the lungs, and a near drowning[84] at various points during his twenty-two years in Guangxi and Guangdong.[85] Louis Byrde wrote of the doctor following his death, "It can be truly said that Dr. Macdonald was without compeer [equal] the most influential foreigner in the Kwang Si Province."[86]

In the years that followed, foreign Wesleyan missionaries departed Guangxi and relocated their ministries to Guangdong. Their ministry in Guangxi, however, including that of the hospital, was carried on by Chinese Christians. In 1907, the English Wesleyan Mission had one chapel with a membership of eighty-four. They also had established a boys' school, a girls' school, and an infant school with a combined total of ninety-two under instruction.[87]

By 1920, the CMA, SBC, Wesleyans, and CMS were well-established in Guangxi. In 1922, seventy-six missionaries from these and other societies were serving in Guangxi.[88] Two-thirds[89] were concentrated in the cities of Wuzhou, Guilin, and Nanning.[90] They had plowed, sown, and reaped. Converts had been made, churches planted, and outstations set up in new territories. However, despite growth in numbers and advances winning the hearts and acceptance of many of the local people, another trial was about to test the missionaries and the young church in Guangxi.

---

84. He was knocked off a boat, trapped underneath, and later pulled out of the water unconscious. Macdonald, *Roderick Macdonald, M.D.*

85. Macdonald, *Roderick Macdonald, M.D.*

86. In Macdonald, *Roderick Macdonald, M.D.*, 293.

87. MacGillivray, *Century of Protestant Missions*, 100.

88. This was comparable to the number in Yunnan (75) and Gansu (72). Guizhou only had 45 missionaries at the time. Those in Guangxi included 7 physicians, 6 nurses, and 276 employed Chinese workers. China Continuation Committee, *Christian Occupation*, 151, 344.

89. 65 percent.

90. China Continuation Committee, *Christian Occupation*, 151. This was no different in 1948 when forty out of a total of sixty Protestant missionaries were located "in four of the large cities." Tubbs, "In Needy Kwangsi," 458.

4

1925–1937

The Anti-Foreign Movement up to the Japanese Invasion

FOREIGNERS AND MISSIONARIES IN China for years had been labeled "foreign devils" or "foreign demons." There were multiple reasons for this. The Chinese had lost Macau to the Portuguese, Hong Kong to the British, and northern Vietnam to the French. They had their ports forced open and their land taken; they were forced to trade and made to sign unequal treaties. All of this resulted in national humiliation. Other foreign provocations which received nationwide attention played a role as well: Germans opened mines and mistreated the Chinese miners; drunk U.S. sailors threw a Chinese man over a bridge to his death; a German steamer traveled up the Yangzi River haphazardly firing its guns; and a garden in Shanghai refused to admit "dogs and Chinese."[1] Mrs. Oldfield remarked, "These ignorant farmers knew nothing of foreigners except stories which pictured them as evil and fierce 'foreign devils' who wants to 'take the precious things out of the earth' and steal and kill their children to make medicine."[2] Pioneer CMS missionary Louis Byrde described how this historical baggage and Chinese perception of foreigners affected the missionaries in Guangxi:

> How tired the foreigner in China becomes of the call, or the quietly uttered words, "Demon," "Foreign Demon." The little children playing on the streets sight the Demon and run in gleefully calling the others to come and see the strange being. When my

1. Byrde, "Foreign Demons"; Wilson, "A City of Rubbish-Heaps."
2. Oldfield, *With You Alway*, 72.

44

wife and I used to go for walks in Kueilin [Guilin], and carry our little girl Christine, the delighted mothers would crowd around to see the "Demonette," or "Little Demon," as they called her. In the above there is little or no malice, as in the case of a worthy Christian woman when conversing with a lady missionary, kept using the words "foreign demon." When politely remonstrated with [challenged] she replied, "Well, after all, what are you but foreign Demons?" Of course in origin the words have a most insulting meaning, but they are often used, simply because no other word is in common use among the Chinese. When the call is shouted out, and the word "Kill" is added, then the intention is bad, but I must admit that only once has the sign "to kill" been made at me in addition, and that was not in China, but in Hongkong.[3]

According to Dr. Bacon in Guilin, after the Revolution of 1911, the use of "foreign devil" greatly decreased.[4] This trend seems to have persisted until around 1924 as John Holden said of Guilin at the time, "The feeling in the city is anything but anti-foreign."[5] However, the following year,[6] a severe wave of anti-foreign sentiment swept through China. There were various causes of the upheaval. One was the fact that the Soviet Union stirred up the Chinese in the aftermath of the Bolshevik Revolution of 1917. Strong anti-foreign sentiment accompanied the Communist movement there and was often directed at missionaries and Christians. The Nationalist Party of China, the "Kuomintang," also played a role. Nationalism was one of its three guiding principles. This often resulted in anti-imperialism directed at foreigners. Its leader, Sun Yat-sen, spoke caustically against the British and made them out to be cruel oppressors of a weak and innocent people.[7] British and Americans alike were labeled "imperialists" and their Christian religion constituted part of what they brought with them.[8] Another cause was an incident that took place in Shanghai when police, under the command of British officers, fired on and killed twelve Chinese

3. Byrde, "Foreign Demons," 38.

4. Bacon, "After the Revolution."

5. Holden, "Bishop's Letter" (September 1924), 539.

6. The September 1925 issue of the CMS's Kwangi-Hunan newsletter began to write of this upheaval. The Oldfields (CMA) left in the summer and returned in the fall. Oldfield, *With You Alway.*

7. Holden, "The Bishop's Letter" (November 1928). Protestants tended to favor Sun while Catholics did not. James E. Walsh, the superior of the Maryknoll China mission, "was the most outspoken in voicing his dislike of Sun." Wiest, *Maryknoll in China,* 321.

8. Latourette, *History of Christian Missions in China;* Bacon, "Iconoclasm in Kwangsi."

protestors.[9] The next month in Guangzhou, some foreigners fired on a crowd of Chinese demonstrators killing fifty-two.[10] These events provoked a great outcry among Chinese, especially the energetic and impressionable student population. Anti-foreign literature was then distributed around China. In Guilin, a poster displayed, "Oppose the Church of Christ."[11] CMA and SBC missionaries in the city sought to remedy the situation by establishing an independent Christian church which would be immune to the anti-foreign movement. However, the local paper wrote an article on this independent church stating that its independence did not change the essential imperialist nature of the Christian religion.[12] The Oldfields (CMA) evacuated to the coast in early summer 1925 and returned in the early fall.[13]

In 1926 and part of 1927, anti-foreign students targeted the Christians around Guangxi. They attacked church buildings and sealed their doors closed. They smashed furniture and tore Bibles and prayer books to pieces. Chinese Christians became known as "foreign slaves"[14] and "running dogs of the foreigners."[15] Students paraded in front of the Catholic church in Pingnan and other locations where they could be heard shouting slogans like, "Down with the Catholic Church!"[16] and, "Down with the foreign devils! Down with America! Down with the Church!"[17] Guangxi managed to pull through the crisis without any calamitous results. In Shanghai in 1927, the Nationalist Party purged and disassociated with Communists. This greatly diminished the Bolshevik movement and its anti-foreign voice. The anti-foreign fervor died out in early 1928.

The effect on the church, however, was long-lasting. Chen wrote, "Although the destroyed and damaged buildings and their furnishings were quickly replaced, it was not so easy to replace the congregations, and to get newcomers to learn about Jesus Christ and follow Him was quite different from before, and very much harder."[18] Many Christians fell away during

9. The May Thirtieth Movement. The occurrence was over the working conditions and incidents (including the death of a Chinese) that had taken place in Japanese factories in China.

10. Strand, *Rickshaw Beijing*, 182.

11. Bacon, "Iconoclasm in Kwangsi."

12. Cannell, "Kweilin Notes."

13. Oldfield, *With You Alway*.

14. A Baptist Christian was branded with *yang* (洋) meaning "foreign" on one cheek and *nu* (奴) meaning "slave" on the other. Oldfield, *With You Alway*.

15. Santler, "A Great Need."

16. Wiest, *Maryknoll in China*, 334.

17. Oldfield, *With You Alway*, 179.

18. Chen, "Kweilin," 10.

this period and church attendance dropped significantly. Christians or Chinese pastors who had been former friends no longer acknowledged one another on the street.[19] The Oldfields experienced one family, one teacher, and another language teacher, all who had seemed like true Christians, turn on them.[20]

The following years were challenging for the urban churches. Mrs. Oldfield remarked, "The Church was smaller, too, but purified by the fire through which it had passed, was more spiritual. Now it increased with greater vigor than before, and self-support made great strides."[21] Outreach to minorities also greatly expanded in the following years (see chapter 8). By the mid-1930s, the Church Missionary Society had an extensive ministry in northeast Guangxi. Guilin was their largest station and the location of their first church, but other stations had opened up in Quanzhou (1922), Xingan (1928), and Guanyang (1932).[22] In 1934, Rev. Gray, who was in charge of the Guilin parish, regularly visited all eighteen villages around Guilin except in the southern part of the city which had been given to another society.[23] Also, in 1936, Walter Oldfield (CMA) reported the work of several other societies in Guangxi:[24] The Church of Christ Mission[25] consisted of two chapels with Chinese evangelists in charge of each. The Assemblies of God Mission served in two locations, one led by a couple and the other by a single lady. The Seventh Day Adventist Mission began work in Guangxi in 1916–1917.[26] They ministered in Guangxi's Cantonese-speaking section where they opened thirteen chapels and had one ordained pastor, eleven evangelists, and a membership of 277.[27] The British and Foreign Bible Society and the National Bible Society of Scotland supported a number of colporteurs and distributed literature throughout parts of Guangxi. The Bible Churchmen's Missionary Society took over the work of the Emmanuel Medical Mission (Dr. and Mrs. Clift), and its principal station was located in

19. Cannell, "Kweilin."

20. Oldfield, *With You Alway*.

21. Oldfield, *With You Alway*, 190.

22. Chen, "Kweilin."

23. Gray, "Kweilin Parish." The other society was probably the CMA.

24. Oldfield, *Pioneering in Kwangsi*.

25. This is probably the "Church of Christ in China," an ecumenical body of Chinese churches formed with the aim to be more self-governing, self-supporting, and self-propagating; also called the "Chinese Independent Church" by the CMA. The Hong Kong Council, "About Us"; Snead, *Missionary Atlas*.

26. Lobenstine, *China Mission Year Book 1917*.

27. Oldfield, *Pioneering in Kwangsi*, 63.

Nanning.[28] By 1937, there were well over a dozen Catholic and Protestant orders and societies serving in Guangxi. And they would all experience the storm that was about to move through Guangxi in the years to come.

28. Tiedemann, *Reference Guide.*

5

1937–1952
War with Japan through the Missionaries' Departure

MANY OF THE EVENTS and uprisings that took place in Guangxi after the arrival of the missionaries were short-lived or limited in impact: floods, famine, epidemics, the Boxer Rebellion, and the anti-foreign 1920s. Not so with the Japanese War. It had a widespread, crushing effect on Guangxi from 1937 until Japan's surrender to the Allies in 1945.

By all accounts, the Japanese were merciless and ruthless in their bombings and invasion of Guangxi (and China as a whole). At the Stout Memorial Hospital, the American flag was flown and red crosses were painted on the roof in hopes they would be spared from Japanese bombs. But spared they were not. On September 17, 1937, the hospital was bombed and a third of Wuzhou was destroyed. By 1938, refugees from the war were streaming into Guangxi from other parts of the country.[1] The following year, the Japanese bombed Pingnan,[2] occupied Nanning,[3] and dropped countless bombs on Liuzhou.[4]

Residents learned at what hours the Japanese planes would come and scheduled their lives and work accordingly. Church services in Guilin were held at 7 a.m. because the raids typically did not begin until 8 or 9 a.m.[5]

1. Stevens, "Bishop's Foreword" (October 1938).
2. On October 23, 1939. Wiest, *Maryknoll in China*.
3. In November. Hutchings, "A Province at War."
4. On December 2. Oldfield, "Amid Falling Bombs," "Fightings and Fears."
5. Leach said the air raids usually occurred from 8 a.m. to 1 p.m. while Stevens said 9 or 10 a.m. to 3 p.m. Leach, "Our Doings and Mis-Doings"; Stevens, "Bishop's Foreword" (March 1940, May 1941).

Whenever the air raid siren would sound, anxiety struck the hearts of the residents. They would then flee to bomb shelters or caves around the city. Three such caves were located behind the CMS hospital in Guilin; one could hold up to three thousand people and the others two to three hundred.[6] Unfortunately, the relentless Japanese targeted the caves and safety zones as well. One lady hid under a banyan tree and saw a Japanese plane separate from the others and head directly for her. She survived, but others were not always so fortunate; they were often unable to make it to safety and were slain by shrapnel or roasted to death in the flames. Even those in underground bomb shelters could be killed by direct bomb strikes.

No Japanese troops were on Guangxi soil the whole of 1941, but Guilin suffered from severe aerial bombings.[7] The following year, heavy bombing continued and Guilin, Liuzhou, Nanning, and Longzhou all took major poundings. The air raids were particularly bad in Wuzhou and Guilin, the latter said to have "seen more planes than any other Kwangsi city."[8] In 1944, Japan executed an all-out offensive in China. The American airbase in Guilin was taken and Wuzhou was captured. Ground troops occupied Guilin and Nanning in November of that year.[9]

The war significantly affected the missionaries and their stations. When fighting broke out in 1937, a number of Church Missionary Society missionaries left the field. From October 1941 to July 1945, publication of their Guangxi-Hunan newsletter came to a halt due to the unreliable postal services caused by the war.

The Oldfields shared some of the CMA's struggles during the war. Mrs. Oldfield reflected in her autobiography, "Our fifth term on the field [beginning in 1938] was to be a stormy one."[10] Her husband Walter, chairman of the CMA in South China at the time, wrote, "Our work and workers in the affected areas are suffering considerably. In the center of the province our work is in complete confusion."[11] In 1943, he noted that the work in Nanning had been at a standstill.[12] During the war, the CMA relocated their headquarters from Wuzhou to Liuzhou. They also sought to keep the Wuzhou Bible School operational. It lost many students who were conscripted

---

6. Bacon, "1930 in the Kweilin Hospital."
7. CMA, "Department of Prayer" (September 27, 1941).
8. Oldfield, "South China under Air Attack."
9. Hutchings, "A Province at War."
10. Oldfield, *With You Alway*, 219.
11. Oldfield, "In the Midst of Alarms," 312.
12. Oldfield, "Our Foreign Mail Bag" (January 23, 1943).

into the army while other students were cut off financially.[13] At one point, the school relocated to a Christian village in Longzhou. However, when bandits began targeting the students, they moved to Jingxi.[14]

Obtaining medicine and supplies posed a great difficulty for the hospitals and medical missionaries. Certain missionaries risked trips through Japanese lines in order to secure medicines. Southern Baptist Rex Ray seemed to delight in these "blockade running" adventures to get medical supplies. He always returned, but when CMS missionary in Guilin Dr. Graham Watt left in the fall of 1941, the Japanese caught him in Hong Kong and placed him in an internment camp.[15]

Nearly all missionaries left their posts at some point during Japanese ground invasions. In Guilin, evacuations were ordered in June and September 1944.[16] Three Maryknollers were still in the city when the Japanese arrived, but they jumped on their bicycles and escaped. All fourteen Maryknoll Fathers in and around Guilin were ultimately driven out.[17] CMA missionaries in the western city of Jingxi, seeing less action than in other cities, were the last to evacuate, leaving December 4, 1944.[18]

By the summer of 1945, the Japanese had departed Guilin, only the second provincial capital taken back by the Chinese.[19] Jean-Paul Wiest commended American Catholics for their wartime service:

> One of the best testimonials Maryknollers gave of their dedication to the Chinese of South China was their decision to remain with them through the war years. Instead of yielding to the advice of the American consul-general in Canton to evacuate, Maryknollers chose to stay in their missions. From September 1937, when Japanese shelling and bombing started along the coastal area of Kwangtung [Guangdong], until December 8, 1941, Maryknollers kept all their missions open. They stayed at their posts in spite of all the difficulties. Instead of curtailing their work because of the Japanese invasion, Maryknollers shouldered more responsibility, accepting the administration of Kweilin [Guilin] prefecture and increasing the number of personnel in Kwangtung and Kwangsi. Between 1937 and 1941, the

13. Oldfield, "Challenges, Opportunities, and Privileges," "Last Minute Foreign News."

14. Oldfield, *With You Alway.*

15. Stevens, "Outline of Events," 8–14.

16. Stevens, "Outline of Events."

17. Wiest, *Maryknoll in China.*

18. CMA, "Work and Workers" (May 5, 1945).

19. Stevens, "Bishop's Foreword" (July 1945), 2–4.

number of Fathers and Brothers expanded from 75 to 97 and the Sisters from 28 to 38.[20]

Before Japan surrendered, CMA missionary in Guangxi William C. Newbern said that he believed Americans would be victorious over the Japanese for the express purpose of world evangelization. He called for Christians to be ready for a window of opportunity to bring Christ to China's millions:

> To the fundamental, missionary-minded churches in America and Great Britain especially, the Holy Spirit is sounding forth the Macedonian call of an unevangelized China. V-E and V-J Days to the Church represent the committing, by a just and loving God, of a sacred trust—the final evangelization of the world.[21]

The end of the war brought tremendous opportunity and wide-open doors. Death, turmoil, and destruction opened the hearts of the people in unprecedented ways. The CMA reported one of its most fruitful years with its second highest number of baptisms ever.[22]

A number of missionaries who left during the war returned afterward to engage in rebuilding efforts. Unfortunately, the period of peace did not last long. With Japan out of the picture, fighting between Nationalists and Communists again took center stage beginning in 1947. By the following year, the number of Church Missionary Society communicants had decreased by 50 percent and two of their Chinese workers had been killed.[23] The year 1949 marked the fiftieth anniversary of their Guangxi-Hunan mission. They had much to reflect on and celebrate since the days that Louis Byrde had lived on a boat and served the people of Guilin. A grand celebration was in the making for this jubilee year; however, the civil war between the Nationalists and Communists interrupted their plans and the highly-anticipated event sadly never took place.

By the second half of 1949, the Red Army had won victory on the mainland. On October 1, 1949, Mao Zedong formally declared their triumph and the founding of the People's Republic of China. The Communists took control of the country, confiscated mission property, and began to expel foreign missionaries. The Church Missionary Society appointed a

---

20. Wiest, *Maryknoll in China*, 362.
21. Newbern, "Custodians of the Unfinished Task," 202.
22. Oldfield, "God's Grace in Kwangsi."
23. Stevens, "Notes of the Bishop's Address."

Chinese bishop in 1950 and all their foreign missionaries were gone by the end of the year.[24] Bishop Stevens wrote,

> And now (December, 1950) there are no missionaries left in the diocese. Is this a matter to be wept over? If we recollect that missionaries went out to preach the Gospel to win converts, and so to found a Church, then we may, in a sense, regard them as scaffolding. We can truly rejoice that the building in Kwangsi-Hunan can now stand without that scaffolding.[25]

Other missionaries and their societies met the same fate, although some later than others. Mr. and Mrs. Kowles (CMA) did not seek permission to leave Guangxi for Hong Kong until early 1951.[26] The Southern Baptists wrote in their annual report from 1952, "For the first time in more than a hundred years, there is now not one Southern Baptist missionary in the field of China proper."[27] An era in the history of missions in Guangxi had come to an end.

24. Stevens, "Peeps into the Past."

25. Stevens, "Peeps into the Past," 20.

26. CMA, "Everywhere Preaching." Yan stated that the last CMA missionary left in April, 1952. Yan, *Guangxi.*

27. SBC, *Annual 1952,* 155.

6

Inter-Societal and Missionary Relations

WHEN HEARING OF THE various missionary societies in Guangxi from different countries of origin and diverse theological persuasions, one may wonder how they related to one another. Were they friendly, divisive, competitive, or did they simply ignore each other? Rev. Gray, CMS missionary in Guilin, said in 1934, "Contrary to what several friends of mine in England have imagined, ancient denominational rivalries here are far from dead—more alive in some quarters than in England, and are a deadweight against advance."[1]

While this was true to an extent, the bulk of evidence from the literature indicates friendly relations between missionaries of different societies. On numerous occasions, missionaries traveled together, prayed together, and showed hospitality toward one another. Here is a sampling:

- When the first CMA (American) missionaries went to Guangxi, they did so in conjunction with the National Bible Society of Scotland.[2]

- Southern Baptist Rex Ray traveled upriver from Wuzhou to Guilin with three Alliance missionaries when Guilin was under siege.[3]

- Dr. and Mrs. Clift of the Emmanuel Medical Mission (British) hosted a missionary of Church Missionary Society (British).[4]

---

1. Gray, "Parish of Kweilin," 14.
2. Oldfield, *Pioneering in Kwangsi*.
3. Ray, *Cowboy Missionary in Kwangsi*.
4. Clift, *Very Far East*.

- Southern Baptists attended the wedding of two CMA missionaries. They also hosted a luncheon and New Year's meeting for the CMA.[5]

- CMA missionaries welcomed Dr. and Mrs. Clift of the Emmanuel Medical Mission when they visited Wuzhou.[6]

- English Wesleyans in Wuzhou welcomed English Presbyterian, CMS, and CMA missionaries on their visits.[7]

- Mr. and Mrs. Oldfield were "welcomed warmly" by the China Inland Mission in Shanghai when returning from furlough.[8] Mrs. Oldfield also noted, "Our relationship with the CIM was always very cordial."[9]

In Guilin, the CMS and CMA displayed particularly warm relations. Some of their missionaries enjoyed tea time together.[10] After Dr. Charlotte Bacon's (CMS) husband was shot and killed, she stayed with the widow of a CMA missionary.[11] These two societies also had a comity agreement whereby they chose different sections of Guilin in which to work.[12] Louis Byrde commented on the relationship between CMS and CMA missionaries in Guilin before the Boxer Rebellion: "Thus we were a party of missionaries of various persuasions, living and working most harmoniously together, and these relations have been consistently maintained ever since, though of course we now have our distinct spheres of work."[13]

While it is impossible to track the history, duration, and involvement of prayer meetings in Guangxi, here is a sampling of the meetings that occurred throughout the years in Guilin:

- The CMA and Emmanuel Medical Mission held a bi-weekly prayer meeting on Wednesday nights.[14]

---

5. Oldfield, *With You Alway.*

6. Clift, *Very Far East.*

7. "Our mutual joys and sorrows cemented friendships that will never be forgotten." Macdonald, *Roderick Macdonald, M.D.*, 167. Fulton, *Inasmuch*; CMS, *Church Missionary Gleaner*; Macdonald, *Roderick Macdonald, M.D.*

8. Oldfield, *With You Alway*, 246.

9. Oldfield, *With You Alway*, 240.

10. Bacon, "Slowly Onward."

11. CMA, "Joseph R. Cunningham."

12. China Continuation Committee, *Christian Occupation*, 149.

13. Byrde, "How We Escaped in 1900," 9.

14. Clift, *Very Far East.*

- Various missionaries gathered on Monday afternoons to pray for God's Spirit to be poured out on the city and district.[15]

- The CMS, Baptists, and the independent Chinese church met on Friday evening to "remember God's glory and China's need."[16]

Catholic relationships with Protestants proved a bit thornier. Catholics expressed grief over losing their Christians to the Protestants despite Catholics having arrived in Guangxi first.[17] Southern Baptists reported an issue between Baptists and Catholics over the distribution of relief supplies in Wuzhou.[18] Americans Catholics (Maryknoll) depended on the Stout Memorial Hospital in Wuzhou for medical care, but it was said that no close relationships had ever developed with the missionaries there.[19] While "close" did not describe Protestant-Catholic relations, they were at times quite friendly. Catholics presented Mrs. Child of the Church Missionary Society a snow-white rabbit in her early days in Guilin.[20] On one occasion, as bandits were approaching, Catholic priests wrote to two American women in a Protestant mission, offering them rooms at the Catholic mission.[21] In Wuzhou, French Catholic priests attended Dr. Macdonald's funeral and burial service to "mark their esteem for one who had won their hearts by his Christian sympathy and professional services to Roman Catholic missionaries of the Kwang Si Province."[22] Even with the slightly more estranged relationship between Protestants and Catholics, as a whole, the letters, biographies, and records show few instances of conflict, slander, or contempt. On the contrary, they evidence many cases of cordial relations between societies and their missionaries in Guangxi.[23]

15. Watkins, "Changes."

16. Leach, "Our Doings and Mis-Doings," 16.

17. See end of chapter 9.

18. SBC, *Annual 1940*.

19. Fletcher, *Bill Wallace of China*, 79–80.

20. Child, "Everyday Life at Kueilin," 48.

21. Cuenot, *Kwangsi*, 227.

22. Macdonald, *Roderick Macdonald, M.D.*, 266.

23. Of course, this does not rule out the possibility that such instances of conflict, slander, or contempt might have gone unmentioned.

7

Notable Missionaries

ROBERT JAFFRAY

ONE OF THE MOST influential Alliance missionaries in Guangxi was Robert Jaffray.[1] Jaffray was a Canadian from good stock. His father was the owner of the Toronto *Globe* and it was said that Robert "had been reared in an atmosphere never free of the smell of printer's ink."[2] Following his teenage conversion, he traveled to hear A. B. Simpson speak where he was influenced by Simpson's passion for missions. He attended the Missionary Training Institute in New York and was sent to South China after his graduation in 1897.[3]

Jaffray first went to Guangxi in 1899, just two years after Wuzhou opened and had a resident foreign missionary. Wuzhou became his base for the next thirty-five years. Jaffray served as principal of the Wuzhou Bible School,[4] his first role in the country. Unsurprisingly, and true to his roots, he later set up a printing press in Wuzhou, the South China Alliance Press, which distributed literature widely throughout the Orient. By 1922, the press had printed some five million pages, and the *Bible Magazine*, which

---

1. Blue, "Jaffray, Robert A."
2. Tozer, *Let My People Go*, Kindle Location 282.
3. Poston, "Jaffray, Robert (1873–1945)."
4. It was founded by Robert H. Glover.

made Jaffray known to a much wider audience, boasted a circulation of three thousand.[5]

Being an adept spiritual leader, Jaffray became the new superintendent of the French Indochina[6] field. His headquarters remained in Wuzhou, but his new role required considerable travel. By 1927, he no longer felt that his work in South China was necessary; he believed Chinese Christians could carry on without foreign help. He remained the chairman of South China but turned his attention to the East Indies, Borneo, Celebes, Malaysia, the Philippines, and other locations in the Pacific.[7] Many students who studied at the Wuzhou Bible School were sent to these locations as missionaries. In 1930, Jaffray withdrew as chairman of South China to focus on his extensive publication work and to superintend the Alliance work in the Dutch East Indies.[8] Mrs. Oldfield, whose husband Walter succeeded Jaffray as chairman, exclaimed, "The exit of the gigantic spirit of Dr. R. A. Jaffray from South China left a great gap which Walter [Oldfield] was asked to fill. But who could!"[9]

During the Sino-Japanese War (1937–1945), Jaffray allowed Alliance missionaries to return to the United States if they desired to do so. He was personally unwilling to leave, however, as long as a single Alliance missionary remained on the field. This was a costly decision. He was captured by the Japanese and imprisoned in a camp on the Indonesian island of Sulawesi,[10] where he died in a weakened, starving state. A. W. Tozer, the famous Christian and Missionary Alliance preacher, wrote Robert Jaffray's biography in 1948.[11]

REX RAY

One Southern Baptist who made his home in Guangxi was Rex Ray, a native of north-central Texas. In his 1964 autobiography *Cowboy Missionary in Kwangsi*, he tells of many storybook-like incidents he faced in his twenty years in Wuzhou. On one occasion (1924), the city of Guilin was under siege with four missionaries trapped inside. Famine conditions arose and people

---

5. China Continuation Committee, *Christian Occupation*, 153.

6. Today's Vietnam.

7. Oldfield, *With You Alway*, 202.

8. CMA, "Change of the Chairmanship."

9. Oldfield, *With You Alway*, 202.

10. Formerly called Celebes.

11. Tozer, *Let My People Go*.

began consuming anything edible, including dogs, cats, and horses.[12] Mr. Ray and three Alliance missionaries decided to travel upriver to Guilin to assist. On the way, they were captured by bandits and marched deep into the mountains where their captors held them for ransom. Two were released to return to Wuzhou with orders to obtain the ransom money while Ray and the other missionary remained as collateral. The two men returning to Wuzhou were unable to secure the ransom money as they were again kidnapped on the way! Ray could do nothing but endure three weeks of limited food as he was marched through the mountains. When he was no longer able to tolerate it, he feigned exhaustion and laid down. The bandits left him momentarily when he fled and managed to get back to safety.[13]

In the 1920s, Rex Ray escaped another crisis when the Communists arrived in Guangxi. He made his way back to the States where he stayed for two years. When he returned to Guangxi, he brought a large tent that had been given to him by his uncle. He spent the next few years traveling around eastern Guangxi holding evangelistic tent meetings. In 1930, he lost one of his daughters to a fever, but that did not deter this "cowboy missionary" and his tenacity to proclaim the gospel to Guangxi's people.

Wherever Mr. Ray went, he distributed literature. Despite the low literacy rate, this did have an effect as illustrated by an encounter he had with a Chinese Christian:

> Oh, you must be missionary Rex Ray. I saw you in the book store. I bought a New Testament there and took it home with me and read it. Now I believe in Jesus and I taught my family and they too believe. We have told others who have believed, until there are forty or fifty people who want to be baptized and form a church.[14]

In the early 1930s, Ray crossed paths with a famous Chinese evangelist who visited Wuzhou. Not mentioning a name, he wrote that this preacher was from northern China, had received his PhD in the United States, and was pronounced crazy while at Union Theological Seminary. Rex Ray was referring to none other than the famous Chinese evangelist John Sung who traveled with the Bethel

---

12. Oldfield, *Pioneering in Kwangsi.*

13. The other missionary was released on a four thousand dollar ransom. After that incident, Chinese soldiers entered the bandit territory and executed some four hundred of them. Ray, *Cowboy Missionary in Kwangsi.*

14. Ray, *Cowboy Missionary in Kwangsi,* 38.

Worldwide Evangelistic Band. In 1932, from late March to early April, the band's members preached in Wuzhou, Guigang, and Yulin.[15]

In 1935, the Ray family returned to China after furlough, this time bringing a car, a Ford V-8, with them. Their new transportation and the newly built roads provided opportunities for a wider scope of evangelism.[16]

In the late thirties and early forties, Ray barely survived the air raids by Japanese planes. Wuzhou was in crisis and the Stout Memorial (Baptist) Hospital in Wuzhou became one of the safest bomb shelters in the city. The Southern Baptists set up a soup kitchen behind their church and Ray did likewise at his place of residence. During one period, he did not see his family for four or five years as they stayed in the U.S. due to the war. His ministry during the famine-like war conditions took its toll. He was told by a doctor that his body had entered a state of starvation and that he needed to return home immediately for treatment. Leaving China, however, was no easy task since Japan controlled most of the coastal waters. Ray managed to hitch rides and flights with whomever he could, including the U.S. Army, and arrived back in Texas in 1944. After recuperating, he again returned to his field in Guangxi. In 1949, Ray left China for good when the Communists took over the country. He was able to catch the last train to Hong Kong before Guangzhou was taken. After his departure from China, he relocated to Korea where he resumed missionary service.

RHODA WATKINS

Rhoda Watkins spent over twenty-five years of her life in Guilin. She was a shy, South Australian country girl sent by the Church Missionary Society. In Guilin, she served as a nurse in the Way of Life Hospital which CMS medical missionary Dr. Charlotte Bacon had established. When Dr. Bacon was away on furlough, Rhoda became the hospital's matron and director. During her time in Guangxi, she lived through three calamitous periods and one particularly nerve-wracking experience. Once when returning from furlough,[17] she was traveling by river back to Guilin with Blanche Tobin, a missionary from New Zealand.[18] Pirates attacked their boat, kidnapped Rhoda, Blanche, and the two daughters of the Chinese boat captain, and fled

15. Lyall, "Biography of John Sung"; Oldfield, *With You Alway*.

16. Oldfield in *Pioneering in Kwangsi* also noted the rapid communication of the gospel taking place due to the roads.

17. In 1928.

18. She was with the Church of England Zenana Mission Society (CEZMS). Cunich, *Women Missionaries*.

with them into the mountains. Rhoda's white dress looked too conspicuous to the bandits so they made her put on her thick winter coat with its fur collar. Rhoda only walked a short way when the bandits released her to obtain the ransom money while they held Blanche hostage. Rhoda made it back to safety, but it took six weeks of searching and negotiations with the bandits before Blanche and one of the captain's daughters were released. The second daughter was never seen again. Rhoda said, "The whole thing seemed like an evil dream."[19]

In 1925, following an incident in which Chinese protestors were shot and killed under orders from British officers in Shanghai, students took to the streets of Guilin. They approached the house of a CMS missionary couple, grabbed them, marched them through the street, and placed them in an office where they were held. The students were aware that other foreigners were at the hospital and quickly proceeded there. Rhoda locked herself in the hospital and prayed. At night, she was escorted in a covered sedan chair to the American mission on the other side of the city. The couple held hostage in the office was later released. They departed Guilin with Rhoda for three months and returned when the situation had cooled down.

During the Sino-Japanese War, Rhoda and the Way of Life Hospital endured numerous trials. Japanese planes attacked and bombed the city multiple times. In the caves in the mountains near the hospital, they set up a makeshift maternity ward where a number of babies were born during the war.[20] In 1944, when the Japanese army was only a few days away from the city, Rhoda and Dr. Bacon evacuated Guilin. After the Japanese arrived, they destroyed nearly all of Guilin and left the Way of Life Hospital in ruins.

Rhoda returned to Guilin after the war where she directed the reconstruction of the Way of Life Hospital. The project required a tremendous amount of human labor as well as millions in Chinese currency. Still, the walls and doors of the little hospital gradually were rebuilt as money came in from various sources. Rhoda took encouragement from Nehemiah who had returned to a defeated Jerusalem to rebuild its crumbled walls.

As soon as life and the medical ministry at the hospital returned to a degree of normalcy, the Nationalists and Communists resumed fighting. The Way of Life Hospital began to see more and more refugees come from Communist-occupied territories. In June of 1949, a directive came from CMS headquarters telling the missionaries and their families to prepare to return home. On October 1 in Beijing, Mao Zedong declared that the Nationalists had been defeated and proclaimed the founding of the People's

19. Watkins, "In Peril of Robbers," 846.
20. Bacon, "Way of Life Hospital."

Republic of China. Rhoda and Blanche remained at their posts, however, until they were the only two foreigners remaining in Guilin. Despite their anxious anticipation, they watched the Communists quietly come into Guilin on friendly terms. After the initial relief, however, the situation began to tense up. Soldiers started to visit the hospital and search for signs of insubordination. They questioned the staff endlessly and required the completion of a vast number of forms. Day-to-day hospital work became increasingly difficult. In addition, there was always a concern that the medical supplies and the silver used to pay the workers would be found and confiscated. Despite the trials, these conditions did allow the opportunity for some unlikely people to hear Good News. On one occasion, Rhoda received a visit from some soldiers:

> "Whose house is this?" they asked.
>
> "It is my house," Rhoda replied.
>
> "How long have you been here?" the young leader asked her.
>
> Rhoda looked straight at him. "I have been here twenty-eight years," she said. "Were any of you here then?"
>
> The young man looked disconcerted, then pointed to another. "He is twenty-eight," he said.
>
> "Why are you here?" one asked her curiously.
>
> "We believe in a God who sent His Son into our world to die for our sins," Rhoda told him. "He told us to go into all the world and preach the good news, to teach and heal the people. I belong to the healing group. Miss [Blanche] Tobin is a teacher."
>
> The young soldiers accepted her explanation rather incredulously and filed out again. As they went the two women heard scraps of their conversation. "She was quite polite," one of them remarked. Another mused, "Twenty-eight years! Why, our movement began then. It's a lifetime!"[21]

When America and China became involved in the Korean conflict in 1950, the CMS again wrote to Rhoda urging her to take an immediate furlough. This time, she sensed her time in China had come to an end. She exchanged tearful goodbyes with her friends and colleagues in Guilin and sailed back to Australia. After a season of rest and restoration, Rhoda relocated to Malaysia where she served for five years as a missionary. Eventually, she contracted Parkinson's Disease which led to her permanent return to Australia and brought her service with the CMS to an end. She was later

---

21. Caterer, *Foreigner in Kweilin*, 120.

presented with the Church Missionary Society's highest honor, the Honorary Life Governor Award.[22]

WALTER OLDFIELD

Walter Herbert Oldfield[23] was born in 1879 in Belleville, Ontario, Canada. He gave his life to the Lord at the age of seventeen and later attended the Missionary Training Institute in Nyack, NY. In 1903, he was ordained and sent to China from the Alliance Tabernacle of Toronto. He began studying Chinese in Guangxi's Pingle County (in Guilin Shi).[24] Following language studies, he relocated to Liuzhou where he started a church. Mr. Oldfield became the head of the Alliance station in Liuzhou which he used as his base for sending out colporteurs and his trips into the more neglected parts of Guangxi. In 1907, his fiancée, Beulah Funk, "always bright and cheery, full of fun and zest,"[25] died of pneumonia.[26] Following the trial, he began to feel a kinship with Mabel Dimock Sherman (CMA) whose husband had died in Guangxi only a month after their wedding.[27] The two were married in Hong Kong in 1910.

Over the next five years, Mrs. Oldfield bore two children, Mildred and Ernest. The kids both battled sickness and at various times, one or both contracted (and survived) bronchial pneumonia, dysentery, malaria, whooping cough, and German measles.[28] Around 1920, the Oldfields were ready to move into the more neglected northwest region of Guangxi. When they had arrived in Liuzhou, there were only four Christians; now there were one hundred as well as a self-supporting, self-governing church. The Oldfields relocated to Qingyuan in Hechi, a three day's journey from Liuzhou. There, they called their dwelling the "Black Hole of Kingyuen [Qingyuan]."[29] In 1922, Mr. Oldfield was kidnapped, robbed, and marched into the mountains. However, when some local soldiers made his captors scurry, he managed to escape.

Mr. Oldfield was at times called upon to serve as a peacemaker for the warring factions in Guangxi. On one occasion, he was presented with

22. Caterer, *Foreigner in Kweilin*.
23. His Chinese name was Chan Fat Yin. Oldfield, *With You Alway*.
24. Hess, "Immediate Evangelization of the World."
25. Oldfield, *With You Alway*, 81.
26. Oldfield, *With You Alway*.
27. Oldfield, *With You Alway*.
28. Oldfield, *With You Alway*.
29. Oldfield, *With You Alway*, 136.

a gold medal for his role in negotiating with the enemy forces who had besieged Liuzhou. By risking his own life, hundreds of Liuzhou residents were spared.[30] In 1929, Mr. Oldfield, due to his extensive travel throughout Guangxi, was honored by the Royal Geographic Society of London with a fellowship. The following year, he succeeded Robert Jaffray as chairman of the South China Mission.[31]

As chairman, Walter Oldfield visited every station in Guangxi at least once a year.[32] He also embarked on regular pioneering trips deep into Guangxi. On one trip, his small boat became the target of a raid while traveling downriver. He and the boatmen hurried to the other side of the river but were chased by the robbers. Oldfield found a hiding spot in some tall grass where he watched the robbers seize his possessions on the boat. He grieved most that they stole his down comforter, his "warm friend" which "had done its best to keep me warm during many a cold night as I have traveled throughout the province." Worse, it had "gone—gone to keep warm a cruel robber."[33] By 1932, including his prior kidnapping, he had been attacked by robbers at least half a dozen times.

Mr. Oldfield lived in Guangxi for over thirty years without any major health issues. But in 1943, probably as a result of the war with Japan, he and his wife began suffering from dysentery and malnutrition.[34] The Oldfields returned to Canada thinking they were saying their final goodbyes to China. However, they both recovered and the two sixty-eight-year-olds returned in 1946 after World War II to direct the rebuilding of Alliance chapels and establishments which had been destroyed by the Japanese. The following year, their health again took a decline and they returned to Canada, this time for good.

In total, Walter Oldfield spent nearly forty years of his life in Guangxi, spread out over six terms. Perhaps more than any other missionary in Guangxi, Oldfield was burdened for the "tribes" (today's "minorities") in the neglected areas of Guangxi where the gospel had not been proclaimed. He was the first to visit many of those tribes as he traveled thousands of miles on foot and horseback. His wife wrote, "Many of the younger missionaries were moved to emulate him, but none were able to outwalk him or outdo

---

30. CMA, "Other Honorees." This seemingly took place in 1922. Oldfield, *With You Alway.*

31. CMA, "Change in the Chairmanship."

32. Oldfield, *With You Alway.*

33. Oldfield, "Attacked by Chinese Robbers," 42.

34. Oldfield, *With You Alway.*

him in his efforts to carry the Gospel into 'the regions beyond.'"[35] Oldfield was also a gifted communicator, having "rare powers of description" and a "keen sense of humor."[36] On furloughs, he frequently spoke at conventions and conferences. His two books, *Kidnapped by Chinese Bandits* (1930) and *Pioneering in Kwangsi* (1936), were widely circulated among Christian and Missionary Alliance churches.[37]

BILL WALLACE

William L. Wallace was born in Knoxville, TN in 1908. His mother died of influenza when he was only eleven. Tall and skinny, his family called him William but most of his adult friends called him Bill. He was quiet by nature and excelled in all things mechanical. He had always assumed he would attend a trade school and become a mechanic. But at the age of seventeen, he sensed the call of God to become a medical missionary. He completed his pre-med studies at the University of Tennessee and later received his MD from the University Medical School in Memphis.

While a resident in Knoxville's General Hospital, Southern Baptist medical missionary Robert Beddoe wrote from the Stout Memorial Hospital in Wuzhou appealing for a surgeon. Shortly after, the Foreign Mission Board of the Southern Baptist Convention received a letter from Bill Wallace indicating his desire to apply as a medical missionary. The Foreign Mission Board saw this as God's answer to Dr. Beddoe's request and Bill was appointed to China in July 1935. He set sail from San Francisco in September.

Dr. Wallace spent a year studying Cantonese in Guangzhou and began his work at the Stout Memorial Hospital the following year. After he joined the hospital, the number of patients went up 50 percent and two families were saved. An example of his character and style was recounted in his biography:

> Dr. Wallace came up one day when a hospital nurse was arguing with two orderlies about the removal of a body. Highly superstitious and convinced that such work was coolie labor,

35. Oldfield, *With You Alway*, 216.

36. Fant, "Publisher's Column," 468.

37. Sources: CMA, "Our Foreign Mail Bag" (October 5, 1918), "Last Minute Foreign News," "Personalia," "Work and Workers" (February 23, 1946), "The Alliance Family: With the Lord," "Other Honorees," "New York, October 1, 1904," "Editorials" (June 21, 1924); Fant, "In Memoriam"; Jaffray, "The Gospel in Foreign Lands," "A General Resume"; Oldfield, "In the Hands of Chinese Robbers," "Attacked by Chinese Robbers," "Pioneering in Kwang Si's Neglected Territory" (August 4, 1928); Snead, "Rev. A. F. Desterhaft," "Walter H. Oldfield: Modern Pioneer."

the orderlies were refusing the task. Dr. Wallace caught the drift of the conversation, picked up the body in his arms, and then walked past the open-mouthed orderlies, down to the morgue. It was the last time a Stout Memorial orderly ever refused to carry a body. If the great doctor could do this, surely it was not beneath them! Drawn by the winsomeness of the doctor's humility and dedication, the Chinese followed him in a way which enabled the hospital to do an excellent job.[38]

Dr. Wallace carried out his first two years of ministry in Guangxi during a time of peace. In October 1937, the American consul urged the hospital staff to evacuate due to anticipated attacks by the Japanese. However, Bill and the hospital staff put the situation before the Lord and decided to stay. The first aid raid came two months later[39] when the Japanese bombed the Wuzhou airport. Additional air raids came the following year in February, late May (or early June), and September. These created an endless supply of patients for the small staff at the Stout Memorial Hospital. However, for Bill, "the busier and more demanding the times, the greater was his sense of fulfillment."[40] Bill treated countless burned and maimed victims as well as those visiting for normal non-wartime ailments. The Stout Memorial Hospital came to mean "the life of China" to Wuzhou's people.[41]

Dr. Wallace returned to Knoxville for a furlough where he took some advanced medical courses, developed an interest in a young lady, and, being a poor public speaker,[42] painfully endured a couple of speaking engagements. Despite having renounced all worldly fame to a small corner of China, he was nonetheless elected as a fellow in the International College of Surgeons. He felt it best not to advance the relationship with the young lady due to the war in China, and he returned to China on his own.

In 1944, the Japanese launched an all-out offensive against China. Air raids occurred almost daily and the hospital staff pushed themselves to the limit to treat the endless number of sick and wounded. In June, the regional director of the Southern Baptist Convention's Foreign Mission Board cabled Dr. Beddoe, asking him to urge all missionaries to evacuate Wuzhou. Dr. Wallace prayed, put the matter before God, and again decided to stay. Bill and the hospital staff did, however, take the hospital equipment and relocate

---

38. Fletcher, *Bill Wallace of China*, 58

39. In December 19, 1937 according to Fletcher, *Bill Wallace of China*.

40. Fletcher, *Bill Wallace of China*, 59.

41. Fletcher, *Bill Wallace of China*, 57, 87.

42. "No one was more aware than Bill Wallace that when God passed out gifts, public speaking was not one of those that came his way." Fletcher, *Bill Wallace of China*, 64.

to a less dangerous part of Guangxi. They navigated the river system, pass-ing through Nanning and into Baise where they set up a makeshift hospital in an empty Confucian temple believed to be inhabited by demons. Bill's mechanical skills were put to good use as he made various contraptions to transport all the equipment through rapids and other difficult sections of the river. They remained in western Guangxi until the end of the war was in sight and then made the river voyage with equipment back to Wu-zhou. Upon returning, they first renovated the old hospital which had been completely destroyed and had even served as a stall for the Japanese army's horses.

For the next few years after the war, the Stout Memorial Hospital, "the life of China," carried out its operations without interruption. Bill made another trip back to the U.S. where he took more medical courses and saw the young lady he had last seen five years before. However, both seemed to sense that she did not have the same calling to missionary life that he had, and he again returned to China a single man.

In 1947, Dr. Beddoe retired leaving Bill with the role of hospital su-perintendent, an administrative position which he never wanted nor felt prepared for. However, the hospital fared well under his leadership. He re-ported back as its superintendent,

> Every effort has been put forth to fulfill the mission of this hos-pital. The blind receive their sight and the halt [crippled] and lame walk; the lepers are cleansed; the deaf hear and the poor have the gospel preached to them. It is our hope and prayer that the medical service in this institution shall be on that high plane befitting the glorious gospel which is preached daily within its walls.[43]

Unfortunately, the following year Bill himself became seriously ill, having contracted paratyphoid which had been widespread in Wuzhou the previous year. Despite being close to death and not having any treatment available, the fever finally broke and he pulled through. While he escaped this trial, another was coming which brought Bill's ministry and the Stout Memorial Hospital to an end.

In the first half of 1949, Communists began to encroach on southern China. CMA missionaries in Wuzhou were ordered to leave Guangxi while

---

43. Fletcher, *Bill Wallace of China*, 109. "He counted medical skills and drugs as God-given resources, but never as the only resources when sickness came. Too many of his cases had inexplicably responded in the face of what seemed inevitable death, for him not to believe firmly in that power just beyond man's exploring fingertips, available only through faith." Fletcher, *Bill Wallace of China*, 110.

the Foreign Mission Board (SBC) left the decision up to each individual missionary. Five missionaries decided to depart while three stayed. Bill, of course, was among the latter. In July, adversity came when the West River flooded in Wuzhou. This brought a new wave of injuries and diseases for the hospital to treat. However, the flooding and its aftermath kept their minds from the approaching Communists. In October, all concern was directed to the Communists. At the time, Wuzhou was the last Southern Baptist station in China that had not been occupied by them. The "Reds" finally came. They first tried to win people's confidence and allowed the hospital to carry out its services. But soon enough, the atmosphere changed. They began making demands on the hospital; they asked for it to house soldiers, required nurses to attend Communist parades, and even imposed a heavy tax. Bill saw an unusual number of stomach ulcer cases during this time.

Before long, Bill himself became the target. A group of Communists came to the hospital and accused him of being a spy for President Truman. A gun was planted in his living quarters as evidence. He was arrested and placed in a prison by the bank of the river where two or three Catholics missionaries were also being held. His captors interrogated him and frequently accused him of incompetence in surgery and of other "crimes" such as performing illegal surgeries and murdering Chinese patients. At night, guards came to his cell with poles to prod and jab him, sometimes to the point of unconsciousness. On one such occasion, something went wrong under this treatment and Bill died at the age of forty-three. The next morning, his body was seen hanging from a beam. The guards claimed that he had hanged himself, but others suspected it was staged since he did not have the physical indications of having been hanged.[44]

Bill Wallace's life had ended, but he was not forgotten. The Chinese remembered him as one who loved and sacrificially served them. In contrast to many other foreigners, they felt that he was similar to them and willing to live and serve on their level. They placed Dr. Wallace's name on a couple of institutions to honor him. Rex Ray, who relocated his ministry to Korea, established the Wallace Memorial Baptist Hospital in the second largest city of Busan. Back in Knoxville, the Wallace Memorial Baptist Church was established and grew to over a thousand members a dozen years after Bill's death.

44. Hefley, *By Their Blood*.

8

Mission to Specific Population Segments

Minorities and Students

MINORITIES

ETHNIC MINORITIES HAVE RESIDED in Guangxi for centuries. Walter Oldfield gave one main reason for their presence: "Tribe after tribe was gradually defeated and finally they were driven back further and further into the wild mountain territories where today they have their homes."[1] The mountains provided security and autonomy for these smaller populations who lacked strength in numbers. Due to the difficulty of outsiders traversing the mountains, they could expect minimal intrusion and could live their lives as they pleased. The mountainous terrain, however, made farming difficult, and there was little incentive to create homes in the mountains from an economic or agricultural standpoint. Mrs. Oldfield noted that corn was their staple food and rice considered a luxury.[2]

The missionaries spoke of these minorities numerous times, calling them "tribes," "tribesmen," and "aborigines."[3] However, little dedicated outreach took place among them. The China Inland Mission's periodical

1. Oldfield, *Pioneering in Kwangsi*, 37.

2. Oldfield, *With You Alway*.

3. One of the oldest references (1850) used the word "savages" but that was not common. Staunton, *Miscellaneous Notices*, 333.

China's Millions mentioned three minorities: the Miao, Lolo, and Zhuang. However, regarding outreach it mentioned, "Among these people very little if any missionary work has been done, except by French Roman Catholic missionaries who have reduced one or two of the tribal languages to writing."[4] Alliance missionary Ada Farmer independently stated the same thing: "With the exception of the efforts of Roman Catholic missionaries, nothing worth mentioning has yet been done to bring to these tribes the knowledge of the Lord Jesus Christ."[5] The neglect was not due to oversight, however. The chairman of the Guangxi Chinese Alliance wrote in 1937,

> In these days when the Lord's return is so near, the taking of the gospel to the unevangelized areas is of prime importance. The tribesmen, Yao, Miao, Chwang [Zhuang], and Tong [Dong], and those living in mountain fastnesses [remote and secluded places] and hitherto unpenetrated areas, who are at present without the gospel, must be reached; therefore we regard the taking of the gospel to these people to be of utmost importance.[6]

If this was such an important task, why was it not carried out? The problem seems to have been twofold: inaccessibility and a shortage of laborers. Many of these minorities lived well beyond river access, where, for the most part, the missionaries were concentrated in the port cities and towns. In addition, and in spite of the overwhelming needs, the sobering reality was that missionaries were in short supply. CMS missionary Elsie Holden compared a field of ministry in Guangxi to that in England:

> A "parish" to dwellers in England suggests either a section of a town, the whole of a country village, or possibly two of the latter at the most. Out here in China, where "the labourers are few," this term has to be expanded to include sometimes more than one "county."[7]

Zhuang

The Zhuang[8] minority was referred to most often in the literature, understandably so since they were also the largest. Today, Guangxi's official

---

4. CIM, *China's Millions*, 4.

5. Farmer, *Ada Beeson Farmer*, 57.

6. Chao, "A Unique Memorial," 327.

7. Holden, "Touring in the Chuanchow Parish," 8. A county included multiple towns and villages.

8. Pronounced *jwong* and commonly Romanized as the *Chwang(s)*, *Chuang(s)*, or *Chung-chia*.

name, the Guangxi Zhuang Autonomous Region, takes its name from this minority. Accurate information about the Zhuang which would satisfy the modern linguist or anthropologist was admittedly lacking. Joseph Cuenot of the Paris Foreign Mission Society held the strange idea that the Zhuang were soldiers from Shandong who came to Guangxi, settled, and intermarried with the local people.[9] Samuel Clarke, in his book *Among the Tribes of Southwest China*, simply lumped them together with the Tai, Shan, and Lao people. He added,

> There seems to be no end to the names by which the various divisions of this race are designated. Who are they? Their history and diffusion, and their relation to other races of southeastern Asia, are very interesting problems which still await solution.[10]

About the only consistent view shared among the missionaries was that the Zhuang were "members of the great Tai race."[11] Few missionaries wrote anything about Zhuang language, customs, or culture. Mr. Oldfield spoke generally of them, saying, "For the most part, the Chwangs [Zhuang] are very illiterate and are bound by witchcraft, devil-worship, and superstitions of various kinds."[12] On an extended trip to northwest Guangxi in 1917, he wrote, "Poverty should be spelled with a capital 'P', and should be doubly underscored when speaking of the condition of these Chwang [Zhuang] tribesmen."[13] Unlike the Miao, Yao, and Dong, however, the Zhuang were not despised by the Han Chinese; in fact, the Han freely intermarried with them.

The CMA was the society that had the most contact with Guangxi's ethnic peoples including the Zhuang. Walter Oldfield spent a night in a Zhuang village in 1915. He wrote of their status and lack of missionary engagement,

> No missionary is Kwangsi speaks their dialect; no Chinese worker is laboring among them; no Christian chapel has been opened in their territories. They live, they die unreached, unhelped, and unheeded. For decades they have been groping in the darkness; for decades more they will have to grope unless some one comes to give them the Message.[14]

---

9. Cuenot, *Kwangsi.*

10. Clarke, *Among the Tribes*, 89–90.

11. Oldfield, *Pioneering in Kwangsi*, 37.

12. Oldfield, *Pioneering in Kwangsi*, 39.

13. Oldfield, "Among Kwangsi's Tribesmen," 232.

14. Oldfield, "A Night in Chwang Village," 361.

The following year, the CMA's South China leadership asked the Oldfields to begin studying the Zhuang language. However, there is little evidence that they were ever able to speak Zhuang. Instead, by 1922, the CMA had "been able recently to reach a number of Tai [Zhuang] people through the medium of its work among the Chinese."[15] By 1928, Mr. Oldfield was incorporating Zhuang speakers in his pioneering trips to northwest Guangxi. On one particular trip, he employed four carriers who could speak both Mandarin and Zhuang. Although some of the Zhuang understood Mandarin, having Zhuang speakers significantly increased the ability to communicate.[16]

In the 1930s, outreach to the Zhuang expanded considerably. Mrs. Oldfield reflected in her autobiography, "In the earlier years individual souls among them had been gathered in, but during this fourth term [1930–1937] whole villages turned to the Lord."[17] In 1934 at a provincial CMA conference, a missionary reported that many Zhuang had heard the message of Christ; he had also received more requests to visit and preach than he could possibly accept. A Zhuang Christian delegate at the conference also represented the Zhuang and appealed for greater outreach to his people.[18] James Poole (CMA) shared about two Zhuang men who had heard a colporteur preach, bought a copy of the Gospels, and took it home and read it. When they read the verse that said, "If any man will come after me, let him deny himself, and take up his cross, and follow me," they made crosses of bamboo and put them underneath their shirts when they walked about the mountains or went to the markets.[19]

The following year (1935), a Zhuang beggar entered the chapel in Liuzhou. The missionaries gave him food, shelter, and work to pay for his boarding. He regularly heard the gospel from them and before long, turned to the Lord and developed a burden for his people. He became a colporteur of the British and Foreign Bible Society and began traversing the mountains to find members of his tribe. Many of his tribesmen were converted and a dozen of them attended the church in Liuzhou as a result of his ministry.[20]

By 1936, a Zhuang convert in the far west part of Guangxi had been witnessing to his people for over a year. He began to feel the need to understand the Scriptures better and applied for the Alliance's Short-Term Bible

---

15. China Continuation Committee, *Christian Occupation*, 350.

16. Oldfield, "Pioneering in Kwang Si's neglected territory" (August 4, 1928).

17. Oldfield, *With You Alway*, 216.

18. Oldfield, "Golden Opportunities in Kwangsi Province."

19. Poole, "The Cross Bearers."

20. CMA, "The Gospel at Work."

School. He sold his cow to pay the fifteen-dollar tuition. After completing the program, he set up a meeting place in a loft and began boldly witnessing for Christ among his people.[21] The same year, the Penningtons (CMA) began studying Mandarin in Liuzhou with a view toward working with the Zhuang.[22] By then, a church composed entirely of Zhuang had been established forty miles from Longzhou.

The next year, over a hundred Zhuang were baptized. Two churches were established and Zhuang converts themselves constructed church buildings. The year after, the CMA reported that over 360 Zhuang had been saved and that an entire village renamed "Revival Village"[23] had professed Christ. Members of a Zhuang church in Hechi were an inspiration as they walked long distances through the mountains to attend. Those who were too far held meetings in their own homes to explain the gospel to their neighbors. Another church was located in Tu'ngan[24] where a number of baptisms followed instances of divine healing. Evangelists sent to the area were so busy with the work that they had little time to eat or sleep. A setback also occurred that year when the CMA's only Zhuang evangelist died.[25]

In 1939, the baptisms of seventy Zhuang converts greatly encouraged the CMA. A year later, two men brought the gospel to a Zhuang village and the whole village believed. The younger of the two men began receiving support from a Christian businessman and entered the Wuzhou Bible School to become a preacher for his people. A place called Chen Pien was also reached in 1940 and became an outreach point for other tribes. In western Guangxi, a Zhuang man bought a Gospel of Matthew and took it back to his village. He read it but did not understand it, so he trekked seventeen miles to Jingxi where he knew a CMA missionary[26] was stationed. The missionary was not there at the time so he hiked another eight miles to a mountainous village where a Zhuang Christian lived. They studied the Scriptures together and the man turned to the Lord. He returned to his village and many members of his family also received the gospel. He set apart half of his house as a meeting room for others to hear the good news of Jesus Christ.[27] Students

21. CMA, "Transformed Lives."

22. Clemmer et al., "Greetings from South China."

23. Named Fuh-Hsing (*Fuxingcun* (复兴村)). Oldfield, *With You Alway.*

24. Seemingly in Du'an.

25. CMA, "Entering New Areas," "From Every Tongue"; Oldfield, "The Tribespeople of South China."

26. The missionary was Al Kowles.

27. CMA, "Our Foreign Mail Bag" (May 20, 1939), "Carrying on in Kwangsi," "Department of Prayer" (June 28, 1941), "Tribesmen Hear and Accept," "The Workings of God"; Kowles, "Ebenezer!"

from the Wuzhou Bible School visited the area around Jingxi that year,[28] held open-air meetings, and did house-to-house visitation. Over fifty were baptized and an additional eleven baptized in another area[29] outside of Jingxi.[30]

In 1941, the CMA wrote that the Zhuang were "most responsive to the gospel at present."[31] Jingxi in the far west of Guangxi also became a center for Zhuang outreach (as late as 1936, Jingxi only had a few believers in the countryside). In 1942, one hundred mostly-Zhuang converts were baptized in Hechi. In Liuzhou's San Fang in northern Guangxi, the first baptismal service was held. The Alliance reported four centers of Zhuang Christianity and outreach that year.[32] The next year was a particularly fruitful year among the Zhuang. Two new churches were established in outstations near Jingxi.[33] Zhuang money and labor built the church buildings, but a Han Chinese led the two groups. In Hechi's Qingyuan, Zhuang Christians traveled from village to village sharing Christ. A Chinese Christian also began serving the Zhuang in the Nandan area. Several times over the next couple of years, the CMA reported that the Zhuang work was "most encouraging."[34] In Hechi, the CMA reported "a great awakening among the Chwang tribes people."[35] Of Jingxi, Walter Oldfield said, "The Spirit of God seems to be doing a work among the Chuang tribesmen similar to the way He is working in other places."[36] In Binyang, a Miss Lee and Miss Su "were doing a marvellously blessed work among the Chuang tribesmen."[37]

In 1946, a group of about one hundred Zhuang in Napo in far western Guangxi asked to be baptized. Three years later, Christians in San Fang had grown from only one in 1936 to one hundred ten. There were also reports of whole families being saved. One boy had received a tract, read it, and decided to visit a nearby "Bible woman." After several visits, he accepted

28. A place called Pa-Mung.

29. Called Lung-pang.

30. CMA, "Tribesmen Hear and Accept," "Tribespeople Won for Christ."

31. CMA, "Department of Prayer" (June 28, 1941), 408.

32. These were not specified, but likely were among Longzhou, Hechi, Jingxi, San Fang, and Liuzhou. CMA, "God's Grace in Kwangsi," "Growing Tall."

33. Called T'ang Mah (seventeen miles from Jingxi) and Peh Chien (thirty miles southwest of Jingxi).

34. Oldfield, "Our Foreign Mail Bag" (January 23, 1943), 57; CMA, "Department of Prayer" (February 26, 1944), 138; Kowles, "Our Foreign Mail Bag" (May 20, 1944), 249.

35. CMA, "Department of Prayer" (July 31, 1943), 490.

36. Oldfield, "In Much Tribulation," 617.

37. Oldfield, With You Alway, 236.

Christ as his Savior. He shared the gospel with his mother, brother, aunt, uncle, and cousins who also believed.[38]

Despite the advances made among the Zhuang, more than fifty years later, Katherine Kaupo, in her book *Creating the Zhuang*, wrote, "Little inroads were made by the missionaries into Zhuang territory."[39] Perhaps Kaup was not aware of the advances the CMA made before 1950, or perhaps she was speaking in terms of scale, for even if there were a thousand Zhuang believers at the time,[40] they still made up only a tiny fraction (0.03 percent) of the total Zhuang population, estimated by the CMA to have been about three million in 1935.[41]

Yao

The literature also regularly mentioned the Yao ethnic minorities. They were said to be "wild,"[42] "simple-hearted"[43] and "one of the least known and most primitive"[44] of the tribes. These unreached tribesmen had "more subdivisions than any other Kwangsi tribe" and were "probably the most strongly 'isolationist.'"[45] According to a couple of missionaries, they lived peacefully until Emperor Han Wudi swept through southern China around 100 B.C. and they were driven into the mountains.[46] After their subjugation, uprisings periodically took place. A large one occurred in Guangxi in 1831.[47] Missionaries described their livelihood by writing, "Extreme hardship is the common lot of the Yao people. Indeed it is a marvel that they have been able to maintain an existence through the centuries of their residence in Kwangsi."[48]

38. CMA, "Blessing in South China"; CMA, "Gospel Fruit in San Fang"; CMA, "God Moves Among the Chuangs."

39. Kaup, *Creating the Zhuang*, 44. Kaup added that this reality "suggests that the Zhuang did not perceive of themselves as marginalized and in need of promotion in relation to the Han."

40. Which is a generous number.

41. CMA, "The Gospel at Work in Foreign Lands."

42. Montanar, "Kwang-Si," second paragraph.

43. CMA, *Atlas* (1924), 88.

44. Snead, *Missionary Atlas* (1936), 94.

45. Snead, *Missionary Atlas* (1950), 114–15.

46. Couche, "Continued from Our Last"; Carter, "Transformations."

47. Falkenheim & Kuo, "Guangxi."

48. Snead, *Missionary Atlas* (1950), 115.

Pioneer CMA missionary Walter Oldfield had the most direct contact with the Yao, claiming they were the "people that I have the honor of being the only white man to ever enter their district."[49] In 1917, after Oldfield preached the gospel in the mountains around Pingnan,[50] two Yao tribesmen came into Pingnan to learn more about Christ. (Over the years, Oldfield maintained that Pingnan was the location in which the gospel had first been taken to this "neglected tribe.")[51] In 1917, Mr. Oldfield traveled to the mountains east of Liuzhou to visit the Yao tribes and found them to be a "timid, retiring race."[52] The next year in northern Guangxi, he came into contact with the White Trouser Yao[53] who are named for the men's white pants.[54] In 1919, a breakthrough came when a Yao chief and his assistant both visited Wuzhou and accepted Christ. However, adversity immediately followed. Robbers attacked new believer Mr. Wang, the Yao chief's assistant, on his way back from Wuzhou. A week later, in an unrelated incident, soldiers beat Mr. Wang and left him for dead. He returned with difficulty to the Wuzhou Bible School but was coughing up blood due to intestinal injuries. He apparently recovered as it was later reported that the Yao chief was a "believer deeply interested in the gospel" and that his assistant was "an earnest Christian who spent two years in the [Wuzhou] Bible School."[55]

In 1921, Mr. Oldfield started a boys' school in a Yao village. Two years later, he baptized three tribesmen in the Yao Mountains. In 1924, the CMA reported on their ministry to the Yao, "A very good beginning has been made and a number of these simple hearted people won to Christ."[56]

Around 1930, Chinese Christians began taking more responsibility for the evangelization of the Yao. A single Chinese lady spent a month in the Yao Mountains, the first time a female had served there due to the danger.[57] About the same time, the Alliance Church in Wuzhou sent a group of Chinese Christians to the Yao Mountains. They were said to have faced strong opposition from the enemy.[58] In 1931, two students from the Wuzhou Bible School began living among and reaching out to the Yao in the

---

49. Oldfield, "A Word of Cheer from China," 659.
50. Guigang, Pingnan (贵港市平南县).
51. Oldfield, *Pioneering in Kwangsi*, 128.
52. Oldfield in Glover, "Our Foreign Mail Bag" (1917), 154.
53. Baiku Yao (白裤瑶).
54. Oldfield, "Pioneering in Kwang Si's Neglected Territory" (August 4, 1928).
55. Poole, "Chinese Tribal Chief"; CMA, *Atlas Showing Mission Fields*, 88.
56. CMA, *Atlas Showing Mission Fields*, 88.
57. Chao et al., "South China Alliance Mission Conference."
58. Christie, "Department of Prayer" (October 25, 1930).

Yao Mountains. That same year, a Chinese pastor itinerated and sent a letter from the "Flower Basket Aborigines," a likely reference to the Hualan Yao[59] in Laibin's Jinxiu Yao Autonomous County.[60] Also that year, three preachers embarked on an extended trip westward from Pingle and spent part of their time among the Yao.[61] At a gathering of Chinese Christian workers, the Alliance enthusiastically noted the presence of a Yao Christian.[62]

In 1932, the Alliance rejoiced that a number of Yao were baptized. Six graduates from the Wuzhou Bible School and twenty-nine others entered service in Guangxi that year, some committed in service to the Yao. The following year, further advancements occurred, and the next year, some Yao Christians attended a Chinese conference in Wuzhou. Despite the progress, however, the CMA continued to write of the "awful need" of the Yao and other tribes "who still sit in darkness."[63]

In late 1932 and early 1933, a Yao uprising took place and made "serious trouble" in parts of Guangxi.[64] A Chinese pastor and Bible woman were unable to go into Guanyang (northeastern Guangxi) due to the turmoil. Bishop Holden (CMS) wrote, "Generally they are quiet, law-abiding folk, but in their simplicity they are easily influenced, and it is generally believed that Communist agitators stirred them up to cause trouble for the authorities."[65] Because the Yao were "unused to modern warfare," they were "easily subdued by Government soldiers and suffered great destruction and loss."[66] Bishop Holden witnessed about 150 of them captured and chained together in groups of five. Miss Law observed a similar scene in Guanyang where forty were roped together and marched off as prisoners. The uprising was finally put down.

In 1935, a Chinese evangelist made his headquarters among a Yao tribe where he discovered "a marked friendliness and interest in the gospel."[67] That same year, evangelistic work was carried out among five Yao tribes in the Yao Mountains where it was reported, "Not a few have been baptized."[68]

59. As Hualan (花篮) literally means "flower basket."

60. CMA, "Touring in South China."

61. Oldfield, "Our Foreign Mail Bag" (June 13, 1931).

62. Newbern, "Impressions"; Oldfield, "A Notable Gathering of Chinese Workers."

63. CMA, "Our China Fields," 832; Christie, "Department of Prayer" (1932); Snead, "Causes for Thanksgiving"; Oldfield, "A Year of Blessing."

64. Couche, "Continued from Our Last," 6–7.

65. Holden, "The Bishop's Letter," (April 1933), 3.

66. Law, "Easter in Kwanyang," 16.

67. Christie, "Department of Prayer" (1935), 330.

68. Turley et al., "South China Conference," 673.

In 1936, Mr. Oldfield cited the names of ten Yao tribes and stated that he had personally visited all of them.[69] At the time, a church had been established in at least one of the Yao villages. In another village, a Christian school for boys was set up. Also that year, the Alliance's Chinese committee[70] accepted the responsibility to evangelize the Yao Mountains.[71]

In 1938, an agent of the National Bible Society of Scotland and an Alliance missionary itinerated in the western part of Guangxi where they were well-received by the Landian[72] ("Indigo") Yao.[73] Trips to the Yao continued to take place over the next couple of years, and in 1940, a new advance began from Jingxi to the Landian and Daban[74] Yao. Wuzhou Bible School students went to the far western part of Guangxi, including Napo, that same year and seven Yao individuals were enrolled as inquirers. The students found a great openness among the Landian Yao whose feet had been cleaned[75] by the missionaries three years before. When the students spoke, one of the Indigo Yao men volunteered to translate the message into their language, the first time they had heard the gospel in their mother tongue. Their Yao hosts knelt to pray for forgiveness from the Lord before these students left.[76]

In 1943, the Alliance wrote that the White Trouser Yao "have remained till the present entirely without the gospel,"[77] but that a Chinese evangelist had begun to take an interest in them. In 1950, the Alliance reported that outreach to the Yao had stalled due to difficulties, some of which were related to the earlier war with Japan. They still maintained, "The Yao people are at present practically unreached by the gospel."[78]

---

69. Oldfield, *Pioneering in Kwangsi*, 128.

70. Termed the "Chinese Conference."

71. "The [Alliance] Chinese Church has accepted the great unevangelized Yao Mountain territory, where live thousands of unreached tribesmen, as their field for evangelization." Snead, *Missionary Atlas* (1936), 97.

72. 蓝靛瑶.

73. CMA, "The Hill Tribes."

74. 大板瑶.

75. Probably medically.

76. Kowles, "Ebenezer!"; Oldfield, "Fruit in Pan-Yang," "Seed Sowing in War Time."

77. CMA, "Department of Prayer" (March 27, 1943), 22.

78. Snead, *Missionary Atlas* (1950), 115. Other section sources: Garrison, Turley, & Carne, "Spiritual Side"; Field, "The Yao Tribesmen"; Poole, "Chinese Tribal Chief"; Foust et al., "Greetings from South China"; Oldfield, "A Word of Cheer from China."

Miao

Several missionaries referred to the Miao minorities.[79] In 1903, Catholics said of the Miao (and Yao) in Guangxi, "There are almost no Christians among them."[80] Walter Oldfield again had the most direct contact with the Miao. He said, "Among the various aboriginal tribes that inhabit the wilder sections of Kwangsi Province, perhaps the lowest in the social scale, as well as the most illiterate, destitute, and inaccessible, is the race known as the Miao. They are the small gardeners, tillers of the soil, and woodcutters, eking out a bare existence by the labor of their hands."[81]

In 1917, Oldfield spent a week among the Miao, Zhuang, and Dong about one hundred kilometers south of the Guizhou border.[82] In 1934, he journeyed among the Miao (and Dong) in northern Guangxi.[83] Two years later, he discovered Black Miao villages of which "none of the inhabitants . . . had as yet heard the first word of the gospel."[84] In April 1938, a Miao believer came from Guizhou Province to Guangxi at the request of the CMA missionaries. He carried his bedding, preached the Word, and sold gospel tracts in all the villages of one particular district of Rongan in Liuzhou.[85] None of the societies indicated any direct, long-term work among the Miao in Guangxi. However, the Miao were (and still are) far more numerous in Guizhou, and a remarkable movement took place among one of the Miao groups there, the Big Flowery Miao, through the ministry of Samuel Pollard of the China Inland Mission.[86]

Dong

The Dong[87] were referred to as one of Guangxi's minorities several times in the literature, although they, like the Miao, were (and still are) more numerous in Guizhou. Reportedly, they worked in the timber industry and were

79. Lowe, *My Daily Prayer Book*; Farmer, *Ada Beeson Farmer*.

80. Launay, *Histoire*, Google translation of the French.

81. Oldfield, *Pioneering in Kwangsi*, 49.

82. Oldfield, "In the Wilds of Kwangsi."

83. Christie, "Department of Prayer" (1934). Oldfield may have taken additional trips to Miao areas between 1917 and 1934.

84. Oldfield, "A God-Prepared Messenger," 489.

85. Clemmer, "God's Advance Provision."

86. See Grist, *Samuel Pollard: Pioneer Missionary in China* and Kendall, *Beyond the Clouds: The Story of Samuel Pollard of South-West China*.

87. Dong was usually spelled "Tung," "Tong," or "Tongs" in the literature.

involved in floating timber down the river to Liuzhou.[88] Oldfield estimated their population to have been about one hundred thousand and said they were the "lumbermen, raftsmen, and boatmen in the northern part of the province."[89] Other missionaries described them as "fearless but peace-loving," "proud and independent," "civilized and easy of [to] approach" and "oppressed and repressed by the Chinese."[90] Religiously, they differed from the Chinese and were said to "know nothing" of Confucianism, Daoism, or Buddhism.[91] Although they did not subscribe to any mainstream religion, they were still "very superstitious and very much afraid of demons."[92]

According to Geary et al., an American missionary established a church among the Dong in Guangxi before relocating to Guizhou's Rongjiang in 1920.[93] However, Rev. and Mrs. Desterhaft of the CMA remarked in 1930, "As far as we know, no Society has ever worked among the Tongs [Dong]."[94] The Desterhafts were the only foreign missionaries to devote themselves to a dedicated and extended ministry to the Dong in Guangxi.[95] While missionaries had brief encounters with the mountainous Dong much earlier, no targeted ministry began until about 1930. In northern Guangxi, the Desterhafts itinerated and distributed thousands of tracts and gospel portions. At the time, the Dong did not have a written script and the Chinese literature probably had a minimal effect on them since only about 10 percent were literate.[96]

On their trips, the Desterhafts were surprised not to see temples in Dong villages.[97] They also experienced the limitations of using the Chinese language to reach the Dong and remarked, "To give them the Gospel, it is absolutely necessary to speak their language."[98] They soon began to study Dong. When they acquired sufficient ability to communicate the

---

88. Broomhall, *Chinese Empire*.

89. Oldfield, *Pioneering in Kwangsi*, 44.

90. Desterhaft, "With the Tong Tribe," 751; Christie, "Department of Prayer" (1936), 620; Desterhaft, "With the Tong Tribe," 748.

91. Christie, "Department of Prayer" (1936), 620.

92. Christie, "Department of Prayer" (1936), 620.

93. Geary et. al, *Kam People*. While this is possible, the present author was unable validate this.

94. Desterhaft, "With the Tong Tribe," 751.

95. This is based on this author's survey of the literature as well as Rev. Desterhaft's comment. CMA, "Work and Workers" (1935).

96. Christie, "Department of Prayer" (1936), 620.

97. Desterhaft, "With the Tong Tribe."

98. Desterhaft, "With the Tong Tribe," 751.

gospel, they relocated to a bungalow in a Dong village in Fulu[99] where they stayed.[100] Fulu thus became the center of Dong outreach in Guangxi and in a portion of southern Guizhou.[101] In 1931, apparently there were still no converts in Guangxi, but the following year, Rev. Desterhaft was encouraged that God was working in the life of one Dong school teacher who knelt and prayed, confessing his sins.[102]

Throughout the 1930s, the meager response among the Dong was a discouragement to the missionaries. The Desterhafts were committed but Dong villages covered a mountainous area of over thirty thousand square miles.[103] The Dong were without a missionary only when the Desterhafts returned to the U.S. on furlough.[104] Chinese Christians and other missionaries traveled several times to the Dong during this period. In the early 30s, Mrs. Oldfield, Mrs. Desterhaft, and their Bible woman visited nearly all the Dong homes in Fulu where they were "kindly welcomed."[105] In 1931, Chinese preachers itinerated in the Dong area, even preaching in one village continuously (in Chinese) from 10 a.m. to 3 p.m. to a crowd of three hundred. Some listened intently the whole time.[106] The following year, Chinese believers from the Alliance's Wuzhou Bible School began to reach out to the Dong.[107]

In 1933, the CMA South China conference was held in Guizhou's Rongjiang, a short river ride across the Guangxi border. The delegates from Guangxi were asked to travel to the conference on foot from Guangxi's Rong'an to Guizhou's Rongjiang so that they could preach the gospel in Dong villages along the way. The journey was much longer and slower than by river, but the CMA intentionally chose the conference's location and route due to the Dong and Miao tribes in that area. At the conference, they agreed, along with the China Inland Mission, to be responsible for the Dong peoples in the vast area from Guangxi's Rongan to Guizhou's Rongjiang.[108]

Over the next few years, CMA missionaries continued to travel to Dong areas. In 1934, Mr. Oldfield itinerated for several weeks in Dong and

99. Fulu (富禄) is east of Congjiang (从江) in northern Guangxi.

100. Oldfield, "A Year of Blessing," "Golden Opportunities."

101. Christie, "Department of Prayer" (1936).

102. Desterhaft, "Our Foreign Mail Bag" (1932).

103. Snead, "Advancing into New Fields."

104. Turley et al., "The South China Conference."

105. Oldfield, *With You Alway*, 207.

106. Oldfield, "Touring Among the Tribesmen."

107. Snead, "Causes for Thanksgiving."

108. Oldfield, "Pioneer Evangelism."

Miao territory in northern Guangxi.[109] The year after, his wife traveled to a Dong area with a Bible woman.[110] In 1936, Mr. Clemmer (CMA) made a trip to Dong area.[111] Two years later, a Chinese Christian couple came from Guangxi to Guizhou's Rongjiang where there were about one hundred conversions, many of which were of the Dong. However, in Guangxi, a major setback occurred. One of the young Chinese preachers specifically serving the Dong died of an illness.[112] Rev. Desterhaft, shocked and confused, said, "I had to bury the man in whom I had staked so much hope for future work among the Tungs [Dong]."[113] Nevertheless, the work carried on and the following year, Rev. Desterhaft had the delight of baptizing his first Dong convert.[114] In 1939, Mr. Oldfield made another trip to search out Dong villages and identify the best routes to take to reach them.[115] The CMA noted that year that work among the Dong was yielding fruit.[116]

By 1942, nearly a dozen years after ministry to the Dong began, Mr. Oldfield wrote, "Although Brother Desterhaft has been putting his entire life and energy into the Master's service for this people, the response has been very discouraging."[117] However, that same year, they started to see "a working of the Spirit of God among the Tung tribespeople."[118] One Dong man who had received a Gospel portion from a colporteur trekked fifty miles to Fulu to seek out the Christian workers. Rev. Desterhaft accompanied a Chinese evangelist back to this man's village where the people showed great receptivity to the message.[119] On one occasion, a crowd of three hundred listened until midnight. None were baptized at the time, but an upper room in a house was dedicated as a place of worship. This greatly encouraged Rev. Desterhaft and word soon arrived that twenty Dong were ready for baptism. Snead wrote, "After years of faithful seed-sowing, reports come of an expected harvest among the Tung tribespeople."[120] Oldfield noted a couple of months later,

---

109. Christie, "Department of Prayer" (1934).

110. Christie, "Department of Prayer" (1935).

111. Clemmer, "Greetings from South China."

112. Christie, "Department of Prayer" (1938).

113. In Oldfield, "The Tribespeople of South China" (1938), 681.

114. Desterhaft, "Our Foreign Mail Bag" (1939).

115. Oldfield, "O'er Mountain Trails."

116. CMA, "Department of Prayer" (1939).

117. Oldfield, "God's Grace in Kwangsi," 441.

118. Oldfield, "Our Foreign Mail Bag" (1942), 265.

119. Oldfield, "God's Grace in Kwangsi."

120. Snead, "War," 201.

A group of Tung [Dong] tribesmen, numbering a little over ten, were baptized recently. While this number may not seem to be large, still to us it is most encouraging, for it means that at this time more Tungs have been brought to the Lord than during the past twenty years—ever since we started work among the Tung tribesmen.[121]

The following year, the CMA spoke of the conversion of the Dong as a "limited awakening." (This was in contrast to the "extensive awakening" that had taken place among the Zhuang.)[122] Rev. Desterhaft was encouraged when he visited the Dong Christians and found them staying true to the Lord.[123] Also that year, a Dong man became a believer, attended the Alliance Bible College in Wuzhou, and became a pastor.

Opposition and persecution were severe for the Dong who turned to Christ, especially from the village leaders. In one case, a Dong Christian named Mr. Su was sharing the gospel around a fire. A military officer saw him, beat him badly, and hung him up by his arms with ropes. Knowing Mr. Su would not last long in this condition, local friends pleaded for him, assuring the officers that Mr. Su was not a traitor. The officers finally let him go, but they displayed their hatred for the gospel through the whole ordeal.[124]

After 1943, the CMA reported little about the Dong work. The reasons seem to be twofold. First, the war with Japan interrupted the work and resulted in many missionaries leaving China. Rev. Desterhaft, too, departed China for a time in the mid-1940s. Second, the CMA experienced a change of personnel in their South China Mission. Mr. Oldfield withdrew to Canada in 1943 due to poor health. He returned three years later, but his health failed again and he relocated to Canada permanently the following year. During Oldfield's leave of absence and later departure, Rev. Desterhaft was made chairman of the South China Mission.[125] Desterhaft's new role and responsibilities likely redirected his time and energy away from the Dong.

In 1950, after the Communist takeover, the CMA reported on their ministry to the Dong:

> Now because of the shortage of missionaries and the dislocation caused by the Japanese invasion, no missionary is working among them. While we cannot feel that we have by any means

121. In Oldfield, "Widespread Witnessing in Kwangsi," 521.
122. CMA, "Department of Prayer" (January 30, 1943), 80.
123. Oldfield, "Our Foreign Mail Bag" (May 22, 1943).
124. Desterhaft, "Mr. Su of South China."
125. CMA, "One for Another"; Snead, "Rev. A. F. Desterhaft."

discharged our responsibility toward them, yet for the present the only way we can help them is by prayer. . . . More than five years the infant church has been without a missionary and is ministered to by occasional visits of a national worker. There is, however, quite a strong Tung [Dong] church across the border in Kweichow [Guizhou], so that there is promise of a harvest if only there were workers to reap.[126]

In 1957, the Mennonite Church reported an exciting movement among the Dong in Guangxi's Tianyang.[127] The background was that a number of Dong had believed in the mid-1940s, but did not receive baptism for the next twelve years. They wrote a letter to some Chinese Christians with the CMA in Nanning asking them to come. Four of these Christians trekked to sixteen of their mountainous villages and baptized 433 "sheep without a shepherd" in a three-day period.[128] They also established a congregation and planned to construct a building by 1958.

Unfortunately, in the following years, church growth among the Dong did not persist. In 2003, Geary et al. wrote, "Today, there is no known church among the Kam [Dong] communities and the influence of Christianity among the Kam remains negligible."[129]

Other Minority Outreach

In addition to the animistic, ancestor-worshiping peoples described above, Muslims ("Mohammedans")[130] were also mentioned in the literature. According to Walter Oldfield, they entered Guangxi during the thirteenth century during the Yuan Dynasty.[131] They established Guilin as a stronghold and were said to have had five mosques there in 1911 and some twenty-three mosques throughout Guangxi in the 1930s.[132] Oldfield wrote of them, "Members of this faith are exceedingly hard to reach with the Gospel."[133]

126. *Missionary Atlas* (1950), 115, 119.

127. In Baise.

128. Erb, "T'ung Tribe Christian Movement," 1079.

129. Geary, *Kam People*, 183. Other sources consulted for the Dong section include: Desterhaft, "With the Tong Tribe"; CMA, "Work and Workers" (1936); Garrison et al., "Spiritual Side"; Oldfield, "The Tribespeople of South China"; Snead, "A People for His Name"; Tubbs, "In Needy Kwangsi"; Yang, "Aspects of the Kam Language."

130. These were presumably the Hui.

131. Oldfield, *Pioneering in Kwangsi*.

132. Bacon, "A Meditation on a Bluff," 7; Oldfield, *Pioneering in Kwangsi*.

133. Oldfield, *Pioneering in Kwangsi*, 56.

However, the first convert of the Church Missionary Society in Guilin was Louis Byrde's Muslim language teacher, Mr. Song.[134]

Catholic outreach to the minorities took place among the Palyu,[135] Zhuang, and Yi. In northwest Guangxi, it was said that conversions among the Palyu took place on a "fairly large scale."[136] Among the Yi, there were a number of Christians and at least one catechist.[137] The Catholics launched a "new venture" among the Yi after Bishop Chouzy became prefect apostolic of Guangxi in 1891.[138] A priest named Matthieu Bertholet visited Yi tribes around the mission in the village of Lung Nui.[139] There was also a "chapel built by the Christian tribe, the Yi, in their village of Tou Yang Tsao."[140] While Cuenot wrote of the Yi, it is not entirely clear to whom he was referring. In one sentence, he seemed to connect them with other minorities when he wrote, "There are other 'Yi' tribes where Christianity has not yet penetrated, and these have their particular language, such as the Pou-la-tse [Palyu], the Chung-kia-tse[141] [Zhuang], the Long-miao[142] [Miao], and the Chang-mao-yao[143] [Yao]."[144]

The Church Missionary Society began to have contact with one unnamed tribe, probably the Yao, in Quanzhou in 1911. They were said to be poor, mountainous, and lived largely on potatoes since rice did not grow well in their areas. The work began with a Chinese colporteur who spent a few days in the mountains.[145] Southern Baptists reported that the China Baptist Women's Missionary Union (WMU) appointed a lady to work with the "tribes" around Guilin before the Communist takeover in 1949.[146]

134. MacGillivray, *Century of Protestant Missions.*

135. In Chinese called the 倈人.

136. Launay, *Histoire*, 51.

137. Cuenot, *Kwangsi*, 58, 116.

138. Cuenot, *Kwangsi*, 7.

139. On French maps, it is about halfway between Pingle and Liuzhou seemingly in today's Luzhai County in Liuzhou (柳州鹿寨县); they were also located nearby in Xiangzhou (象州). Cuenot in *Kwangsi* mentions that they later migrated to Yongfu County in Guilin (桂林永福县).

140. Cuenot, *Kwangsi*, 94. Tou Yang Tsao is an unidentified location.

141. The Zhuang.

142. A Miao subgroup.

143. A Yao subgroup.

144. Cuenot, *Kwangsi*, 167.

145. Byrde, "The Aborigines of China."

146. SBC, *Annual 1950.*

No society indicated any missionary work among the Maonan people of Guangxi, one of China's fifty-five nationally-recognized ethnic minorities.[147]

An evaluation of missions to the minorities before 1950 leaves the strong impression that it was still in its infancy. Of the literature consulted, only one society, the CMA, shared any statistics on missions to minorities. In 1936, after nearly four decades in Guangxi, the Alliance reported a mere sixty converts among three (unspecified) minorities.[148] The following year, the chairman of the CMA's Chinese committee in Guangxi petitioned on behalf of the Yao, Miao, Zhuang, and Dong and declared they were "at present without the gospel."[149] George Tubbs (CMA) wrote a year before the Communist takeover, "The only conclusion we come to is that the real need of the unevangelized areas is not being met. Very little is being done for the neglected tribes."[150] In 1971, a seasoned CMA missionary to Laos appealed for prayer and the gospel to be taken to the neglected, remote peoples of the earth. In his appeal he included the following:

> Rev. W. H. Oldfield was considered a pioneer to the tribespeople of Kwangsi, South China. Mr. Oldfield felt that while there were apparently many missionaries available for work among the Chinese and in the cities of China, the tribal peoples were being bypassed, neglected and forgotten. These tribespeople, numbering about seven million, made up half the population of Kwangsi Province. At the time of the Communist takeover in 1949 missionary work among them was really just getting started. . . . May a burden of prayer rest upon us until earth's remotest people have heard of Jesus.[151]

STUDENTS

In addition to schools for boys and girls that were associated with the mission societies, some missionaries conducted a specific outreach to university students. The CMS longed to develop an effective ministry to students in Guilin in their early years, but the desire was only partially fulfilled.[152] In Tokyo, they set up a Chinese church in 1907 where four international

---

147. 毛南族.

148. Oldfield, *Pioneering in Kwangsi.* They termed these minorities "aborigines."

149. Chao, in CMA, "A Unique Memorial," 327.

150. Tubbs, "In Needy Kwangsi," 458.

151. Tubbs, "To Earth's Remotest People," 6.

152. Cannell, "The Revolution."

students from Guangxi were baptized before 1913.[153] In Guilin in the 1920s, students sought out missionaries for English Bible classes. A decade later, a missionary held a New Testament study in English on Sundays with about fifteen students attending. The head of the CMS's Chinese committee commented in 1931 that student work was one of the most promising prospects in the near future.[154] In the 1940s, the CMA noted that God was at work among students of Guangxi University. The university was established in Wuzhou but had moved to Liuzhou and Guilin during the war with Japan. In Liuzhou in 1943, Oldfield spoke of a "real opening" among the students.[155] Three years later in Wuzhou, students were meeting weekly at the Wuzhou Bible School (CMA) for services. The students organized the services but invited the missionaries to give the messages. In 1947, at a branch of Guangxi University twenty miles north of Guilin, Southern Baptist, CMA, and CMS missionaries from Guilin took turns conducting a weekly Bible class and speaking at the Sunday services.[156] About a hundred students attended one Sunday morning to hear a CMS missionary speak on Luke 7. Walter Oldfield baptized five students in Guilin that year and noted that the wife of the university's president in Guilin, President Ma, was a Christian.[157] There were as many as forty Christians among the seven hundred students (6 percent) at the Guilin branch of the university.[158]

153. Bondfield, *China Mission Year Book 1913.*

154. Hsu, "My First Trip."

155. Oldfield, "Our Foreign Mail Bag" (May 22, 1943), 330.

156. Rogers, "Resurrection."

157. Oldfield, "Baptismal Service."

158. Rogers, "An Open Door."

9

Missionary Methods and Ministries of Compassion

MISSIONARY METHODS

Despite a few differences in Catholic and Protestant methodology, the methods employed by the various mission societies shared a great deal in common. They included evangelistic preaching, literature distribution, the use of native workers, medical ministry, church planting, and instruction and training for believers. These methods were not used in isolation but were integrated into a systematic whole.

Evangelistic Preaching

The preaching of the gospel was conducted openly, boldly, and in a variety of settings, including on bridges, on butchers' blocks, and in caves.[1] Missionaries sometimes used spacious preaching halls when available. Otherwise, they preached in the open air. Oldfield described the Alliance's gospel ministry: "From the first, God's blessing rested upon the message whether preached on the streets, gossiped in the teashops, spoken on the roadside, or carried by the colporteurs and evangelists into hidden hut and hamlet."[2] He wrote of the pioneer evangelistic bands,

1. Parker, "Kweilin Notes"; Leach, "And as He Sowed."
2. Oldfield, *Pioneering in Kwangsi*, 170.

Sometimes meetings were held among the timber rafts on the riverside, where raftsmen and boatmen could be easily reached; sometimes in open spaces along the busy street, where merchants and traders had an opportunity to hear; sometimes under the shadow of a spreading banyan tree at the outskirts of the town, where villagers and near-by gardeners gathered to listen to the strange news; sometimes the group assembled within the precincts of the crumbling walls of the ancient city, where soldiers and local residents were reached with the message.[3]

Missionaries used a number of methods to draw crowds. One was the use of the "magic lantern" or "stereopticon," an early type of slide projector (see figure 3). These could be used to show pictures as an aid to gospel presentations. They always attracted a crowd who were greatly amused at the projection of color pictures. Another method was the use of sound. Instruments such as the organ, concertina, and accordion were commonly mentioned (see figures 4, 5a, and 5b). The organ was often played inside a chapel to draw people inside. In contrast, the concertina and accordion could be carried. They were called the "push and pull instrument(s)" by the Chinese. They were definite attention-getters and were used both indoors and out.[4] The latter two were commonly used by the CMS, CMA, Wesleyans, and even Chinese evangelists. Rev. and Mrs. Louis Byrde lost both an organ and a concertina in one of their boat wrecks.

Figure 3: A magic lantern. (Credit: Andreas Praefcke, "Laterna magica Aulendorf. jpg," Wikimedia Commons, CC BY 3.0.)

3. Oldfield, "Pioneer Evangelism," 280.

4. Child, "A Journey to Yungchow"; Oldfield, "Touring Among the Tribesmen of Kwangsi, South China."

Figure 4: A Bastari Anglo concertina (Credit: Wikimedia Commons. Photographed by Wiki Taro on 20 November 2007. https://commons.wikimedia.org/wiki/File:Anglo-concertina-40button.jpg).

Figures 5a and 5b. Piano and button accordions. Figure 5a (Credit: Photo via https://goodfreephotos.com/). Figure 5b (Credit: Photo via https://www.maxpixel.net/).

Missionaries and evangelists also drew attention through the use of bells and loud whistles.[5] CMA evangelistic bands made door-to-door invitations during the day; in the evening, they played the accordion and sent a runner boy with a banner and bell to notify the people of a meeting.[6] In some cases it was not the Christians who were trying to get people's attention. A local official was the instigator in one location in the far west of Guangxi. He set up a platform for the speaker and commissioned a runner

---

5. Leach, "And as He Sowed."
6. Poole, "South China Evangelistic Band."

to travel the streets banging on a gong to announce a meeting about the "Jesus Doctrine."[7]

The mere presence of foreigners created interest and drew people in as well. CMS missionary Frank Child took his son into Guilin two to three times a day, drawing crowds to whom the native evangelists would preach.[8] In Guanyang,[9] Blanche Tobin wrote, "As we near a village, the sound of a bell and the sight of a foreigner immediately attract attention, and the men of the party call out, 'We have come to speak holy words. Come and listen.'"[10]

Opportune times and seasons for evangelism were given particular attention. When golden opportunities presented themselves, missionaries wrote home pleading for more workers. The CMS noted an "autumn offensive" after the blazing summer heat subsided.[11] They also held an "intensive week of evangelism" during the Chinese New Year featuring nightly magic lantern shows.[12] The Religious Tract Society provided posters for use throughout the country for Spring Festival outreach.[13]

The goal of bringing salvation to the those who had never heard was always in view. Even in locations where people had heard and showed an interest in the message, the missionaries felt compelled to move on so others could hear. CMA missionary J. A. Poole's report of a three-month trip covering 665 miles exemplifies this:

> This trip has brought us into contact with thousands of Chinese men and women, many of whom had never heard the Gospel before, but now they have heard. Some have rejected it. Some have only gone so far as to become interested. Some have believed. What is going to happen to the latter two classes? If we could go back again soon, those who are interested might become believers, and those who have believed might have a better chance to make progress, but alas! in most of the places a return visit is not possible for a long time, as we have to go on to other places still more needy.[14]

CMS missionary Robert Bland questioned the wisdom of that approach:

7. Oldfield, "Official's Friendliness."

8. Child, "The Women of Kweilin."

9. In Guilin Shi.

10. Tobin, "Evangelism in Kwanyang County," 4.

11. Leach, "Our Autumn Offensive."

12. Wilson, "Fellowship in the Gospel"; Leach, "Sowing the Seed."

13. Blenkinsop, "New Year Evangelism."

14. Poole, "South China Evangelistic Band," 798.

Often one felt impatient to get finished with one house so as to get on to the next and finish a whole street in the time available, but where a good opening occurred it was the wisest plan to concentrate on that, even if only two or three places could be visited in one morning. To work out [start] from the church members first is probably a sound method, for when we go straight to new people we have to start with material which is so ignorant and superstitious, and so sunk in sordid ideas that it is impossible to get far in a short time.[15]

Literature Distribution

To the preaching of the gospel, A. W. Tozer added a second component:

The methods employed were simple and direct. Missionaries would go into a town and select a suitable spot, a market place or some corner where people gathered. They would try to back up against a wall to prevent attack from the rear. Then they would preach the Word for a while, and if they were able, would sing a few gospel songs. Whatever else might be done, though, they would always sell Scripture portions and hand out gospel literature to the crowds that gathered to hear them.[16]

Literature, whether in the form of tracts, Bibles, Bible portions, or booklets was a vital part of the ministries of most societies. CMS missionary Louis Byrde wrote in the early years, "As the Chinese are such lovers of books we feel that a great work can be done by providing good literature for them."[17] C. J. Lowe described the approach of the Southern Baptist ministry:

A missionary from another mission passed our chapel when one of our special meetings was in progress and asked "How do you do it?" I replied, "Through Christian Literature." We have literally sown this City down with Gospel seed and they are bound to grow and bring forth fruit.[18]

15. Bland, "Some Thoughts," 16.

16. Tozer, *Let My People Go*, Kindle Locations 318–321. Tozer distilled the work of missions to four things: contacting, evangelizing, organizing, and instructing. To achieve the fourth, Tozer said a Bible school and printing press were needed. Tozer, *Let My People Go*.

17. Byrde, "Two Pressing Financial Needs," 5.

18. Lowe, "Evangelism on the Kwei Lin Field," 4.

Walter Oldfield once found a man reading the Gospel of Matthew in a remote, mountain village and remarked,

> How the Word of God travels! Closed districts do not prevent its entrance; rough roads cannot keep it back; toilsome climbs over rugged mountains do not weary it in its journey. Sold in one district far removed from the neglected regions lying to the West, it finds its way through the mountain passes, across turbulent streams, over mountain ranges, and finally settles down in a little country district far removed from the place where it first started its journey. Then in its new environment it begins to tell its life-giving story, and to the people who accept its message it manifests its transforming power in heart and life.[19]

But literature distribution had its limits. While on a scouting trip before the Chinese New Year, CMS missionary W. R. Cannell noted,

> I tramped [walked, trekked] from village to hamlet distributing literature with the purpose of discovering a likely field for our New Year week of evangelism. . . . As we travelled we noted in a number of places large scripture posters which had been pasted up ten or more years ago by an evangelistic band. The characters were still quite clear and distinct, bearing their silent message to all who can read. "To all who can read." That has been one of the great hindrances to fruitfulness on the part of the "seed sown." For in spite of the honoured place of "learning" in the estimation of the Chinese people for many centuries past, "learning" has been confined to a very small percentage of the population, whilst the masses, from economic and other pressure, have remained uneducated.[20]

Gustave Woerner added,

> One of the sad phases of colportage work is the fact that hundreds who buy Scripture portions cannot read even the simplest characters, and one can only hope and pray that somehow God will use these scattered printed pages in spite of such pitiful conditions.[21]

Women were particularly at a disadvantage. Mrs. Child (CMS) estimated that in 1932, only 1 percent could read. Ms. Pim said of Guilin's women,

19. Oldfield, "Pioneering in Western Kwangsi," 313.
20. Cannell, "On Sowing Seed," 12.
21. Woerner, "Present Evangelistic Opportunities in Kwangsi," 698.

> The womens' hearts are hardened in a very real way by millenniums of utter ignorance, and by being regarded by most people as utterly incapable of learning anything outside ordinary home duties; they themselves often remark, "I *can't* possibly learn anything, I have *no* memory, it's *no* use my learning, I don't understand *in the very least*."[22]

To compensate for this, missionaries used other creative methods. Women memorized scriptures, learned to sing hymns, and listened to oral presentations. Blanche Tobin wrote in 1935,

> Here again [in Guilin's Xingan County] there was a good opportunity among the women. Whether in their homes, or in the Church premises, they seemed ready to listen. Since most of them cannot read and economic difficulties would prevent many from finding time to study Chinese "characters," listening seems, humanly speaking, their one way of learning.[23]

Missionaries sometimes carried large picture posters as an aid in explaining the gospel. In Wuzhou, Father Bernard Meyer published an illustrated catechetical series in 1937. The first edition used Westerners in the scenes, but the 1939 edition depicted Chinese landscapes, buildings, and even Chinese people. Pictures in both editions were drawn in such a way that they could be colored at the end of the lesson.[24]

Native Workers

Despite the limitations caused by illiteracy, the China Continuation Committee in 1922 believed that the developing postal agencies in Guangxi would mean wider literature distribution and greater Christian advance.[25] But literature distribution in Guangxi was always carried out predominately on foot by colporteurs. And it is here that we find another characteristic feature of missions in Guangxi: the deployment of native workers. John Bacon wrote, "We do want men and women from the Homeland, but it has long been accepted that the work they should chiefly give themselves to is to train

---

22. Pim, "Quiet Roads," 15.
23. Tobin, "A Visit to Hingan Parish," 15.
24. Wiest, *Maryknoll in China*. It was called *Our Holy Religion*.
25. China Continuation Committee, *Christian Occupation*, 149.

and teach natives, who will in turn extend the Native Church."[26] In 1922, 276 native workers were employed by different Protestant societies.[27]

Colporteurs, frequently utilized by the Protestant societies, were Chinese Christians who traveled both selling and freely distributing literature. Margaret McRae Lackey wrote, "Our Baptist work in the Mandarin-speaking section of Kwang Si Province was really started by colporteurs going through the country selling Gospels, Christian tracts, New Testaments, and telling the simple Gospel story."[28] The colporteurs were the spearheads and pioneers. Dr. Macdonald employed six to take the gospel to outlying villages while he was occupied with his medical, evangelistic, and hospital construction work in Wuzhou.[29] Walter Oldfield regularly sent colporteurs weeks or months before his trips for the purpose of seed sowing. Occasionally when he arrived in a remote location, he found literature that had been distributed by the colporteurs who had gone before him. For the colporteurs themselves, the joy of being the first to take the gospel to new areas also meant considerable difficulties, and many of them suffered dearly. Walter Oldfield wrote,

> The colporteurs are the missionary vanguard in every pioneer field. . . . God bless the colporteurs! They are a self-sacrificing set. They tramp [trek] around the country, over mountains and through the valleys, eating the poorest food, undergoing great privations, and sometimes, overcome by sickness or disease, they lie down upon the roadside and give up their life for the preaching of the Gospel.[30]

These Chinese ambassadors, unsupported by Western powers and carrying few possessions, did not provide a lucrative prize for the bandits. On one occasion, a colporteur was captured, marched over mountain after mountain, and finally released because he was not worth a ransom.[31]

Other native Protestant workers included preachers/evangelists, catechists, and "Bible women."[32] For the CMS, evangelists were the first grade of workers. They could advance to become catechists and later clergy.[33] Bible women often accompanied female missionaries on trips and in-home

---

26. In Tobin and Cannell, "Student Work in Kweilin," 9.
27. China Continuation Committee, *Christian Occupation*, 344.
28. Lackey, *Laborers Together*, 55.
29. Macdonald, *Roderick Macdonald, M.D.*
30. Oldfield, *Pioneering in Kwangsi*, 65, 173.
31. Oldfield, *Pioneering in Kwangsi*.
32. Usually written as a single word: Biblewomen or Biblewoman.
33. Gray, "The Parish of Kweilin."

visits.[34] They also functioned as personal assistants, literature distributors, girls' school teachers, and preachers to those waiting in the hospitals. One report stated that "the pastors find that they can do little without the Bible-women to carry on in the homes what they do in the church."[35] Mrs. Clift asserted that Bible women were "absolutely essential"[36] and noted that one could be hired for six pounds a year.[37]

In the 1930s, several native Chinese evangelistic bands were organized to go to unreached areas in Guangxi. A look at their daily schedule illustrates their commitment and diligence:

> The daily schedule for the Bands was as follows:
> 5:30 a.m.   Rising bell.
> 6:00 to 8:00 a.m.   Private prayer and Bible study.
> 8:30 to 9:00 a.m.   Concerted Bible study and prayer.
> 9:00 a.m.   Breakfast.
> 10:00 a.m. to 4 p.m.   Going out two by two for house-to-house visitation, when every home within a radius of ten miles was visited, a brief Gospel message given, and tracts and booklets handed to those who could read. Before the workers passed on to the next home or hamlet, a pressing invitation was given to attend some of the meetings that were being held every evening at the center where the Band was located.
> 5:00 p.m.   Supper.
> 7:00 p.m.   Evangelistic service.

Figure 6: Daily schedule for evangelistic bands.
Oldfield, *Pioneering in Kwangsi*, 203.

Catholic native workers included priests and catechists. Priests visited Christians, preached, and heard confessions. They were "not only useful,

---

34. Tucker, "Role of Bible Women."

35. MacGillivray, *China Mission Year Book 1910*, 274. The text (274–75) goes on to say, "Another refers to their labours as 'not noised on earth, praised more in heaven.' And again we are told that 'the Bible-women are doing honest work; miles and miles have been travelled through heat and cold, visits have been made in homes, prayer meetings held, the Gospel preached, personal talks given; and as a result lives are being transformed.'"

36. Clift, *Very Far East*, 112.

37. According to the Bank of England's inflation calculator, this would equal £679 ($840) in 2017. Bank of England, "Inflation Calculator." Interestingly, twenty-five years later, Bible women could still be hired for five pounds a year. Couch, "The Rear Guard."

but necessary" and enjoyed "freer entry into pagan homes"[38] than European priests did. Catechists also fulfilled a vital role. They taught, led prayer, shepherded believers, and brought encouragement to Christians in districts far from the mission centers. Female catechists performed a necessary service in teaching other women due to a Chinese custom which did not allow male priests to teach women.[39] Joseph Cuenot said that without the catechists, "little progress could be made in converting a pagan country."[40] He also reported that catechists earned an average salary of about eight dollars a month while Maryknoll mentioned they earned fifteen U.S. dollars a month.[41]

Securing Locations

Attempting to secure physical property as a "beachhead" in new areas was another characteristic feature in mission methodology in Guangxi. It was connected with the strategic placement of workers as explained by the CMA:

> The plan followed by our mission in South China for the evangelism of the country districts has been to locate a foreign missionary in some large, central, strategic city as a main station, and endeavour as rapidly as possible to open therefrom outstations to be visited regularly by the missionary. Also, itinerating trips by the missionary, with native evangelists and colporteurs, are arranged throughout the district from this main centre.[42]

Upon entering a new location, missionaries would preach, distribute literature, and attempt to find a place to buy or rent.[43] The type of building (or its condition) did not seem to matter as long as it could serve as a chapel, preaching point, base for a colporteur, or medical clinic. Unfortunately, the task of securing property was fraught with difficulties. Local residents were often unwilling to deal with foreigners. In Wuzhou, a Southern Baptist girls' school was held in an old ancestral temple. Money was available to purchase land, but the Baptists found it "impossible" to buy.[44] Missionaries in

38. Cuenot, *Kwangsi*, 100.

39. Cuenot, *Kwangsi*.

40. Cuenot, *Kwangsi*, 101.

41. Cuenot, *Kwangsi*, 106; Wiest, *Maryknoll in China*, 83.

42. Lobenstine, *China Mission Year Book 1916*, 209.

43. Upon their arrival in Liuzhou, early pioneers Walter Oldfield and Mr. Farmer "went to a public inn, until such time as they could rent a house which they could clean, renovate, and make into a chapel." Oldfield, *With You Alway*, 110.

44. Lackey, *Laborers Together*, 46. They added, "However we are trusting in the Lord to open a way for a suitable location very soon."

Yulin used a room in a Buddhist temple since temples were the closest thing to public property.[45] The only house that pioneer Alliance missionaries in Wuzhou could obtain was thought to have been haunted by demons. The landlord happily sold it, and it later served as an Alliance chapel.[46] Dr. Macdonald had nearly secured a site for the future headquarters of the Guangxi Wesleyan mission when "the landlord withdrew, on account of a superstitious fear lest the erection of a foreign-looking building should interfere with the 'fung shui' (wind and water influences) of the neighboring hill and the family graves situated there."[47] Walter Oldfield shared an illustrative experience in Liuzhou:

> Our first week in Liu-Cheo [Liuzhou] was spent distributing Gospels on the street and looking for houses, but although the city abounds in empty dwellings, we found great difficulty in renting, as the Chinese in their hatred of the foreigner seemed to band together to prevent us [from] getting a house. . . . North, South, East and West were faithfully traversed. Location now had lost its charm. Anywhere to get a footing. We were willing now to live in an alley; on a back street, or down by the river side.[48]

Maryknoller James E. Walsh wrote from Wuzhou,

> Father Dietz and I are well but getting no converts. I don't hope to do much in Wuchow until we can get a larger property with room enough for a school and a reception hall. Our present home is so small that we could not invite the people here even if they wished to come. I have been dickering [bargaining] for a property for a long time but without success. After a hunt I settled on what I considered the most desirable site, a hill lying between the business section and the foreign section. This would make a fine mission and is suitable on every count. But the price! I was so disgusted that I dropped the whole matter. One could buy the same land in Hongkong itself for a good deal less money. Well, that's the way it goes. We shall have to wait and see what we can do as time goes on.[49]

---

45. Oldfield, *With You Alway.*

46. Oldfield, *Pioneering in Kwangsi.*

47. Macdonald, *Roderick Macdonald, M.D.*, 108. The explanation of "fung shui" is original.

48. Oldfield, "Immediate Evangelization" (December 1, 1906), 344.

49. Walsh, in FMSA, *Maryknoll Mission Letters, China*, 286.

On one occasion, it was the kindness and mercy of the missionaries that led to the opening of a place of residence. It happened that a local mob had attacked the missionaries and even struck the women. When the death penalty was suggested for the perpetrators, the missionaries asked that the offenders only be lightly punished and released. This warmed the hearts of the people toward them and the location in which the attack occurred became an outstation with a chapel.[50]

Securing property in frontier locations was a method also employed by the native evangelistic bands. Mrs. Oldfield illustrates:

> The method of Bands such as this was to hire [rent] a house in a village, and to work the whole district to a radius of fifteen or twenty miles, visiting every home, scattering tracts and Gospels, and preaching every evening and on Sunday in the central village. By very early rising, they themselves were able to spend much time in Bible study and prayer.[51]

Medical Ministry

In order to break down barriers of mistrust, open doors for evangelism, and carry out Christ's command to heal the sick, missionaries commonly engaged in medical ministry. At the time, many Chinese attributed illnesses to the work of evil spirits or deceased ancestors. Accordingly, some of the methods used to treat sickness and disease sound astonishing to modern readers. In one case, a cancer-stricken woman placed a piece of rotten pork on a wound on her side. It was thought that the pork would attract the worms in the wound and draw out the disease. When she finally neared death, her husband and children left her by herself, fearing the evil spirits that might befall them when she died.[52]

Medical ministry not only met a felt need, it also opened the hearts of the people to the missionaries and to the Good News. As previously mentioned, the first Church Missionary Society pioneers to Guilin[53] lived in their boat and conducted medical work in their first few months. This brought Mr. Song who came seeking medical help for his father. Mr. Song later served as their language teacher, helped them rent a place in the city,

---

50. Oldfield, *Pioneering in Kwangsi.*

51. Oldfield, *With You Alway,* 208.

52. Macdonald, *Roderick Macdonald, M.D.,* 178.

53. Rev. and Mrs. Byrde.

and also became their first convert. Arnold Foster told another insightful story:

> One morning, in the interior of the province of Kwang-si, Mr. Andersson and I managed to slip ashore without the soldiers. We walked for a considerable distance along the banks of the river, and at length came to a large town, which we entered. The people of the town were a ruffianly [violent-looking] set, who had probably never seen a foreigner before. We had not been long in the town before we wished we were safely out of it, or that we had the soldiers with us. The people crowded round us in a most menacing manner, and the cry, "Kill the barbarian devils!" was heard on every hand. A tradesman standing in the doorway of his shop caught sight of us struggling through the mob toward the river, and at once called out, "Dr. Wenyon." "What!" I said, "Do you know me?" "I should think I do," he replied. "You cured my arm at the hospital in Fatshan [Foshan, Guangdong]. Come in and have a cup of tea!" That simple episode acted like a spell, and changed at once the conduct of the mob from riot and ridicule to order and respect, and we got back safely to our boats.[54]

Dr. Charlotte Bacon shared what resulted from caring for a Muslim shopkeeper's daughter who had been stricken with malaria:

> By God's grace she recovered, and that meant that Mohammedan homes all over the city were opened to me. I could go in anywhere, and they sent for me right and left, and always after the patient had been seen, came the long earnest upholding of Jesus Christ by the bedside. . . . Now and again in Mohammedan homes has it been said to me in the case of serious illness, "We have been calling on Jesus all night." Our leading catechist, an ex-Mohammedan, was first made an inquirer through seeing a missionary attending to the sick. . . . We can say definitely, however, that the homes of the city, heathen and Mohammedan, can be entered far and wide by the medical staff, and *visiting is not possible otherwise.* We can say that an entrance and a welcome entrance will be accorded to any member of our staff, foreign or native, far and wide throughout the villages around Kweilin, because here is a man healed of trachoma, there a woman cured of cataract, here a boy delivered from stone in the bladder. Oh that we had the men and the means to enter these open doors! . . . So once more it has proved true that healing and preaching

54. Foster, "Christian Progress," 178.

must be one, that ministry to the body is opening the door to the soul, that medical work is the Gospel in action.[55]

As already illustrated in chapter 3, Southern Baptists successfully combined medical care and evangelism at their hospitals in Guilin and Wuzhou. They knew that people were unlikely to come to church but would visit a hospital to have their bodily ailments treated. At the CMS hospital in Guilin, the Bible woman, armed with pictures and tracts, preached to the outpatients in the mornings and taught in the wards in the afternoons.[56] Dr. Bacon wrote, "This 'Way of Life' Hospital is as you know here for one purpose only, that is to proclaim the Way of Life through Jesus."[57]

The medical missionaries themselves evidenced a deep conviction in the importance of their work. Dr. Clift, medical missionary in Nanning, declared, "The channels made use of [in spreading the Gospel] are various, but the Medical Mission is one of the most important."[58] American Presbyterian Mary Fulton commented, "Medicine seems to be the key that is opening all the doors to high and low, rich and poor."[59] The early newsletters of the Church Missionary Society also expressed this conviction. For their first twelve years in Guilin, they lacked a doctor. Their Guangxi-Hunan newsletter frequently mentioned the urgent need for a doctor, and they pleaded for readers to pray. "A medical mission is our great need, and would have untold influence in reaching the people,"[60] wrote Frank Child. Finally, in 1911, the prayer was answered in the arrival of Dr. Charlotte Bailey.[61] Walter Oldfield likewise felt that such a ministry could have aided him in his pioneering trips to the ethnic minorities:

> When traveling, among the tribespeople especially, I frequently meet with such cases and almost invariably it arouses a desire to be a medical missionary. It does seem that going around helping suffering humanity as Jesus did, arouses in the hearts of those helped a sense of appreciation and confidence, and opens the heart to receive the spiritual healing we have come to bring them.[62]

---

55. Bacon, "Five Years' Work in Kweilin," 43–44.

56. Bacon, "Kweilin Medical Work, 1932," "Out-Patients."

57. Bacon, "A Letter from Kweilin Hospital," 5.

58. Clift, *Very Far East*, 8.

59. Fulton, *Inasmuch*, 32.

60. Child, "Kueilin Notes," 47.

61. Bailey, "Kweilin at Last!" She married and became Dr. Bacon.

62. Oldfield, "Uncle Eight," 333.

While Catholic medical ministries in Guangxi did not develop to the degree of that of Protestants, they too spoke of its value:[63]

> Although no conversions were attributed directly to the work of the dispensary, still this charitable enterprise proved of great value, as it helped to win the good will of the people, and at the same time it gave the missioners many opportunities to explain to the poor pagans Christ's commandment of love: "Thou shalt love the Lord thy God with thy whole heart."[64]

Modern Chinese scholar Yan Xiaohua counted at least eighteen hospitals and leper colonies established by missionaries in Guangxi.[65] He also noted some of the positive effects on Guangxi's development which included helping the suffering, training nurses and doctors, encouraging medical education, advancing medical equipment, and improving the overall healthcare system.[66]

Church Planting

Church planting comprised another component of the work of missionaries and their societies. It was an expected outcome of evangelism but received much less emphasis than in present times. All mission societies started churches. When a nucleus of believers existed in a location, a church was birthed.

Main stations usually were associated with a church. This was not always the case with outstations; they were often supervised by female missionaries whose primary ministry centered on women, children, or the profession of nursing. It was common for believers to gather on Sundays at outstations where missionaries or clergymen traveled to preach or conduct Mass or the Lord's Supper.

A church led and supported by indigenous believers was the goal, at least for Protestant agencies. The Church Missionary Society reflected the "three-self"[67] formula drawn up in the nineteenth century by its former general secretary, Henry Venn. In the early 1900s, Louis Byrde (CMS) wrote

---

63. However, Cuenot in *Kwangsi* (239) added that while operating a dispensary was a "considerable advantage," schools were a "vital necessity."

64. Cuenot, *Kwangsi*, 239.

65. Seven Catholic and eleven Protestant. Yan, *Guangxi*.

66. Yan, *Guangxi*.

67. Self-governance, self-support, self-propagation.

that they paid no "native agents."[68] Their reasoning was that they wanted "to instil into the minds of the converts that it is *their* business to support the Church *and* to evangelise the heathen."[69] Early CMS missionaries *were* willing to pay for a personal Chinese ministry helper, but hesitant to go beyond this. In 1928 they wrote, "The Synod made the best use of its time in discussing and devising plans for the progress of the whole work, especially toward the ideal of a self-governing and self-supporting Chinese Church."[70] A cursory search in their Guangxi-Hunan newsletter results in over fifty instances of "self-support" or related terms.

The Christian and Missionary Alliance spoke much more frequently of self-supporting churches. This goal was further solidified following the anti-foreign period. Mrs. Oldfield wrote, "The experiences under Communism [in the 1920s] had shown both the missionaries and the Chinese leaders that a self-supporting, indigenous Church would stand the test far better than one dependent on foreign leadership and money."[71] The CMA even reported the degree to which churches were self-supporting and had plans of tapering off support (by time and percentage) for those that were not. Walter Oldfield reflected the views of the CMA and its missionaries in Guangxi when he wrote,

> Twenty-six missionaries . . . are earnestly laboring to establish on Chinese soil indigenous churches that will be self-supporting, self-managing, and self-propagating. Success is measured, not by the number of missionaries maintained on the field, nor by a row of statistics, however encouraging, but by the degree in which foreign missionaries may be dispensed with, and the church under Chinese leaders still remain spiritual at heart and aggressive in work, extending her evangelistic operations until all the tribes and people still unreached have had at least one opportunity of hearing the Gospel.[72]

Education and Training

Education and training combined to fulfill a final component of the missionary methods used by the societies and their missionaries. Catholics and

---

68. Byrde, "Kueilin Native Church Funds," 19.
69. Byrde, "Kueilin Native Church Funds," 19.
70. Hsu, "Chinese View," 807.
71. Oldfield, *With You Alway*, 215.
72. Oldfield, *Pioneering in Kwangsi*, 191.

Protestants established over 120 schools between 1874 and 1949.[73] The types of schools varied, however, and included boys' schools, girls' schools, Sunday schools, nursing schools, evening Bible classes, schools for cat- echists, preparatory seminaries, and Bible schools. Boys' and girls' schools taught subjects including French, Latin, English, Bible, science, geography, physical education, teamwork, and practical skills.[74] In the early twentieth century, these schools, with their advanced, practical, and broad range of courses, stood in stark contrast to Chinese schools which focused predomi- nantly on the Chinese classics.[75]

French Catholics opened a preparatory seminary in Guigang in 1895 which relocated to Nanning in 1901. There, the candidates studied Latin among other subjects. Those who persevered transferred to the "major seminary" in Penang, Malaysia.[76] Maryknoll established a catechist school in Pingnan in 1935.[77] The CMS operated primary schools in several outsta- tions, a boys' high school and two girls' schools in Guilin, a girls' school superintended by a catechist in Guanyang, and a training school for Bible women.[78]

The largest Protestant training school was the CMA's Wuzhou Bible School.[79] It developed into a launching pad for many of Guangxi's Chris- tians to enter fields of ministry at home and abroad. In 1915, A. B. Simpson remarked, "Perhaps the most valuable agency of the mission in South China is the Bible Training School in Wuchow."[80]

In 1927, the mission schools faced a crisis following the anti-foreign movement. The southern government in Guangzhou began introducing new regulations for private schools. Sun Yat-sen's nationalistic book became required reading and registered schools came under increasing control by the local governments. Bible teaching was allowed but could not be made compulsory; students could choose whether or not they attended Bible

---

73. Catholics established 36 and Protestants 88. Yan, *Guangxi*.

74. Different societies often taught or emphasized different courses (for example, Latin was usually taught in Catholic schools).

75. Yan, *Guangxi*.

76. Cuenot, *Kwangsi*.

77. Wiest, *Maryknoll in China*. It only lasted six months but was reestablished again in 1931 (if not before).

78. Bland, "Kweilin Students"; Couche, "Biblewomen"; Pim, "Yellow Ox Market," "In Touch with China's Young People."

79. Which was called by various names.

80. Simpson, "Annual Survey," 172.

classes or worship services. Other new regulations concerned the school property and staff.[81]

By 1929, the CMS Guangxi-Hunan diocese had closed down all its middle schools, the more prominent ones being located in Hunan.[82] By 1935, authorities had introduced additional regulations. The CMS operated a school in Guilin which was the center for work among women and girls in the city. Issues at the school drew the attention of the local government. The school's leaders were given the choice of registering or shutting it down. Registering meant that they could no longer teach the Bible during school hours or on school grounds and that leadership would pass to a non-Christian principal. The CMS decided to close its doors feeling that its purposes could no longer be served under such restrictions.[83] In some of the villages, Catholics continued to run schools but only taught Christian doctrine during the evening.[84]

MINISTRIES OF COMPASSION

In addition to medical care, missionaries and their societies also engaged in other ministries of compassion.[85] CMA missionaries Mr. and Mrs. Smith opened a school for the blind in Guiping. There, they taught over fifty blind girls skills such as weaving and knitting.[86] Catholics opened orphanages in Nanning, Guigang, Fangchenggang,[87] and in other locations.[88] The CMA established two orphanages in Wuzhou, one for boys and one for girls.[89]

In times of famine, many missionaries and their societies raised money and engaged in famine relief.[90] In 1902, during a serious flood on the West River, English Wesleyans housed sixty-two servants and refugees (and

---

81. Ibbotson, "Flight in Winter."

82. Blenkinsop, "Reconstruction."

83. Tobin, "End of a Chapter."

84. Wiest, *Maryknoll in China.*

85. These were called "corporal works of mercy" by Catholics. Wiest, *Maryknoll in China*, 199.

86. CMA, "Our Foreign Mail Bag" (March 31, 1917); Field et al., "South China Conference."

87. "Chang-se" appears to be Fangchenggang.

88. Launay, *Histoire*; Cuenot, *Kwangsi*. Oldfield mentioned in *Pioneering in Kwangsi* that the Paris Society had two orphanages with twenty-one orphans at that time (1936).

89. Oldfield, *Pioneering in Kwangsi.*

90. CMS, *Church Missionary Gleaner*; Ray, *Cowboy Missionary in Kwangsi.*

twenty of their neighbors' pigs!) on their mission compound.[91] Also that year, CMA missionaries distributed rice gruel to the "starving multitudes" and rice seed to many impoverished farmers.[92]

The CMS rescued a number of young girls from slavery.[93] Such compassion was unheard of in a land which engaged in the trade of human lives. Louis Byrde wrote, "The benign officials have for months forbidden the export of cattle, etc., for fear of impoverishing the country, but the lives of the people seem to be the last thing that 'fathers and mothers of the people,' i.e., the officials, seem to care about."[94] In one case, after a mistress beat her slave girl, the girl poisoned herself to death with opium. However, the mistress was far more concerned that the girl's dead spirit would torment her than the fact that the poor girl died, so she ordered her coolies to move the girl's body far away.[95]

At least a couple of societies served lepers. Wesleyans carried out a ministry to lepers on a small island near Wuzhou.[96] The CMS established the Church Leper Mission in Beihai which was "carried on most efficiently and is one of our very real contributions of hope and healing to Chinese life."[97] To understand how such a ministry to this outcast segment of society stood out, two accounts illustrate how lepers were otherwise perceived and treated:

> In 1911, a decade after the Boxer outbreak, when China was beginning to take her place among the nations, an official of Kwang Si [Guangxi] province, by fair promises, gathered a large number of lepers in an open compound. When all the lepers were crowded in one great compound, his soldiers were ordered to shoot. Dead, dying, maimed, wounded, alike, [they] were thrown into a large pit, covered with oil and burned. A proclamation was issued rebuking the Christian missionary for furnishing food and medicine to these "outcasts who menace the life of the community"; and extolling the work the Governor

91. Macdonald, *Roderick Macdonald, M.D.*, 169. Dr. Macdonald wrote, "Led by her [Margaret's] gentle example the boys and I have agreed to give up butter, jam, and sugar, so that we may put more rice and meat in the little children's 'chuk'—it will do the boys no harm to self-deny a little for the sake of others." Macdonald, *Roderick Macdonald, M.D.*, 171.

92. Oldfield, *With You Alway*, 69.

93. Tobin, "An Unfinished Story."

94. Byrde, "The Evil Arrows of Famine," 8.

95. Holden, "A Door to Be Opened."

96. Oldfield, *Pioneering in Kwangsi*.

97. Donaldson, *The Call*, 53.

had done "for the preservation of the health of his fellow-countrymen." Most native peoples now recognize the desperate condition of the leper. Children sent to the missionary physician are told by their parents, if the diagnosis is leprosy, to go and drown themselves.[98]

Rhoda Watkins, ministering in Guilin, provided a second account:

> Now I would like to tell you the story of the leper woman to whom I was giving the injection. Her son came that morning to thank the doctor for treating his mother, and to beseech her to completely heal her, and this is the story concerning her as he tells: A wealthy man of his native village contracted leprosy, but would not admit that he had this terrible disease. He had money and influence, and so remained on in the village unmolested. Later on four other people contracted leprosy, amongst the number was our patient. The villagers became alarmed at the way the disease was spreading and ordered the lepers to leave the district. The first woman who was told to go refused. The villagers took that woman and burned her alive. The other three lepers fled. Two of them have since died, not of the disease, but from starvation—no provision was made for them. The other, our patient, some Buddhist nuns took pity on and helped, also the son did what he could for her. . . . Stories as of the burning of the poor leper woman fill one with horror, and unfortunately others have shared the same fate as this woman. It makes one realise just how dark heathenism can be. The villagers were filled with fear for themselves, and they had not that love which made provision for the afflicted. It is only the love of Christ which will make men and women concerned for the welfare of others. It is only a knowledge of Him that will enforce laws that are now only on paper and are not in force.[99]

During the Guangxi-Guangdong conflict in 1920 and 1921, Maryknoll missionaries in Wuzhou willingly received those fleeing the fighting and bombs. James E. Walsh wrote, "We had many demands made on us to take people in, and we gladly admitted into our little compound whoever asked to come. The place was crowded with men, women, children, chickens, dogs, baggage, boxes, and household furniture, and we had indeed as much privacy as gold-fish."[100]

98. Halsey, "Go and Tell John," 36.
99. Watkins, "Hospital Stories," 11–12.
100. Walsh, in FMSA, *Maryknoll Mission Letters, China*, 288.

During the Sino-Japanese War, the doctors, nurses, and hospitals operated around the clock. Several non-medical ministries emerged during this time: visiting wounded soldiers, mending their clothes, helping them to write letters back home to their friends and relatives,[101] digging out bomb shelters, and distributing rice and other goods to the impoverished.[102]

Refugees began pouring into Guangxi from other parts of China during the war. The population of Guilin swelled from 150,000 to 350,000 in just five years.[103] A ministry to the refugees arose. The Missionary Service League met in Guilin to unpick cotton material, cut, and sew to make clothing and shoes for them.[104] The CMS made an agreement with the Hong Kong government to look after sick Hong Kong refugees from 1942 to 1944.[105] In Quanzhou, one church designated half of its collection monies to benefit refugees; the refugees used the money to buy mosquito nets, soap, money, and clothing. At Christmas, the refugees received gifts. For a few desperate individuals and families, housing was provided.[106]

The CMS had a station in Xingan (northeast of Guilin). On one occasion, a bus from central China passed through. It dropped off four girls with cholera who were left under the blazing sun. One died within a matter of hours. The other three lingered for two or three days with parched, cracked, and bleeding lips, moaning for water. While they were under the jurisdiction of the local magistrate, it was the Church Missionary Society's head Chinese nurse who helped them. The girls were brought to the missionaries' house where they stayed until strong enough to be transferred to the CMS hospital in Guilin. They recovered and later revisited the Christians in Xingan "looking so well and strong, fat and rosy, full of life and fun."[107] In another case, a fourteen-year-old boy was found lying in a wet field on some straw. He was barefoot and clothed in rags, having walked a thousand miles from Nanjing to Xingan. The Christians helped connect him with his brother who was constructing bridges in Guangxi who began to care for him. In another case, a mother and her three children, ages one, three, and

---

101. Oldfield, "National Christian Service."

102. Yan, *Guangxi*.

103. Bacon, "Way of Life Hospital." Yan said it rose from 80,000 in 1937 to 275,000 in 1942. Yan, *Guangxi*.

104. Tobin, "Child-Refugees."

105. Bacon, "C.M.S. Medical Mission in Kweilin."

106. Prentice, "Refugees."

107. Waterson, "Joy at Hingan," 7.

four, traveled by road from Hankou[108] and fell ill. Missionaries took them in until they were strong enough to move into a refugee camp.[109]

After the war, American Catholics (Maryknollers) helped refugees return to their homes. They set up shelters and soup kitchens near major roads and railroad stations. They also distributed food, clothing, and medicine which were provided by various relief agencies and friends from the United States.[110] Others missionaries took care of orphans and helped out in the rebuilding projects.

Throughout the history of missions in Guangxi, ministries of compassion were predominantly directed at the sick, wounded, disadvantaged, and refugees. But Southern Baptists in Guilin carried out a ministry of another kind—a campaign against cigarette smoking.[111] C. J. Lowe explained,

> We put up posters and give out thousands of circulars condemning this dreadful curse that has come upon China and tends to weaken her as a nation. . . . Even though this is not direct evangelistic endeavor it has opened many doors of opportunity for us because it has shown to the people that we want to get rid of the things that are injuring them as a nation. . . . When they pass us on the street some of them try to hide their cigarettes.[112]

Foot binding received some attention from the missionaries. Although they did not address the issue in any public, large-scale way, they did sometimes address it with individual converts. Couling wrote, "Christian missionaries strongly discouraged foot-binding among their converts, in many cases making unbinding a condition of receiving pupils into their boarding schools, and in a few places, a condition of entering the Church."[113]

Maryknoll historian Jean-Paul Wiest commented that their ministries of compassion (called "corporal works of mercy") had three characteristics: first, they focused on the needs of the community, giving priority to the

---

108. Hubei Province.

109. Waterson, "Joy at Hingan."

110. Wiest, *Maryknoll in China.*

111. Dr. Macdonald of the Wesleyan Methodist Mission himself was a smoker. While in Guangdong in 1889, he wrote in his journal, "Gave up smoking for a time; no habit should be indulged in without a break occasionally." Macdonald, *Roderick Macdonald, M.D.*, 51. Six months later, he again wrote, "Stopped smoking for self-discipline." Macdonald, *Roderick Macdonald, M.D.*, 57. The following year, after a time of special communion with the Lord, he lost the desire to smoke and was able to stop without self-discipline or effort. Macdonald, *Roderick Macdonald, M.D.*, 157.

112. Lowe, "Evangelism on the Kwei Lin Field," 4–5. For an interesting parallel, see footnote 49 on page 119.

113. Couling, *Encyclopedia Sinica*, 30.

poor and defenseless; second, they contributed to the modernization of rural China; and third, they countered China's traditional attitudes toward females and gave new status to women.[114]

While a plethora of practical ministries were carried out, they were not ends in themselves or the ultimate goal; they were usually connected in some way with the proclamation of the gospel.[115] As an example, the Faith and Love Mission discovered the needs of blind girls whom they observed while preaching from house to house, on the city streets, or in villages. They went on to operate a school for blind girls in Guigang where they cared for one hundred blind children. Ada Farmer's comment expressed a view that would have raised no objection among her contemporaries:

> Beloved, it is true the aim of the missionary is not civilization, Westernization, learning, reform, not even the alleviation of pain and the breaking off of awful habits, such as the opium habit and foot-binding, but it is winning men and women to Christ, saving their souls, leading them from the kingdom of Satan to the kingdom of God; yea, bringing men back into harmony with God, so they may glorify Him here and enjoy Him throughout eternity.[116]

Similarly, Rev. Charles Bone said of Dr. Macdonald who treated thousands of patients and started a ministry to lepers,

> No sketch of the life of Dr. Macdonald would be correct without a reference to his strong evangelical sympathies. Though he was a doctor, and a successful one, too, yet it has been abundantly clear that from his advent [arrival] in China, the healing of the body, the enlightenment of the mind, the improvement of the social surroundings of the Chinese, were all sacredly subservient to that aim which is greater than them all. It was his joy, his passion, that men should be turned "from darkness to light, and from the power of Satan unto God, that they might obtain forgiveness of sins, and a lot among those that are sanctified." And lately his mind has been drawn more and more toward the vocation of the preacher, who shall minister to minds diseased, and teach them to find and walk in the way everlasting.[117]

Catholics, too, placed a high priority on salvation. James E. Walsh wrote,

114. Wiest, *Maryknoll in China*.

115. Little is seen of today's sharp division between ministries of social justice and evangelism.

116. Farmer, *Ada Beeson Farmer*, 223.

117. In Macdonald, *Roderick Macdonald, M.D.*, 276.

Missioners who convert pagans in any numbers know that the way to do so is to find some human, and usually more or less material, need that is pressing upon them, and when found, to proceed to find some way to relieve it. . . . Any sincere attempt to help the people in any of their little needs will usually be appreciated and may indeed result in conversions. . . . From the very beginning, the missioner must make his motives plain to the people, explaining and repeating and harping upon the fact that his chief object is not so much to help their bodies as to save their souls.[118]

Finally, in regards to missionary methods and ministries, Catholic Joseph Cuenot's comments are insightful. His criticism of Protestants in Guangxi touches on many of the aforementioned methods as well as the sentiments Protestants and Catholics had for one another:

Protestantism is better known among the upper classes than Catholicism, and gradually the missioners of the former have influenced the lower classes. . . . Owing to their large financial resources, they have been able to establish schools which, placed on an equal footing with the government schools, and well attended because of the eagerness on the part of the Chinese to learn English, have inculated [instilled] into the youth certain principles not always in accordance with the Gospel teaching. Their fine hospitals, staffed with many doctors, have given them prestige, and the local newspapers which they control, even when they have not founded them, publish in every number at least one page of Protestant propaganda. Their missions are established, not only in the towns, but even in country villages. Although their chapels, where they preach every market day, are not filled with practicing converts, they attract the peasants through decoys who pass out propaganda pamphlets, tracts, or pictures. The students who leave their schools and do not pursue higher studies are practically assured of having the help of their pastors in finding positions in the post office or customs. Well-printed notices in large characters are placed in full view along the roads and in meeting places of ever so little importance,

---

118. Wiest, *Maryknoll in China*, 131. Wiest added, "To reduce these corporal works of mercy to a simple strategy is misleading. The approach was founded on the belief that service and the exercise of charity were the essence of Christianity and that they exerted a magnetic attraction to nonbelievers to investigate the motivating force behind such works. . . . These concrete expressions of Christian charity projected the Gospel's message that concern for other people, especially those in direst need, was the true mark of someone's love for God and a path to salvation." Wiest, *Maryknoll in China*, 132.

to recall to the pagans that Protestantism is the only road to salvation and true happiness. If their European and American ministers do not generally attack Catholicism, this cannot be said of the native pastors or catechists, who use every occasion to vilify. . . . Many possible converts flock to their churches, but not all are equally serious and, although admission to baptism is easy, many of them go as quickly as they come. There are, however, some fine individuals among these converts, who are lost to Catholicism once they are caught in the net of Protestantism. . . . The old man told the fathers that the other Christians in his village had become Protestants, because "the Protestants have schools and the Catholics have none."[119]

119. Cuenot, *Kwangsi*, 163–66, 226.

10

Challenges, Costs, and Martyrs

THE HISTORY OF CHRISTIAN missions in Guangxi is one of sacrifice. The costs affected every facet of life: physical, material, social, emotional, psychological, spiritual, and every combination thereof.[1]

Several physical challenges and dangers—hazardous boat travel, bandits, pirates, and disease—have already been described. The oppressive weather warrants a few more comments. Modern readers would do well to imagine a day and age before air conditioning and electric fans. Scottish missionary Thomas Cochrane wrote of Guangxi's weather, "The moist heat from May to September is very trying."[2] When two of the pioneer Christian and Missionary Alliance missionaries entered Guangxi, they returned to Guangzhou when it grew too hot and left their Chinese associates to preach. The heat also made language study difficult during summer months. Writing from Guilin, Mrs. A. B. Child declared,

> There is nothing in the least amusing to tell you about that, it's just grind, grind, grind, until one feels half dazed, and all the time one is being simply melted with the awful heat. . . . Now don't exclaim "Oh! how lazy to go to sleep in the middle of the day." Indeed in this hot climate it is absolutely necessary, so for one and a half hours we are all invisible [asleep].[3]

1. Broomhall in *Chinese Empire* boiled these costs and challenges down to four causes: (1) Chinese attaching themselves to the church for political reasons; (2) A "commercial spirit" affecting all who were accepting new ideas; (3) The methods used by Roman Catholics causing bitterness among the Chinese; (4) Unrest and uprisings.

2. Cochrane, *Survey*, 4.

3. Child, "Everyday Life at Kueilin," 50.

Two years later, she wrote,

> Though it is the first week in September, it is an intensely hot day, with the temperature already over ninety degrees. Every door and window is wide open, and one and all are armed with fans of every shape and kind, from a palm leaf to the prettily painted and gaily coloured round gauze fan.[4]

Mrs. Clift said in Nanning,

> It has been terrifically hot the last week—life was something of a struggle, and I felt wickedly lazy, but we both feel we are ending the week with the comfortable consciousness that we have got through a fair amount of work today.[5]

Bishop Holden (CMS) even said the weather affected writing newsletters:

> This letter is being written at a date later than I had hoped, but various circumstances have conspired to make this inevitable. Pressure of insistent duties, and very hot weather, make it almost impossible to attempt anything beyond what was absolutely necessary until a few days ago. . . . Hot weather certainly is not the best time for writing.[6]

Some missionaries engaged in an "autumn offensive" after the hot summers. Rev. Joe Leach of the CMS wrote,

> Poetically speaking, Autumn is the time when the golden glory of summer begins to wane and decay, but for us in China the waning of the sun is the signal for offensive action. If you inferred from this that we had been idle during the summer, the inference would be wrong.[7]

Guangxi's mountainous landscape introduced another physical challenge. The mountains manifested God's splendor, but they also presented a great obstacle. Walter Oldfield personally experienced the challenge of the mountains when he took pioneer trips into the "neglected territories." He completed journeys of 300, 335, 700, 800, and 2,000 miles at various points,[8]

---

4. Child, "Sunday in Kueilin," 42.

5. Clift, *Very Far East*, 193. As a contrasting view, Dr. Macdonald in Wuzhou wrote, "I keep very well, and in spite of the heat can sleep and work with great comfort." Macdonald, *Roderick Macdonald, M.D.*, 213.

6. Holden, "The Bishop's Letter" (October, 1931), 2.

7. Leach, "Our Autumn Offensive," 9.

8. In 1916, 1931, 1915, 1928, and 1934, respectively.

much of which passed through mountainous territory.[9] On one of his trips, the pain and swelling from blisters was so bad that he cut a piece of wood and tied it to his heel to keep the sole of his foot off the ground.[10] He put a missionary's perspective on the mountains when he wrote,

> In places their rugged grandeur reminds one of the Canadian Rockies, but to the Gospel pioneer who has to climb them they lose much of their attractiveness by the blisters they raise, and the groans of weariness they entail, before the other side is reached.[11]

Joseph Cuenot of the Paris Society cited two other challenges he categorized as physical. The first was the fact that suitable locations were hard to obtain and that missionaries were physically spread out. The second was that Guangxi was on the border of Tonkin (French-Indochina). The French defeat of China there in 1885 resulted in a deep hatred for anything French in neighboring Guangxi.[12]

Material costs took various forms but primarily involved the destruction of property and the loss of personal possessions. Bandits looted mission stations and took everything of value on mission compounds, in mission hospitals, and from the missionaries themselves. Pirates pillaged boats and robbed numerous missionaries on their river voyages. The early Presbyterian hospital in Pingnan was destroyed by a mob. Mr. and Mrs. Louis Byrde lost an extensive collection of books and Bibles after a river voyage accident.[13] In 1932, a fire destroyed the Alliance printing press in Wuzhou.[14]

The anti-foreign period of the 1920s resulted in the destruction of a considerable amount of property. The Alliance chapels in Wuzhou and Longzhou were looted.[15] The CMS mission residence in Guilin was decimated by fire. The hospital, too, was badly damaged and its microscopes smashed.[16] Furniture, Bibles, and songbooks in the churches were also destroyed.

9. Glover, "Our Foreign Mail Bag" (April 29, 1916); Oldfield, "Pioneering in Kwang Si's Neglected Territory" (August 25, 1928), 555; Oldfield, "Attacked by Chinese Robbers," "Golden Opportunities"; Simpson, "Annual Survey," 172.

10. Oldfield, "After Ten Years," 826.

11. Oldfield, *Pioneering in Kwangsi*, 17.

12. Cuenot, *Kwangsi*.

13. CMS, *Church Missionary Gleaner*.

14. Snead, *Missionary Atlas* (1950).

15. CMA, "Editorials" (May 15, 1926); CMA, "Recent Cablegrams."

16. Holden, "The Bishop's Letter" (September 1926); Bacon, "Report of the Kweilin Hospital."

The most widespread and severe destruction of property occurred during the war with Japan. Guilin was 90 percent destroyed. Everything but the walls and chimney of the hospital which Dr. Bacon had spent so long in building came down. The mission house, schools, and all three CMS churches—except the walls of St. John's Church—were gone. CMS Bishop Stevens wrote, "Of all the fine blocks of buildings belonging to the Mission there was not so much as a room with a roof on where we could go to reside even for a time."[17] In Wuzhou, all that was left of the CMA headquarters was some broken walls.[18] In several outstations, the churches and mission residences were destroyed. In some cases, brick churches remained standing, but windows were knocked out and the insides burnt out or ruined.[19]

The harsh reality was that despite years of hard work, labor-intensive buildings and valuable medical supplies could be lost in a matter of minutes.[20] But the missionaries managed to maintain a proper perspective on material goods. After their boat wreck, Louis Byrde wrote, "We must take joyfully the spoiling of our goods."[21] In Guilin after the Japanese occupation, Eric Hague spoke of a "religion in ruins" but no "ruin in religion."[22] Bishop Stevens said essentially the same thing: "'The work of many years gone, and the labour wasted!' . . . True enough of material things, but not of the spiritual, for work had been done that no bombs could destroy."[23]

While God allowed the temporal to be destroyed, at times missionaries spoke of miraculous intervention. Mrs. Oldfield told a story in which a Chinese Christian helper, a lady, was bringing a missionary's belongings on a small river craft. Bandits emerged but perceived that the boat was full of soldiers and cried out telling the others to turn back. The believers concluded that God had sent heavenly soldiers to protect the lady and the belongings.[24] In 1931, government troops once again besieged Guilin in an attempt to drive out a rebel army. After the troops bombed the city, some of those who had fled returned to an Alliance chapel asking about the "men in white" on the roof. They assumed they were foreigners putting up a bomb-resistant roof. The local evangelist stationed at the chapel replied that no

---

17. Stevens, "Peeps into the Past," 18.

18. Oldfield, *With You Alway.*

19. Stevens, "Bishop's Foreword" (December 1946); Stevens, "Peeps into the Past"; Hague, "Religion in Ruins"; Law, "Impressions."

20. Farmer, *Ada Beeson Farmer.*

21. In Stevens, "Bishop's Foreword" (January 1937), 4.

22. Hague, "Religion in Ruins," 15–16.

23. Stevens, "Peeps into the Past," 18.

24. Oldfield, *With You Alway.*

one had been on the roof. After a subsequent bombing, they again returned to the chapel asking about the men in white on the roof. It occurred to the evangelist that God had sent his angels to guard over their little chapel. From that point on, many of the local residents fled to the chapel during the bombings where they listened intently to the local evangelist preach the gospel.[25]

Lack of funds constituted another material challenge. Catholics cited a lack of money for schools and other establishments as a hindrance to their ministry.[26] The CMS and Wesleyan Missionary Societies also expressed limitations on their ministries due to finances. Times of war exacerbated this financial problem as inflation drove up prices. During the war with Japan, the price of an egg, which normally cost two cents, rose to one hundred dollars.[27] Medical missionaries like Dr. Clift and Dr. Macdonald, however, were not as limited by funding from overseas as they both conducted self-supporting medical work.[28]

Socially and emotionally, the costs included separation from loved ones, struggles in cultural adjustment, and the death of family members on the field. Facing persistent dangers also caused anxiety and emotional stress. This was more acute during Japanese air raids, confrontation with robbers and bandits, and in times of war. Walter Oldfield noted another "burden of the work, which presses so heavily on the missionary."[29] He was referring to the public executions he witnessed: beheadings, a woman strangled to death in the death cage, and three criminals who were thrown alive into a burning pit and shot.[30] According to Mrs. Child in Guilin, such horrors happened "almost daily."[31]

Missionaries also experienced rejection due to the anti-foreign climate. The foreign devils[32] were viewed with a deep sense of superstition and fear.[33] The results of the Franco-Chinese War of the 1880s caused the Chinese hatred of the French, but the local people could not distinguish the

25. Woerner, "An Angel Guard."

26. Cuenot, *Kwangsi*, 183.

27. Stevens, "Outline of Events."

28. It was said those who could pay did so but that the poor were never turned away. Macdonald, *Roderick Macdonald, M.D.*

29. Oldfield, "Immediate Evangelization" (September 22, 1906), 185.

30. Oldfield, "Atrocities in Kwangsi."

31. Child, "Some Needed Changes," 58. Crucifixions were said to take place just across the border in Hunan in Yongzhou.

32. "It was known all over the city that the 'foreign devil' had gone to Kweilin [Guilin] to bring his wife, the 'foreign devil woman,' to reside at P'ingloh [Pingle]." Farmer, *Ada Beeson Farmer*, 127.

33. Fulton, *Inasmuch*; Farmer, *Ada Beeson Farmer*.

French from any other Westerners.[34] Protestants were guilty by association with the Catholics. This context made entry into the province very difficult. Mrs. Clift wrote,

> It is a fact that we have to face—THEY DON'T WANT US. I think of the beautiful and often touching hymns we sing at home in our missionary meetings—"Come over and help us, we die in our anguish"—and many others. And they are *true*—the NEED of the people criest to us with an exceeding bitter cry, but they don't *know* that they need us and they certainly do not *want* us.[35]

This social rejection often involved physical and material consequences. In Pingnan County, when pioneer Presbyterian missionaries tried to enter, they were struck with stones. When one of the early Baptists tried to enter Guilin, his boat was burned, and he was sent back down the river on another boat.[36]

During the anti-foreign period, even Chinese Christians became antagonistic toward the work of foreign missionaries. Some of these native believers withdrew from their churches and formed a Chinese church independent of foreign influence.[37] Robert Jaffray noted that the positive result of this withdrawal was an increasingly indigenous church.[38] But in general, missionaries were vulnerable in such uprisings. Latourette wrote, "Missionaries were more widely scattered than were foreign merchants or diplomats and so bore the brunt of the anti-foreign outbreaks."[39] During the 1920s, the situation grew so dangerous that most missionaries fled and stayed in Hong Kong or other locations until the anti-foreign zeal cooled off.[40] While it did simmer down for a while, it did not disappear. Three years later, Woerner wrote, "To be anti-Church in Kwangsi has been and still is popular. The local papers are constantly featuring some phase of 'down with Christianity.'"[41]

Language acquisition created another difficulty for the missionaries. In Guangxi, three languages were common: Hakka, Cantonese, and Mandarin. However, when moving from one region in Guangxi to another, the languages differed. Additionally, a multitude of tribal languages existed. Cuenot claimed,

---

34. Latourette, *History of Christian Missions in China*.
35. Clift, *Very Far East*, 176.
36. Lackey, *Laborers Together*.
37. Oldfield, *Pioneering in Kwangsi*.
38. Tozer, *Let My People Go*.
39. Latourette, *History of Christian Missions in China*, 429.
40. Tozer, *Let My People Go*.
41. Woerner, "Impressions," 10.

"Far more difficult [than Mandarin, Hakka, or Cantonese] is the learning of the aboriginal languages."[42] Gustave Woerner (CMA) remarked of this difficulty, "This literal 'Babel' of languages is one of Satan's most effective means to retard the progress of the Gospel. Kwangsi is not exempt from this curse."[43]

George Wiseman added another dimension to the costs of missionary service when he said, "Many understand that missioners have to endure material hardships; but not many know about the trials and disappointments of a more spiritual nature."[44] Catholics cited several such difficulties. These included grief over seekers who returned to paganism,[45] sorrow over believers dying without having had the sacraments, angst over enslaved girls or women, and anxious concern for Christians with whom the missionary had invested much. Chinese Catholics who converted to Protestantism also brought grief to Catholic missionaries. Cuenot called the "active propaganda of the Protestants" one of the three main obstacles to their work. He added, "Although they [the Protestants] did not come until 1900, after the Catholic missioners had blazed the trail, we must admit that since then they have lost no time."[46] One village called Tai Yung four hours from Pingnan was once entirely Catholic "until the Protestants came and bought over half the number by taking a member from a family here and another there, and giving them positions with attractive salaries."[47]

Protestants and Catholics alike encountered the ministerial difficulty of making the gospel comprehensible. Superstition and cultural differences created formidable barriers. R. A. Kowles (CMA) remarked, "In bringing the gospel to them, as pioneers, we must first clear away the thorns, briers, and weeds of superstitious beliefs in cramped, darkened minds while at the same time trying to sow the seed of the Word."[48] Many people were simply complacent with their lives. They remained content to worship idols, sacrifice to demons, and make offerings to ancestors to the chagrin of the missionaries.[49] "They don't want Jesus, but oh! how they need Him!" said Mrs.

---

42. Cuenot, *Kwangsi*, 166–67.

43. Woerner, "Present Evangelistic Opportunities in Kwangsi," 698.

44. Wiseman, translator's preface in Cuenot, *Kwangsi*, vi.

45. Due to a lack of catechists.

46. Cuenot, *Kwangsi*, 163. The reference to the year 1900 should probably be taken as a general or rounded year.

47. Cuenot, *Kwangsi*, 221.

48. Kowles, "Marketing for Souls," 505.

49. Cuenot in *Kwangsi* said that some catechumens (those being taught in the faith) would hide their idols when the catechist (teacher) came. They would bring them back out when the catechist left.

Clift.[50] "If ever China needed the Gospel, she needs it now, at this great crisis in her history. She needs it, but she doesn't want it."[51] She also lamented, "When you remember that this is only one of hundreds and hundreds of superstitions in which these women fully believe, you can see how hard it is to get them to listen seriously to the Gospel."[52]

To bridge the cultural gap, some missionaries adopted native styles of architecture and dress. Mrs. Clift said, "It has been our ambition to have a chapel which would not strike the Chinese as very strange and foreign."[53] Some Protestant missionaries found greater acceptance by wearing the local dress. However, this brought its own complications. Mrs. Clift wrote, "It's very funny what a sore point Chinese dress is even among missionaries. Those who don't wear it always seem to have an irresistible desire to attack those who do."[54] French Catholics in Guangxi required the use of the black and white cassock. However, James E. Walsh permitted Maryknoll (American) missionaries to wear a Chinese gown over a Chinese shirt and trousers.[55]

Catholics used Chinese forms of hospitality. They extended "strict Oriental courtesy" to those who came to their missions. Native catechists greeted guests with a pipe, cigarettes, or tea.[56] One priest noted the benefit that came from holding a housewarming party for local officials, merchants, and other notable individuals. After that, he "was given the key of the city, and [his] miseries were at an end."[57]

In addition to the barriers of understanding and acceptance, missionaries dealt with people who harbored ulterior motives. Neither Catholics nor Protestants were immune to this issue. Some Chinese wanted to associate with foreigners for material gain.[58] Joseph Cuenot of the Paris Society said, "The hope of material aid and financial assistance, as we have seen, often draws pagans to religion."[59] In one location it was said that "many families desired to become Catholics because they thought that the missioner

---

50. Clift, *Very Far East*, 64.

51. Clift, *Very Far East*, 155.

52. Clift, *Very Far East*, 64–65. The superstition was believing that the illness of a son was caused by a demon making off with his soul.

53. Clift, *Very Far East*, 236.

54. Clift, *Very Far East*, 96.

55. Wiest, *Maryknoll in China*.

56. Cuenot, *Kwangsi*, 105.

57. Cuenot, *Kwangsi*, 121.

58. Oldfield, *Pioneering in Kwangsi*.

59. Cuenot, *Kwangsi*, 151.

had come to open silver mines and that he had a capital of $100,000 to invest in the project."[60] Other missionaries contended with those who wanted to practice English but had no interest in the gospel. Mrs. Oldfield commented that inexperienced missionaries without discernment permitted a few with ulterior motives into the Church.[61] Joseph Cuenot shared one (not recommended!) way he and perhaps other Catholics sought to remedy this difficulty:

> We must appeal to motives other than the glory of God and the salvation of souls. For example, such motives are the desire to convert a pagan family with the hope of a later union in marriage, or the desire to bring an influential individual into the Catholic community because his assistance would be valuable. . . . Motives of temporal interest are needed to draw an individual or a group to the Church.[62]

A second way Catholics and the Church Missionary Society dealt with ulterior motives was to delay baptism, often for long periods of time. They believed this would reveal the seeker's (the "inquirer's") true motives.[63] Mrs. Child (CMS) wrote,

> So you see it is only after real testing that the Chinese are baptised in Kueilin. This is why our numbers are but few, for we feel it is far better to be strict and have only a small Church, and those truly converted, than to have a long list of baptized who may soon leave us or dishonour the name of Christ.[64]

Discipling native believers posed a real ministerial challenge for the missionaries. One problem was the native believers' lack of availability. Many worked hard during the day and in the evenings, showed little desire to study. In addition, many worked on Sundays just like any other day of the week. Joseph Cuenot said, "Anyone can readily understand the difficulty of training Christians under such conditions."[65] He added,

> It is almost impossible to obtain regular attendance at classes: one boy must tend the water buffalo; another is kept at home to mind his little sister, or, if he does come to school, he will arrive

60. Cuenot, *Kwangsi*, 127.

61. Oldfield, *With You Alway*.

62. Cuenot, *Kwangsi*, 110–11, 126.

63. "The length of time required before baptism varies with the individual; except in rare cases, a year is necessary." Cuenot, *Kwangsi*, 131.

64. Child, "Drops of Blessing at Kueilin," 5.

65. Cuenot, *Kwangsi*, 131.

with her strapped to his back; a third must prepare the meals for his parents and wait for their return, and so it goes. Further, classes worthy of the name are impossible since, as a result of irregular attendance, no two of the pupils will be studying the same book or the same chapter. The only way to assure regularity would be to feed every pupil at the mission.[66]

Cuenot further stated that for this reason, those who lived near stations usually grew more spiritually; conversely, those in remote areas were in greater danger of falling away.

Another problem for Catholics and Protestants in discipling and training native Christians concerned marriage. Many believers committed apostasy over issues of marriage. For Protestants, marriage to non-Christians was the primary issue. Single Christians faced the temptation of marrying outside the faith. Christian parents were likewise tempted to give a child in marriage to a non-believer.[67] The CMS hospital in Guilin lost its senior nurse who married a non-believer and later drifted away from Christ.[68] Before 1940, the CMS had a rule, albeit not always strictly enforced, to excommunicate Christians who married non-Christians. In 1940 they overturned the rule and replaced it with a rule to simply exhort Christians to marry Christians. However, for paid workers who arranged their children to marry non-Christians, they could no longer be employed by the church.[69] Catholic issues with marriage were related to teachings on priestly celibacy. They opened a school to train catechists, but it did not succeed because "the young neophytes . . . found difficulty in keeping the vow of chastity."[70]

Third, the loss of potential leaders in the church discouraged missionaries in their attempts to disciple native believers. Men sometimes left ministry jobs to work in the higher-paying public schools. Cuenot commented, "The desire for a position which brought more financial returns was stronger than the zeal and gratitude toward the faith that had educated them. Once more the devil had raised a barrier against the evangelization of Kwangsi."[71]

---

66. Cuenot, *Kwangsi*, 133.

67. Whether to a believer or not, daughters had little power to resist. Mrs. Oldfield said, "A Chinese girl's only weapon against an unwelcome engagement is tears." Oldfield, *With You Alway*, 55.

68. Bacon, "Kweilin Hospital Sorrows and Joys."

69. Stevens, "Bishop's Foreword" (September 1940).

70. Cuenot, *Kwangsi*, 101.

71. Cuenot, *Kwangsi*, 100.

Fourth, a lack of zeal and courage marked many native believers. Cuenot cited this as one of the limiting factors in their work. In regards to evangelism, which he called "introducing religion in pagan homes," he said,

> We must admit that, with a few exceptions, they are timid in this regard, if they are faced with danger. . . . The limitation of zeal to the salvation of the souls of relatives or friends, is one reason why the number of Christians in our various districts is so small. . . . it remains generally true that the Christians of Kwangsi [Guangxi] seem not interested in the eternal salvation of their relatives or pagan friends.[72]

Louis Byrde had a similar experience. He cited the lack of evangelistic zeal as one of the top three reasons[73] for the CMS's slow growth. He wrote,

> Our converts are young men of no position, and they hesitate to take a prominent position in witnessing for Christ, chiefly through fear of man, but also due to an inherent love of ease, and a "don't bother me" kind of spirit.[74]

While some Catholic and Protestant Christians alike were timid in sharing their faith,[75] many exhibited extraordinary boldness and a willingness to suffer for the gospel. Oldfield wrote, "One often hears of the hardships and trials which the missionaries bear; of the horrors of robbery and kidnaping which some are called upon to suffer, but we hear comparatively little of the persecutions and sufferings which our devoted Chinese Christians are frequently called upon to bear."[76] Colporteurs undertook great hardship to take Christian literature to new territories. By 1928, a third colporteur working with the CMA went missing and was pronounced dead.[77] In 1939, three colporteurs were falsely accused of being spies and faced five horrid months in appalling prison conditions.[78] Dr. Charlotte Bacon wrote in 1924,

---

72. Cuenot, *Kwangsi*, 100, 111, 168.

73. The second reason was the fact that Chinese people were exclusive and suspicious; the third was that they longed for western wealth and position but not religion.

74. Byrde, "Kueilin Notes," 46.

75. Bible women often took volunteers with them on trips into the countryside. This was said to have encouraged the spirit of evangelism among the volunteers. Oldfield, "From Village to Village."

76. Oldfield, "Preaching Amid Persecution," 386.

77. CMA, "Old Missionary Mail Bag."

78. Oldfield, "Five Months in a Chinese Prison."

How we thank Him, too, for the progress in the Church, both in town and country, in spite of all the changes and chances of the particular time. For the stedfastness and bravery of the cat- echists and evangelists, continuing in their posts and doing their work in continual peril of robbers.[79]

One Chinese Christian, Leo T. Chao, had the opportunity to go to America in 1913 to study at the expense of the Chinese government. At the time, that was one of the greatest ambitions and highest honors for a Chinese student. However, before leaving, Mr. Chao, despite fierce opposi- tion from family and friends, felt the call of the Lord and decided to stay in Guangxi to preach to his people. Mrs. Oldfield commented, "Some are called to leave home, country and friends to preach the Gospel in a foreign land. Leo T. Chao was called to stay at home! In the circumstances, his sac- rifice was the greater."[80] He went on to become the chairman of the CMA's Chinese division in Guangxi.[81]

Chinese believers, as a matter of fact, were often the ones who often suffered *the most*. During the Boxer Rebellion, thirty thousand Chinese Christians died while less than two hundred foreign missionaries met the same fate.[82] In Guangxi, a single Frenchman (Chapdelaine) was martyred, but two Chinese Catholics died with him. Many Chinese had to endure the ridicule by their own people who accused them of becoming slaves of the foreigners or selling themselves to the French.[83] After the Communist take- over in 1949, the foreign missionaries left while Chinese Christians had to stay to "fight the good fight of faith" under Communism.[84]

But the foreign missionaries certainly experienced their share of trials. Walter Oldfield's summary of the hardships faced by the CMA missionaries in Guangxi reads not unlike that of the Apostle Paul:[85]

Missionaries have been persecuted; they have been stoned by the people; mobbed by hostile crowds; driven out of various cit- ies by angry mobs. They have passed through riots, not know- ing what would be the outcome. They have faced the dangers of civil war, when homes have been struck by shot and shell; they

79. Bacon, "Bluffers and Bandits in Kweilin," 495.

80. Oldfield, *With You Alway*, 188.

81. Oldfield, *Pioneering in Kwangsi*; Cunningham, "The Work in Kweilin"; Field, "A Rice Christian?" This was often called the "Chinese conference" or "Chinese committee."

82. Farmer, *Ada Beeson Farmer*.

83. Cuenot, *Kwangsi*.

84. This included the Cultural Revolution from 1966 to 1976.

85. Compare with 2 Cor. 11:24–27.

have passed through the horrors of famine and pestilence when confined in besieged cities. They have been robbed, kidnapped by cruel bandits and forced to endure the harrowing experience of being held for ransom in mountain caves and robber dens and being dragged night after night from one hiding place to another, not knowing how or when the awful ordeal would end.[86]

Mrs. Clift echoed the sentiments of many when she stated, "No one would exactly choose to make their home in an inland Chinese town if they could live elsewhere, unless it were because God called them there."[87] But God's calling and its accompanying hardships brought great reward. In 1928, Walter Oldfield remarked, "Frequently the greater the trials the missionary has to encounter, the greater the obstacles he has to meet, the greater the blessing when he presses through."[88] Mrs. Oldfield stated in her autobiography, "Praise God, the joy of being in His will makes all these inconveniences seem as nothing."[89] She later added, "Praise the Lord, I would not be anywhere else in all the world but right here, for I know I am in His will, and that brings peace and rest in spite of circumstance."[90] John Fee reflected on his 1895 pioneering trip into Guangxi by saying, "In my ten years in China I have at no time had more blessed fellowship with God, or more joy in the work, than in those trying days."[91] Southern Baptist Ida Taylor declared,

> I had rather walk in old Wuchow with its problems, dirt and misery, and be of service there, than to have the luxuries that surround you here in this country.[92] There is joy in working where you realize there is such a great need.[93]

MARTYRS AND DEATHS

Many Christians paid the ultimate price for their service in Guangxi: their lives. Some were killed directly for their Christian witness while others died of secondary causes. While some would only consider the former true

86. Oldfield, *Pioneering in Kwangsi*, 208.
87. Clift, *Very Far East*, 225.
88. Oldfield, "After Ten Years," 826.
89. Oldfield, *With You Alway*, 43.
90. Oldfield, *With You Alway*, 63.
91. In Oldfield, *Pioneering in Kwangsi*, 76.
92. Country unspecified, but probably the United States.
93. In Lackey, *Laborers Together*, 33.

martyrs, it is still the case of the latter that it was their faith that brought them to Guangxi in the first place.

Catholic

The deaths of Andrew Xavier Koffler in 1651 and Auguste Chapdelaine in 1856 have already been noted. Others followed. In 1881, Father Eugene Creuse of the Paris Foreign Mission Society disappeared on the river around Baise. The details are lost to history, but he was "probably murdered either by pirates or by the owner of the boat on which he was traveling."[94] In 1897, Father Mazel was killed. He was on his way to a new post when alarming reports came that bandits were marauding ahead of him. Mazel stopped in a small town in Baise's Lingyun where a Catholic mission house was located. In the middle of the night, the bandits entered the house and shot him.[95] Bishop Chouzy responded to his murder with this observation: "The crime was committed principally out of hatred for the name 'European' and 'French.'"[96] Bishop Chouzy himself died in Wuzhou in 1899.

Another priest, thirty-two-year-old Matthieu Bertholet of the Paris Society, carried out a ministry to the Yi. He was killed by bandits armed with lances in Laibin's Xiangzhou in 1898.[97] In 1921, native Chinese priest Father Louis Tsin was taken captive and killed by bandits. In 1940, during the Japanese air raids, the French priest Father Seosse hid in a dugout, contracted pneumonia, and died. He had served in Guangxi for thirty-six years.[98]

Protestant

Protestants also had a number of missionaries who died serving in Guangxi. In 1905, five American missionaries were killed in Beihai, Hepu (although Beihai was still part of Guangdong at the time). The following year, pirates shot Dr. Roderick Macdonald of the Wesleyan Mission Society as he returned by ship to Wuzhou. The year after, Walter Oldfield's fiancée Beulah Funk died of pneumonia. A decade later, G. L. Hughes died in Baise of a fever which affected his pre-existing heart condition. In 1924, CMA

94. Cuenot, *Kwangsi*, 6.

95. Cuenot, *Kwangsi*.

96. Cited in Cuenot, *Kwangsi*, 37.

97. Cordier, "Martyrs in China"; Latourette, *History of Christian Missions in China*; Cuenot, *Kwangsi*.

98. Cuenot, *Kwangsi*.

missionary Joseph R. Cunningham was killed by a stray bullet in Guilin after having served in South China for twenty-seven years (see figure 6 for additional Alliance missionaries who died).[99] In 1925 during the anti-foreign uprising, the wife of Rev. Cannell (CMS) died of burns the day after the mission house was destroyed by fire.[100] In 1951, Southern Baptist Dr. William Wallace, who served many years at the Stout Memorial Hospital in Wuzhou, also "joined the martyrs in heaven."[101]

Missionary	*Cause of Death*	*Date*	*Place*
Mr. Clarence H. Reeves	Smallpox	Mar. 5, 1898	Wuchow
Miss Agnes Cooney	Fever	Aug. 1, 1900	Macao
Mrs. Mazie Doner Hess	Fever	Sept. 22, 1902	Wuchow
Mr. Henry Zehr	Smallpox	Apr. 11, 1904	Kwaiping
Miss Theodora H. Campbell	Fever	Nov. 6, 1904	Wuchow
Mr. George T. Sherman	Smallpox	Mar. 7, 1907	Pinglo
Mrs. Ada Beeson Farmer	Dysentery	Mar. 12, 1907	Kwaiping
Miss Beulah Funk	Fever	Nov. 21, 1907	Kweilin
Mrs. M. C. Allward	Smallpox	May 22, 1911	Hongkong
Mr. G. Lloyd Hughes	Heart failure	Aug. 25, 1911	Hongkong
Miss M. Edith Dyer	Smallpox	Dec. 31, 1916	Pinglo
Mr. Alvin W. Field	Malignant malaria	Aug. 29, 1919	Hongkong
Mr. Isaac L. Hess	Heart failure	July 26, 1923	Wuchow
Mr. Joseph R. Cunningham	Accidental	Apr. 26, 1924	Kweilin

Figure 6: CMA missionaries to Guangxi who died.
Oldfield, *Pioneering in Kwangsi*, 208. George T. Sherman, Mrs. Oldfield's first husband, actually died the following year. Oldfield, *With You Alway*.

99. CMA, "Editorials" (June 21, 1924).

100. Holden, "The Bishop's Letter" (September 1926).

101. Ray, *Cowboy Missionary in Kwangsi*, 85.

11

Receptivity, Results, and Evaluation

RECEPTIVITY LEVELS AND RESULTS

RECEPTIVITY LEVELS WAXED AND waned throughout the history of Christian missions in Guangxi. Protestants experienced greater resistance in early years as the pioneers plowed in hard soil. Mrs. Child (CMS) wrote from Guilin in 1908, "Very many of these people don't want to hear about Jesus, they want to make money and get rich, and they haven't any time to think about God and heaven."[1] By the time that Protestants had gained an established presence in Guangxi in the early twentieth century, however, Roman Catholic membership had already reached the thousands. In 1905, Catholics had 3,201 members; four years later, membership had risen to 3,610; by 1916 it had reached 4,700.[2] For the CMS, they had baptized fewer than forty-five people by 1909.

After the Protestants served Guangxi's people and won their hearts, they became more open to the gospel. The period from 1910 to 1925 was one of steady growth. In 1914, the CMS reported over 350 baptisms and four years later over 500. Southern Baptist church membership in 1921 in Guilin reached 686, up from only 12 in 1913. There were also 1,196 Christians in

1. Child, "The Women of Kweilin," 24.

2. Broomhall, *Chinese Empire*, 288; Wolferstan, *Catholic Church in China*, 448; Planchet, *Les Missions de Chine*, 302–3. These numbers differ somewhat from those in Montanar.

the greater Guilin region.[3] The CMA experienced its most fruitful year in 1922. However, it was not explosive church growth like in other fields as CMS bishop John Holden's reflection in 1920 indicates: "It is evident that we are not confronted by any Mass Movement similar to those which our brethren in India and Africa have to deal with."[4]

In the years following the anti-foreign outbreaks of the mid-1920s, receptively levels plummeted in Guilin. In the CMS "Way of Life" Hospital, they plodded along faithfully without seeing much fruit. In 1929, Dr. Charlotte Bacon wrote,

> The nurses in the surgical dressing room, the dispenser dispensing medicines, the nurses in the wards, the morning prayers, the outpatient preaching, the teaching of inpatients, the nightly evangelistic children's and inpatients' meeting, all have their part in making it (the hospital) what it so often is called in Mrs. Chang's Prayers, "*Chu tih I uen*"[5] —"The Lord's Hospital." But how few results we see![6]

Receptivity levels did not change for the CMS in Guilin in the early- to mid-1930s. Rhoda Watkins wrote in 1932, "Sometimes we in [the] hospital feel very discouraged as to the few who are baptised here as a result of what they hear. We seem to be continually 'sowing the seed,' but the people come and go and we do not know the result."[7] However, the spiritual climate was different in an outstation of Guilin. Blanche Tobin shared, "Every time we entered a house a crowd followed us in, and I found I was expected to begin preaching immediately—a welcome change after Kweilin [Guilin], where people so often turn a deaf ear to the Christian message."[8] Miss S. E. Law wrote, "In this part of China there has been no vast mass movement, no great revival, but as one looks I think we can see 'the stirrings of the wind in the tree tops' and thank God and take courage."[9] Dr. Bacon noted the "very poor"[10] spiritual results of the hospital. M. B. Pim added, "Decisions to follow Christ are very few."[11] Two years later (1936), J. R. Wilson bemoaned,

3. Lackey, *Laborers Together.*
4. Holden, "A Big Dose," 259.
5. *Zhu de yiyuan* (主的医院).
6. Bacon, "Medical Work, Kweilin," 7.
7. Watkins, "Kweilin Hospital," 13.
8. Tobin, "Visit to Hingan," 15.
9. Law, "An Itineration," 13.
10. Bacon, "Kweilin Medical Work, 1932," 11.
11. Pim, "One by One," 16.

"Twenty to thirty years of evangelistic work, and yet how few had been reached! . . . What are the chief causes of failure?"[12]

Walter Oldfield reported some statistics of many of the mission societies in 1936 leading up to the Sino-Japanese War:

- CMS: 20 churches, 670 members.

- English Wesleyans: 5 churches, 217 members.

- Pentecostals: 2 churches, 85 members.

- CMA: 16 stations, 65 churches, 2,000 members.

- Faith and Love Mission: 11 churches.

- Chinese Independent Church: 6 churches, 200 members.

- Bible Churchmen's Missionary Society (formerly the Emmanuel Medical Mission): 130 members.

- Southern Baptists: 31 churches, 1,756 members.

- Seventh-Day Adventists: 13 churches, 277 members.[13]

The Japanese advance ushered in a new spiritual climate. Air raid sirens, whistling bombs falling out of the sky, explosions, loss of home, limb, and loved ones caused many otherwise complacent people to begin to look outside of themselves. The war conditions were, of course, not conducive to Guangxi's economic development. But spiritually, a new openness prevailed and the CMA reported a record year in 1941. In the aftermath of the war, the opportunities for spiritual work were unprecedented. Freda Rogers observed in 1947, "As far as I can judge at this early stage, the Church is full of enthusiasm and eagerness to preach the Gospel to those who are still in ignorance of the Good News."[14] Joe Leach remarked the same year, "Speaking of our part of China, I think it is true to say that not since the days of the Nestorian Christians, and the days of the Mongol king who asked the Pope for two hundred workers to teach the Christian religion, have the opportunities been so great."[15]

In 1949, the Communists took over the country, but this did not immediately constrain the church. In 1950, Rev. Desterhaft (CMA) wrote,

> The present circumstances have, in most districts, caused the attendance at Sunday worship services to increase instead of

12. Wilson, "When the Mists," 7.
13. Oldfield, *Pioneering in Kwangsi.*
14. Rogers, "An Open Door," 14.
15. Leach, "On the King's Business," 15.

decrease. In some churches, there has been an increase of nearly fifty per cent, and in all churches at least a twenty-five per cent increase. The reason for this is, as one speaker said, "People's hearts are suffering bitterly and they now love to listen to the Word of God." ... One of the brethren stated that he definitely believed that this present situation was being allowed by God in order to force the Chinese churches to stand on their own feet, as it were. ... Thus far there has been no ban on literature going into China so we are taking advantage of this opportunity to send in all the Bibles, tracts, posters and other literature that we possibly can.[16]

Before the founding of the People's Republic of China, Catholics numbered around thirty-five thousand and Protestants seven thousand.[17] In the last year in which the CMA reported statistics (1949), they had established eighty-six churches around Guangxi.[18] Their two most fruitful years were 1922 and 1941, both of which exceeded five hundred baptisms.[19] Throughout their half-century in China, their goal was always the complete evangelization of the province and self-supporting Chinese churches.[20] The Church Missionary Society also sought self-supporting churches, but their ministry was more limited to eastern and southern Guangxi. The growth of their Guangxi-Hunan mission is outlined in table 2.

1914	485 church members (Donaldson, *The Call*)
1918	Guilin: 39 baptisms that year and a total of 214 in the Christian community; 4 outstations and 7 organized congregations (CMS, "Statistics")
1923	1,757 church members (Donaldson, *The Call*)
1931	159 baptisms (Holden, "The Bishop's Letters" [1933])
1932	196 baptisms (Holden, "The Bishop's Letters" [1933])
1935	St. John's Church in Guilin totaled five hundred baptisms (Bacon, "Meditations")
1936	20 churches, 670 members (Oldfield, *Pioneering in Kwangsi*)
1948	Work in 12 cities, 40 outstations (Hsu, "Turn Again Our Captivity, O Lord")
1950	40 churches (Stevens, "Notes")

Table 2. Statistics of the Church Missionary Society's Guangxi-Hunan mission/ diocese (including stations across the border in southwest Hunan).

16. Desterhaft, "God Is Still Working in China," 587.

17. Yan, *Guangxi*.

18. Newbern, "The China Bible Seminary," 12.

19. Oldfield, "God's Grace in Kwangsi."

20. Oldfield, *Pioneering in Kwangsi*.

EVALUATION

Catholics arrived in Guangxi in the sixteenth century. By 1910 they had established a convent, planted churches, started schools and orphanages, and seen several thousands of Guangxi's people convert to Catholicism. Yet in the 1920s, they maintained that the work in Guangxi was unfinished.[21] They spoke of a huge triangular mass of land with points at Xilin (northwest), Nanning (south central), and Guilin (northeast) that remained unevangelized. By 1936, they numbered thirty-one churches and nearly five thousand Christians.[22] But in 1942, they wrote that their laborers had been "extremely few" and added, "Among the fourteen missions in China, Kwangsi [Guangxi] is one of the most difficult to evangelize."[23] Joseph Cuenot's overall assessment of Catholic impact in Guangxi: "Notwithstanding fifty years of effort, few of Kwangsi's [Guangxi's] inhabitants have been attracted to the beauty of the doctrine of our Blessed Lord."[24]

Walter Oldfield begins the conclusion of his biography of the Christian and Missionary Alliance's mission in Guangxi with, "Costly indeed has been the price of the Mission's success."[25] The costs have been well-noted, but what of their "success?" In 1929, CMA missionary Gustave Woerner said that gambling, brothels, and opium smoking had "repeatedly been stormed by the gallant army of the cross, but with apparent[ly] very little success."[26] In 1936, the Christian and Missionary Alliance mission had established dozens of stations and churches in Guangxi through sweat, blood, and tears. However, Oldfield clearly did not understand "success" to mean that the job was done. He wrote of the "vast interior," "great hinterlands," and "large areas" of Guangxi that were "absolutely neglected" and "largely unreached." He added, "There, millions of human beings, mostly tribesmen, are still waiting for the Gospel."[27] In 1950, in their last detailed report on their South China mission, the CMA wrote,

> From all over the province come reports of unprecedented opportunities challenging the Alliance Church—crowded evangelistic meetings; large classes of interested high school students studying the Bible (often in English, but nevertheless studying

21. Cuenot, *Kwangsi*, 13.

22. Oldfield, *Pioneering in Kwangsi*.

23. Cuenot, *Kwangsi*, 183, 189.

24. Cuenot, *Kwangsi*, author's preface, xv.

25. Oldfield, *Pioneering in Kwangsi*, 208.

26. Woerner, "Present Evangelistic Opportunities," 697.

27. Oldfield, *Pioneering in Kwangsi*, 167, 199.

God's Word); well attended Sunday schools and young people's meetings; deepened interest among university students; many Christians desiring Bible study; scores of tribespeople seeking the Lord; but a lamentable insufficiency of workers to buy up these marvelous opportunities. In some places there are only five or six workers including missionaries, for more than a million people. . . . One-half of the county seats in the province are still without any Christian meeting place.[28]

28. Snead, *Missionary Atlas* (1950), 120.

12

Conclusion

1952 to the Present

AFTER THE COMMUNIST TAKEOVER, missionaries wrote little of what transpired in Guangxi, although Chinese Christians from inside the "Bamboo Curtain" wrote letters indicating their situations.[1] Southern Baptist reports in the years that followed hardly mentioned anything about Mainland China,[2] except that the Christians were being faithful in difficult circumstances.[3] The CMA reported in 1964,

> Too little information has filtered through to make possible
> an accurate assessment of present-day Alliance interest in Red
> China. There is reason to believe that the church continues on
> and that at least a remnant stand true to Christ Jesus despite
> the overwhelming opposition of an atheistic materialistic
> government.[4]

After the departure of the foreign missionaries, the Chinese churches learned to be independent of foreign influence. Some joined the Three-Self Patriotic Movement, ultimately under the authority of the government, while others chose to remain unregistered. From 1966 to 1976, China

---

1. Statistics on the Three-Self Church do exist, but many more Christians are involved in non-registered churches.

2. Other than the Hong Kong-Macao Mission which was the last Southern Baptist "beachhead" on the mainland. SBC, *Annual 1955*, 162.

3. SBC, *Annual 1954*.

4. King, *Missionary Atlas* (1964), 135.

regressed during the Chairman Mao-initiated Cultural Revolution, a period in which Christians experienced considerable persecution. In the late seventies, churches in Guangxi began resuming services at the same time that China began making policy to open up its doors to the outside world under the reforms and leadership of Deng Xiaoping. In the years that followed, a remarkable phenomenon was observed around China: despite the Communist takeover and three decades of oppression, Christians were vibrant and growing. And yet in Guangxi,[5] the situation paralleled that which followed the decades of service of Catholic of Protestant missionaries: definite progress but large gaps and vast remaining needs.

In the eighties and nineties, the Alliance gained more information on what had taken place since the missionaries had left. Thousands of letters arrived at the Alliance radio broadcast station in Hong Kong from believers in China. One sixty-nine-year-old Chinese Christian, Mr. Chu, gave an encouraging testimony:

> I was a student of the Alliance Bible Seminary when it was in Kwangsi. During my four years there I studied under Dr. Robert A. Jaffray, Rev. Philip Hinkey, Dr. W. C. Newbern, and also some Chinese teachers. During the Cultural Revolution (1965–68)[6] I was attacked and put in prison. The Lord was gracious to me and after eleven years my case was restudied and I was released. I was so thankful, for I had been named a "false religion revolutionist" and sentenced to life imprisonment. Now my health is better than before I was put in prison. Indeed, I experienced Himself during those years. It was for my good. My faith is much stronger, for I have seen the salvation of the Lord. I will continue to preach until I go to see the Lord. I now work hard at personal evangelism and preaching in family meetings. I listen to the broadcasts every day. During the years of persecution all the books, notes and Bibles were burned. In the battle against Satan I could only use the verses I had memorized. But in every problem the Lord has helped me to stand firm. [Signed] God's servant, Chu.[7]

In 1986, Rev. James Bollback, the son of a CMA missionary, returned to his childhood home in China. He visited Wuzhou and Nanning where many Alliance missionaries had served before 1949. He reestablished contact with Chinese believers who were leaders in Alliance churches and

---

5. And much of the rest of the country.

6. The dates are quoted from the original. The years of the Cultural Revolution were 1966–1976.

7. CMA, "Bible School for China."

schools. He discovered that the Alliance churches had since become aligned with the Three-Self Patriotic Movement. In Wuzhou, the church remained active. It had a seating capacity of three to four hundred, and Sunday, Wednesday, and Saturday services were reportedly always full. In Nanning, Bollback attended the fifth annual conference of the Guangxi Autonomous Region Christian Protestant Church. He learned that fifteen of the forty-two delegates were graduates of the Wuzhou Bible School and that 70 percent of the delegates had been baptized in Alliance churches. He also met with Pastor Yu of the Zhongshan Road Church in Nanning (neither were associated with the CMA). Pastor Yu reported that there were eighteen thousand baptized believers[8] in Guangxi and an additional four thousand baptized minority peoples. Bollback also learned that six former CMA pastors were still serving in Guangxi in the cities of Yulin, Nanning, Wuzhou, Baise, and Liuzhou.[9] The oldest pastor was eighty-three years old.

Thirty-four Catholic and sixty Protestant churches, all government-registered, were located in Guangxi in 1992.[10] Dr. Maurice Irvin, former editor of the *Alliance Life* magazine, visited Guangxi the following year. He met the sixty-three-year-old daughter of a Guangxi resident who had become a Christian in the late 1890s. Her father had been a teacher in the Wuzhou Bible School for nearly fifty years. In 1953, he was accused of being a British spy and his family was continually harassed and berated. He died in 1974, six years before services resumed in the Wuzhou Church. His daughter expressed some disappointment in the church and its leaders. She felt that the church was too small and lacked zeal. She said there were only two hundred adult baptized believers and only ten to twenty attending weekly youth services. It could not compare to the days she had remembered in Alliance churches before the Communist takeover.[11]

Currently (2020), churches exist in every major- and medium-sized city in Guangxi. While not every city or town (and certainly not every village) has a church, a small number of Christians can usually be found in areas of sizeable population. To the unaware visitor, however, Guangxi still shows little evidence of having been impacted by the gospel. In 2009, it had one of the lowest percentages of believers among all the provinces of China, a mere 0.26 percent according to estimates by a Chinese sociologist at Baylor

---

8. This is probably an official Three-Self count since Bollback also learned there were only six million Christians in all of China at the time, a very low number.

9. Bollback, "China Journal."

10. Yan, *Guangxi.*

11. Irvin, "The Persecuted Professor's Daughter."

University (see figure 17).[12] That number did not change much by 2017 if Chinese scholar Yan Xiaohua's estimation of eighty thousand Christians (0.2 percent) is correct.[13] In addition, Guangxi's residents are often unaware that churches or Christians exist among them. Regarding the minorities, Guangxi's "tribes," the Zhuang, Yao, Miao, Hui, and Dong all still remain on lists of China's unreached or unengaged peoples.[14] The hope remains that believers both inside and outside Guangxi, following the example of the missionaries and Christians who served before them, will continue to pray and labor sacrificially to make Christ known among all the peoples, tongues, and tribes in Guangxi, China.

12. Wang, "Explaining Christianity in China." See also the distribution maps at https://www.epm.org/resources/2010/Oct/18/map-showing-distribution-christians-china and https://www.businessinsider.com/new-religious-breakdown-in-china-14.

13. Yan, *Guangxi*. This includes both Protestant and Catholic.

14. Yan estimated twenty thousand Zhuang (0.14 percent), ten thousand Yao (0.56 percent), two thousand Miao (0.47 percent), eight hundred Yi, and six hundred Jing believers. Yan, *Guangxi*.

Appendix A

Statistics

To tabulate these parts then, we find in March, 1884, there were :—

PROVINCE.	AREA.	POPULATION.	MISSIONARIES.	
1. KIANG-SI ...	61,580 square miles	... 15 millions	... Only 5 men	and 0 women
2. GAN-HWUY ...	54,002 " "	... 9 "	... " 4 "	" 4 "
3. HO-NAN ...	66,928 " "	... 15 "	... " 1* "	" 0 "
4. SHAN-SI ...	65,950 " "	... 9 "	... " 14 "	" 4 "
5. SHEN-SI ...	81,215 " "	... 7 "	... " 4 "	" 6 "
6. KAN-SUH ...	166,000 " "	... 3 "	... " 2 "	" 1 "
7. SĬ-C'HÜEN ...	185,052 " "	... 20 "	... " 8 "	" 5 "
8. YÜN-NAN (including Bhamó) ...	122,461 " "	... 5 "	... " 6 "	" 0 "
9. KWEI-CHAU ...	66,758 " "	... 4 "	... " 3 "	" 0 "
10. KWANG-SI ...	77,856 " "	... 5 "	... NONE	" 0 "
11. HU-NAN ...	83,214 " "	... 16 "	... " 1* "	" 0 "
TOTALS	1,031,016 " "	108 "	Only 48 men	and 20 women

Figure 7: The area, population, and numbers of CIM missionaries by province in 1884. Guangxi is number 10 and spelled "Kwang-si." Taylor, *China's Spiritual Needs and Claims*, 36.

Statistics of the C. M. S. Central China Mission

	KUEI-LIN 桂林. 1899.
Foreign Missionaries.	
Men	...
Wives	...
Native Workers, Men	1
Baptized Christians	9
Catechumens	4
Adherents, Total	13
Native Communicants	6
Baptized during the year.	
Adults	...
Children	2
Total...	2
Native Contributions	$30

Figure 8: Early statistics (1899) of the Church Missionary Society in Guilin ("Kuei-Lin"). MacGillivray, *Century*, 44.

ROMAN CATHOLIC STATISTICS FOR 1905

Members	.	.	.	3201	Chinese catechists .	40
Chapels	.	.	.	50	Schools	45
Bishop .	.	.	.	1	Scholars . . .	510
Priests .	.	.	.	24	Dispensaries . . .	5
Lay brothers .	.	.	.	...	Baptisms, heathen . .	611
Sisters .	.	.	.	3	„ heretics . .	9
Chinese priests	.	.	.	4	„ children . .	198

Figure 9: Roman Catholic statistics for 1905.
Broomhall, *Chinese Empire*, 288.

Statistics of Canton District, W. M. S., 1905.

Principal Stations.	Chapels.	Other Preaching-places.	English Missionaries, Ordained and Lay.	Chinese Ministers.	Subordinate Agents.				Membership.		Schools.				Scholars attending Sunday or Day-school or both.			Average attendance at Public Worship	
					Paid.		Unpaid.				Sunday.		Day.						
					Catechists.	Day-school Teachers.	Sunday-school Teachers.	Local Preachers.	Full Members.	On Trial.	Schools.	Scholars.	Schools.	Scholars.	Male.	Female.	Totals.		
Canton	2	1	1	1	1	6	1	2	297	15	1	50	5	195					
„ Institution	...	...	...	1	...	...	...	...	...	...	...	...	...	...					
Fatshan: Tai Ki Mi	1	2	1	...	1	1	1	2	124	15	1	31	1	31					
Fatshan: Man Cheung Station and Hospital	2	...	2	...	1	1	1	2	61	5	1	9	1	9					
Wuchow Mission and Hospital ...	1	...	2	...	7	3	2	...	84	18	1	92	4	92	No Returns.	No Returns.	No Returns.	No Returns.	
San Ui	5	2	...	...	5	1	1	2	219	5	1	20	1	20					
North River	17	2	3	1	17	1	...	11	958	85	...	...	...	...					
Hongkong, *English*	1	...	2	...	...	...	4	6	70	5	1	30	...	...					
„ *Native*	...	1	...	2	...	7	...	8	57	2	...	...	5	177					
Heungshan	3	...	...	...	2	1	1	1	151	5	1	10	1	10					
Totals for 1905	30	10	12	5	34	20	11	34	2,051	158	7	242	18	534	...	...	...	...	
Totals for 1904	29	12	10	5	35	21	13	27	1,943	307	6	222	14	607	...	...	...	...	

THE WESLEYAN METHODIST MISSIONARY SOCIETY.   103

Figure 10: Statistics of the Wesleyan Methodist Missionary Society in 1905 (see "Wuchow Mission and Hospital"). MacGillivray, *Century*, 103.

The latest report of this Mission includes the following figures: —Stations, 11 ; out-stations, 2 ; chapels, 14 ; missionaries, 39 ; native workers, 35 ; church members, 227 ; catechumens, 47 ; native church offerings for the year, $324.00.

Figure 11: Christian and Missionary Alliance statistics in 1907. MacGillivray, *Century*, 364.

KWANGSI

Kweilin.—C.M.S. ; C.M.A.
Kweiping (Sünchow).—C.M.A.
Lungchow.—C.M.A.
Nanning.—C.M.A.
Tangan.—C.M.A.
Tungtsun.—C.M.A.
Wuchow.—A.S.B.M. ; C.M.A. ; C.M.S. ;
W.M.S.

Figure 12: Mission societies in Guangxi by location in 1906. Stanford, *Atlas*, xii.

KWANGSI.

FOREIGN MISSIONS OF PARIS.

Prefect-Apostolic—R. R. MGR. J. M. LAVEST.

Missionaries.

Priests—European	.	.	27	Religious, European . .	4
Chinese	.	.	4	Nuns—European, 6 ; Chinese, 1	7
				Schoolmistresses . .	6
				Catechists . . .	31

Educational.

1 Seminary for training Clergy   26 Schools—Scholars   .   297
   —Students   .   20

Charitable.

7 Orphanages or Asylums—   Hospitals and Dispensaries .   6
   Inmates .   .   .   54

In Mission, 1907.

Estimated Population   10,000,000   Chinese Catholics (exclusive
Churches and Chapels, 55 ;   of Catechumens) .   . 3,610
    Stations ?   .   .   ?55   Catechumens .   .   . 4,312
                      Baptised in 1906—Adults . 511
                         Children of Christians . 135
                         Children of heathen . 330

Figure 13: Statistics of the Paris Foreign Mission Society in Guangxi from 1907.
Wolferstan, *Catholic Church*, 448.

KWANGSI.

Population, 6,500,000 ; No. of Prefectures, etc., 104 ; Mission Centres, 9

Kweilin

C A

*‡Cunningham, J. R., and wife.

C M S

‡Bacon, J. L., and wife.
Gardner, Miss.
§Parker, J., and wife.
Santler, Miss.
*White, Miss K.

S B C

‡King, W. D., and wife.
*‡Lowe, C. J., and wife.

Liuchowfu

C A

*Charles, Miss A. L.
*Lewis, Miss E. M.
‡Oldfield, W. H., and wife.
Poole, J. A.

Lungchow

C A

Allen, R. N.
‡Worsnip, T. P., and wife.

Nanning

C A

‡Christopherson, F. A., and wife.

C M S

*‡Mackenzie, C. N. R., and wife.
‡Upsdell, G. E. S., M.A.

E M M

Clift, H. L., M.B., Ch.B., and
   wife.
*Mitchell, Miss M. S.

Pinglo

C A

Dyer, Miss M. E.
‡Field, A. W., and wife.

Pingnamyun

C A

Oehme, Miss L. E.
*Rolle, Miss M. E.

Sünchow (Kwaiping)

C A

‡Smith, W. G., and wife.

Tengyün (Tang-ün)

C A

Holmes, Miss B. N.
Rudy, Miss E. N.

Wuchow

C A

‡Cowles, R. T., and wife.
*‡Hess, I. L., and wife.
‡Hinkey, P., and wife.
‡Jaffray, R. A., and wife.
March, Miss E. K.
Rudy, Miss S. M.

S B C

Hayes, C. A., M.D., and wife.
Leavell, G. W., M.D., and wife.
*Meadows, Miss J.
Rea, Miss E. E.
Scarlett, Miss L.
‡Tipton, W. H., and wife.

S D A

‡Law Keem, M.D., and wife.

W M M S

*‡Anderson, H. E., and wife.
‡Marris, C. C.
Vickers, B. R., M.B., and wife.
Wamsley, W. B., M.B.

KEY:

CA: Christian and
Missionary Alliance

SBC: Foreign Mission
Board of the Southern
Baptist Convention

CMS: Church and
Missionary Society

EMM: Emmanuel
Medical Mission

WMMS: Wesleyan
Methodist Missionary
Society

SDA: Seventh-Day
Adventist

Figure 14: Protestant societies and missionaries in Guangxi in 1916.
Boynton, *Directory*, 166.

3. Nombre de Chrétiens par Province en 1916.

			Chrétiens.
Province du Tchely (6 Vic. Ap.)			500.655.
»	» Kiangsou (1 V. A.)		175.621.
»	» Setchouan et Thibet (5 V. A.)		141.834.
»	» Chantoung . (3 V. A.)		135.160.
»	» Mongolie (3 V. A.)		94.877.
»	» Houpé (3 V. A.)		91.298.
»	» Kwangtoung et Hongkong (3 V. A.)		87.602.
»	» Kiangsi (3 V. A.)		71.886.
»	» Foukien (2 V. A.)		59.481.
»	» Anhoui (pas de V. A.)		59.100.
»	» Chansi (2 V. A.)		56.849.
Province de Mantchourie (2 V. A.)			53.265.
»	» Tchékiang (2 V. A.)		47.058.
»	» Honan (4 V. A.)		46.487.
»	» Chensi (4 V. A.)		46.180.
Evêché de Macao (dont partie en Chine)			40.000.
Province du Kouitchow (1 V. A.)			32.858.
»	» Hounan (2 V. A.)		20.412.
»	» Yünnan (1 V. A.)		17.714.
»	» Kansou et Ily (3. Miss.)		6.360.
»	» Kouangsi (1 Vic. A.)		4.700.

Figure 15: "Number of Christians per Province in 1916" from the Paris Mission Society. The last entry is Guangxi (spelled "Kouangsi").

Planchet, *Les Missions de Chine*, 302–3.

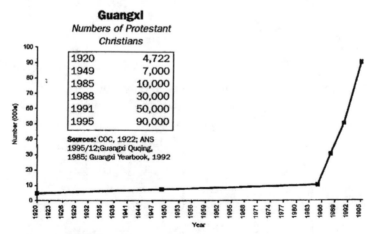

Figure 16: Number of Protestant Christians in Guangxi, 1920 to 1995.
Lambert, *China's Christian Millions*, 228. (Used with permission.)

Table 2

Percentage of Christianity in Province, 1918 to 2009

Province	1918	1949	1999	2004	2009	Marketing index-05	Emigration	Ancestor worship[a]	Culture Isolation
Fujian	0.87	1.62	1.91	3.4	3.50	8.33	0	31.31	90%
Jiangsu	0.77	1.16	1.39	2.11	2.64	8.63	0	16.67	30%
Shanxi	0.72	1.29	0.63	0.61	2.17	5.13	0	15.61	80%
Shaanxi	0.67	0.96	0.97	1.27	1.57	4.46	0	7.58	36%
Shandong	0.66	1.89	0.91	1.30	1.21	7.52	0	25.28	45%
Guangdong	0.51	0.78	0.28	0.3	.	10.06	0	43.71	72.8%
Guizhou	0.49	0.36	0.98	1.13	0.99	9.36	1	31.18	92.5%
Zhejiang	0.46	1.41	2.92	3.92	2.62	9.77	0	23.02	70.4%
Jiangxi	0.39	0.76	0.71	0.97	2.31	5.76	1	24.05	70%
Sichuan	0.29	0.36	0.47	0.63	0.68	6.38	1	10.6	90%
Hebei	0.23	0.89	0.45	0.59	3.05	6.05	1	5.52	48.1%
Hunan	0.18	0.28	0.31	0.47	0.77	6.11	1	20.19	70.2%
Gansu	0.16	0.29	0.27	1.02	.	3.95	0	3.51	40.8%
Henan	0.16	0.7	5.38	5.4	9.33	5.64	1	7.94	44.3%
Guangxi	0.1	0.15	0.19	0.25	0.26	5.42	0	40.48	70.8%
Anhui	0.09	0.62	4.85	5.01	5.30	5.99	1	4.64	60.7%
Northeast[b]	0.38	0.43	1.13	1.44	2.15	5.97	0	7.73	60%
Yunnan	0.49	0.87	1.93	2.75	.	481	1	32.22	84%
Inner Mongolia	[c]	0.77	0.64	0.72	2.0	5.12	0	2.36	20.9%
beijing	.	0.19	0.16	0.28	0.78	8.19	.	.	62%
Tianjin	.	0.17	0.16	0.20	1.51	7.86	.	.	7%
Hainan	.	.	0.49	0.50	0.48	5.41	0	.	25%
Chongqing	.	.	0.65	0.97	1.05	7.20	1	26.63	97.6%
Hubei	0.49	.	0.25	0.83	0.58	6.11	1	6.5	55.5%
Xinjiang	.	0.015	0.23	0.68	1.00	4.76	0	.	.
Ningxia	.	.	0.18	1.17	.	4.56	0	.	61.4%
Qinghai	.	.	0.59	0.76	.	3.10	0	.	69.9%
Shanghai	.	.	0.95	1.12	1.95	9.81	.	.	0
Tibet	.	.	.	.	.	1.55	.	.	.

Note. [a] The percentage of believing in ancestor came from the data of China Spiritual Life Survey conducted by Horizon Company in 2007. Based on the question "Do you believe in the existence of ancestor spirit?", the percentage of respondents answering yes was calculated by province, which was used as a variable measuring the strength of ancestor worship tradition. The higher the percentage of this variable, the more solid traditional culture embedded in this province or region.

[b] Northeast region includes Heilongjiang, Jilin and Liaoning provinces. In 1921, it was called Manchuria. Because their similarity in history, natural and social demographical factors, I merge them together in the table.

[c] . no data available

Figure 17: Percentage of Christians by province from 1918 to 2009.
Wang, "Explaining Christianity in China," 15. (Used with permission.)

Year	Location	Number of Christians
1992	Guangxi	60,000 Catholics 40,000 Protestants
2007	Yulin	3,221
2017	Guilin	20,000
2017	Nanning	3,500

Table 3: Various statistics from Yan, *Guangxi*.

Appendix B
Living in Guangxi: Comments from Some Missionaries

VARIOUS MISSIONARIES TO GUANGXI wrote the following comments, many of them over a century ago. However, they still likely resonate with foreigners living (or who have lived) in China, and especially Guangxi.

"I had no idea Chinese food could be so good."[1]

"I think there is some rubbish talked about the trials of missionaries in China having to eat Chinese food. Of course on the boats when they give you nothing but pork, etc., it is horrid, but the food they give at feasts is much more cleverly cooked than our English food, and really very good."[2]

"The absence of light had its bright side, for when eating in the Miao huts we were constantly in a dilemma. If we ate in the dark we could not see what we were eating, and if we had a light, we saw too much."[3]

"And yet we prefer not to eat more than two or three Chinese meals a week."[4]

"When one can speak the language, life becomes ever so much more varied and interesting."[5]

"Perhaps you would like to know exactly what learning Chinese is like. You must bear in mind that the 'teacher' is merely a machine for producing Chinese sound, which you endeavor to imitate. The meaning of the sounds you wrestle with later in a quiet room, if you can find any such place in China."[6]

1. Clift, *Very Far East*, 25.
2. Clift, *Very Far East*, 133–34.
3. Oldfield, *Pioneering in Kwangsi*, 51.
4. Oldfield, *With You Alway*, 63.
5. Clift, *Very Far East*, 29.
6. Couche, "Chinese Language Lesson," 26.

"Our Chwang [Zhuang] vocabulary was so meager, and most of the knowledge we possessed was contained in a note book which we carried, that it was with grunts, and groans, and grim articulations that we tried to inquire the way of strangers whom we met along the road. One morning we learned the sentence, 'Going to ____ which road should we take[?],' and later in the day we came to converging paths. Seeing a tribesmen coming along, we thought, 'Now is the time to practice our sentence,' and so with more than ordinary effort made ready to ask the way. Smiling, we started, 'Going to ____' the rest of the sentence would not come out. It seemed stuck in our throats. Again we tried to speak, but the second attempt almost choked us. The tribesman looking startled and started to pass by, but we detained him with uplifted hand, while the other hand delved deep into our coat pocket for the treasured note-book and the rest of the sentence. Our actions seemed to startle the man more than ever, and before we could get out our notes and the sentence rightly framed, the stranger was going, going, had gone, while we were still at the cross-roads, perplexing and perspiring, but with plenty of time to string the forgotten words together before the next man came along."[7]

"One missionary, meaning to say, 'I greatly love the Chinese,' declared to his audience, 'I greatly love to slaughter men.'"[8]

"Never believe anything you hear in China!"[9]

"Oh, happy Chinaman! who can travel with only a little bundle of belongings."[10]

"It is something utterly new and strange [for the Chinese] to see any one die in perfect peace, to have no loud wailing or wild demonstration of grief at the funeral, just a gathering of Christians standing round the strangely-fashioned coffin."[11]

"The crafty little wretches of mosquitoes wait their chance, and then when you have tumbled into bed worn out and just longing to go to sleep, you hear a vicious little sharp singing noise, which tells you that some mosquitoes have crept inside and have been waiting in some hidden corner to attack you."[12]

---

7. Oldfield, "Among Kwangsi's Tribesmen," 232.

8. Oldfield, *With You Alway*, 52.

9. Clift, *Very Far East*, 36.

10. Clift, *Very Far East*, 13.

11. Clift, *Very Far East*, 41.

12. Clift, *Very Far East*, 66.

"There was a restaurant across the narrow street from us, where fowls were killed over the gutters. The odors that drifted up to us from across the way were not the fragrance of honeysuckle and roses."[13]

"I have heard a child of two years old repeat page after page of this book from memory. He would probably go on repeating the same words for years, without an attempt on the teacher's part to explain the meaning. Then at the age of eight or nine, having been thoroughly grounded in this parrot-like method of learning, he is supposed to stop and think of the sense of the dreary words. . . . this is the time of the Awakening and surely we may hope better things of the future generation, if they are allowed to think, as well as to memorize the wonderful Chinese characters, which their forefathers literally worshipped."[14]

"After Mass we go to our correspondence or books, according to circumstances. We are practically recluses, but there is one advantage in that we have ample time for study. One of the 'indoor sports' is to make out [identify] street cries, some of which are distinctively striking. Needless to say we know every peddler's voice by this time, but when we meet one or the other while out walking, often enough 'he' happens to be a woman."[15]

"In China people do not take furtive glances at one another—they settle themselves comfortably for a prolonged stare at the object of interest."[16]

"There was a long street outside the city wall, to be traversed before one could enter the city, and down this I limped, my feet by this time being in a very uncomfortable condition. I had scarcely entered this street when my presence became known, and in a minute or two the street was lined with spectators, old, young, rich and poor, pushing and squeezing and scolding to get a good view of the 'foreign devil.' Many were not satisfied with one look at me; as soon as I had passed they would run on ahead and again take up their position to have another look. It was amusing to see elderly well-dressed men running ahead in this manner to get a view."[17]

"It is the Chinese New Year's Day tomorrow, and everybody is in a state of great excitement—so missionaries are compelled to take a holiday. No one has time to listen to the Gospel."[18]

13. Oldfield, *With You Alway*, 144.
14. Clift, *Very Far East*, 150.
15. Dietz, in FMSA, *Maryknoll Mission Letters, China*, 283.
16. Clift, *Very Far East*, 158.
17. Child, "A Trip to Hunan," 146–47.
18. Clift, *Very Far East*, 167.

"We have heard of a house, a shop in a busy street, which would suit our purpose excellently, but the man, knowing a foreigner wants to rent it, is asking far too big a price. We assure him in vain that we are not rich Westerners. The idea is firmly rooted in the Chinese mind that every foreigner is rolling in wealth, and lawful prey in the matter of house rents and land purchases."[19]

"Did I tell you of the student who was walking about Kuei Lin [Guilin] with an English straw hat on, and round the hat band in English lettering was writ large—MY HAT? We met another one the other day, labelled 'Chinese Student.' I think they feel that in this style they are in the height of English fashion! It would be certainly very interesting if only it was the fashion in England; we could go and stand, say at London Bridge station in the morning, and watch the business men pouring out, each with a hat label denoting his particular occupation!"[20]

"Perhaps the best way of conveying an idea of what [bi]cycling in Kweilin [Guilin] is like would be to ask the readers of these lines to exercise their imaginative faculty and come for a ride. Our objective is a quiet country ride on a road outside the South Gate. . . . Having prepared the machine, we wheel it through the compound to the main entrance and into the street. A few country folk, on their way back to their villages, are passing the door at the time. The cycle catches their attention. They look! They stare! They stop, turn round and gaze at the machine as it goes out of sight. They then stare at one another, shake their heads, and silently pass on, wandering[sic] what next thing these Westerners will import into their country. Further down the street is a group of children playing. They see the machine, cease their games, clap their hands with excitement, jump for joy and shout '*Iang chae lai, iang chae lai*'[21] (Foreign cart comes, foreign cart comes). . . . A good deal of dodging and steering has to be done, and the breaks [sic] applied every few yards. . . . But now the street is unridable, being much narrower and more uneven, and it is necessary to dismount. Our followers are delighted, for it gives them an opportunity of examining the machine at close quarters. The bell is tried, then the brakes, the seat and accessory bag are handled. But what astonishes them most is the noiselessness of the cycle, bearing in mind no doubt the truly noisy 'rickshaws,' which were introduced into Kweilin about two years ago. The tyres are therefore felt. 'That's elephant skin,' says one. 'No' says the Westerners, 'that's tree fluid [sap used for making rubber].' 'Elephant skin,' quietly murmurs an old man, refusing to be instructed or

19. Clift, *Very Far East*, 171.
20. Clift, *Very Far East*, 47.
21. *yang che lai, yang che lai* (洋车来，洋车来).

corrected by foreigners. Their ancestors called that material elephant skin, and therefore it must be elephant skin. 'How much did it cost?' is another question. 'Can it go as quickly as a horse?' 'How many miles can it walk a day?' Then we are asked to ride on and give them more excitement. Our method of mounting provokes great mirth, and it is increased when we put on a sprint and leave them behind."[22]

"Transportation has always been a problem in China, but it is a more serious one now. The best accommodation we could get on a two weeks' trip was on top of a truck load of old dried animal bones, on the way to be made into fertilizer. It was like riding on a load of hay, except that it neither felt nor smelt like hay! It was neither soft nor comfortable. But for all the stench, it was far better than the regular passenger bus. In the ordinary bus the cargo is loaded on the floor to a height of about eighteen inches before the passengers are allowed to enter. Then five-inch planks, notched so that they cannot be moved, are placed across the cargo. These planks are spaced about fourteen inches apart, leaving neither leg nor foot room, and one sits hunched up with his chin touching his knees. There are no springs, and the roads are rough. These planks are eight feet long, and eight passengers, with first-class tickets, fight and scramble to find space while the man who sold the tickets declares there must be plenty of room as nine people occupied the same space on the last trip, and did not complain! The baggage and bundles are stacked high on the roof of the bus, together with whatever cargo is left over. Overloading a bus thus has caused many a one to capsize on the short turns of the narrow mountain roads, and many persons have been killed or injured. However, the bus company assumes no responsibility for life, limb, or baggage. The last often catches fire from the sparks of the charcoal-burning contraption on the side of the bus. In comparison with this, riding on the load of old bones was not too bad. I wished, however, that I could have exchanged places, for about five minutes, with one of the 'Homeside' passengers riding on a Greyhound."[23]

"If you belong to the unhappy class of mortals who cannot 'keep smiling' in the face of small discomforts or real hardships, then try some other field—China is no place for you."[24]

Bill Wallace posed a question to a doctor friend in Chongqing:

> "How do you ever get used to the idea that you are going to be able to make such a small impression upon all this suffering—even

22. Bacon, "Kweilin's First Bicycle," 37–38.
23. Lang, "Itinerating in China," 570.
24. Couche, "Dining Out," 52.

in a lifetime?" His friend smiled. "You're tackling a problem that almost did me in, my first term of service. I believe every missionary faces it. A kind of crisis of compassion. You can either narrow your eyes against it and harden your heart—and all of us do that to a degree—or you can let it drive you to a frenzy that will break you. These are the extreme reactions, of course. I finally had to face the fact that God is fully aware of my limitations, and he brought me here for a purpose. I must do what my hand finds to do to the best of my ability. But, I must leave the statistics up to God, even as I have to leave the course of history up to him." Bill said gloomily, "I am more aware of my limitations than I have ever been. I guess my problem is that I have been imposing my limitations on God." "Each of us has to make this adjustment by himself. Some never do. It's a time when a missionary's faith is tried to its foundation and his emotional strength is tested to its core." Bill pondered his friend's words for a long time.[25]

"To me, living in China is like living on the slopes of a slumbering volcano. You may be safe for years, and then, suddenly—. But our path is clear. We must go on doing our duty day by day, and leave the rest with God."[26]

"People who think missionary life is hum-drum ought to come to South China, to the wilds of Kwangsi. Here there is enough excitement and danger to satisfy the most venturesome."[27]

25. Fletcher, *Bill Wallace of China*, 40–41. Bill Wallace's biography is written as a narrative so the quote may not be an exact one.

26. Macdonald, *Roderick Macdonald, M.D.*, 277.

27. Oldfield, "In the Hands of Chinese Robbers," 151.

Bibliography

Bacon, Charlotte. "1930 in the Kweilin Hospital." *The Kwangsi-Hunan Diocesan Newsletter* 93 (March 1931) 31–34.

———. "Back in Kweilin." *The Kwangsi-Hunan Diocesan Newsletter* 128 (May 1941) 6.

———. "Bluffers and Bandits in Kweilin." *The Newsletter of the Kwangsi Hunan Mission of the C.M.S. & C.E.Z.M.S.* 67 (January 1924) 490–95.

———. "C.M.S. Medical Mission in Kweilin." *The Kwangsi-Hunan Diocesan Newsletter* 134 (May 1947) 5–9.

———. "Five Years' Work in Kweilin: A Retrospect." *The Newsletter of the Kwangsi Hunan Mission of the C.M.S. & C.E.Z.M.S.* 46 (July 1916) 42–45.

———. "Iconoclasm in Kwangsi." *The Newsletter of the Kwangsi Hunan Mission of the C.M.S. & C.E.Z.M.S.* 76 (January 1926) 691–93.

———. "Inasmuch." *The Kwangsi-Hunan Diocesan Newsletter* 102 (July 1933) 13–14.

———. "Kweilin Hospital Sorrows and Joys." *The Kwangsi-Hunan Diocesan Newsletter* 92 (January 1931) 16–18.

———. "Kweilin Medical Notes." *The Newsletter of the C.M.S. Kwangsi Hunan Mission* 35 (August 1914) 41–60.

———. "Kweilin Medical Work, 1932." *The Kwangsi-Hunan Diocesan Newsletter* 101 (April 1933) 10–12.

———. "A Letter from Kweilin Hospital." *The Kwangsi-Hunan Diocesan Newsletter* 104 (January 1934) 4–6.

———. "Medical Work, Kweilin." *The Kwangsi-Hunan Diocesan Newsletter* 88 (December 1929) 5–8.

———. "Meditations of Twenty-Five Years." *The Kwangsi-Hunan Diocesan Newsletter* 111 (October 1935) 12–15.

———. "Out-Patients—'Way of Life' Hospital, Kweilin." *The Kwangsi-Hunan Diocesan Newsletter* 107 (October 1934) 16–18.

———. "Pulling down and Putting Up." *The Kwangsi-Hunan Diocesan Newsletter* 108 (January 1935) 5–7.

———. "Report of the Kweilin Hospital." *The Kwangsi-Hunan Diocesan Newsletter* 90 (June 1930) 14–18.

———. "Slowly Onward." *The Newsletter of the C.M.S. Kwangsi Hunan Mission* 35 (August 1913) 41–60.

———. "Way of Life Hospital." *The Kwangsi-Hunan Diocesan Newsletter* 132 (May 1946) 12–13.

Bacon, John L. "After the Revolution." *The Newsletter of the C.M.S. Kwangsi Hunan Mission* 31 (August 1912) 130–32.

———. "Farewell to Kweilin." *The Newsletter of the Kwangsi Hunan Mission of the C.M.S. & C.E.Z.M.S.* 45 (February 1916) 17–19.

———. "Kweilin's First Bicycle." *The Newsletter of the C.M.S. Kwangsi Hunan Mission* 26 (May 1911) 37–39.

———. "A Meditation on a Bluff." *The Newsletter. C.M.S. Central China Mission* 25 (February 1911) 7–8.

———. "A Short Overland Journey." *The Newsletter of the C.M.S. Kwangsi Hunan Mission* 28 (November 1911) 68–72.

Bailey, Charlotte. "Kweilin at Last!" *The Newsletter of the C.M.S. Kwangsi Hunan Mission* 26 (May 1911) 35–36.

Bailey, H. S. "The Green One: An Introduction." *The Newsletter of the Kwangsi Hunan Mission of the C.M.S. & C.E.Z.M.S.* 68 (May 1924) 530–31.

Banister, W. "Appeal for Kweilin." *The Newsletter of the C.M.S. Kwangsi Hunan Mission* 32 (December 1912) 140–41.

Benigni, Umberto. "Sacred Congregation of Propaganda." In *Catholic Encyclopedia: An International Work of Reference on the Constitution, Doctrine, Discipline, and History of the Catholic Church*, edited by Charles G. Herbermann, vol. 12. New York: Appleton, 1911.

Bland, Robert N. "Kweilin Students." *The Newsletter of the Kwangsi Hunan Mission of the C.M.S. & C.E.Z.M.S.* 101 (December 12, 1925) 643–45.

———. "Some Thoughts on Aggressive Evangelism." *The Kwangsi-Hunan Diocesan Newsletter* 101 (April 1933) 14–16.

Blenkinsop, A. P. "New Year Evangelism." *The Kwangsi-Hunan Diocesan Newsletter* 124 (May 1939) 15–16.

———. "Reconstruction." *The Kwangsi-Hunan Diocesan Newsletter* 132 (May 1946) 10–12.

Blue, J. R. "Jaffray, Robert A." In *Who's Who in Christian History*, edited by J. D. Douglas, Philip W. Comfort, and Donald Mitchell, 350. Wheaton, IL: Tyndale, 1992.

Bollback, James A. "China Journal: An Alliance MK Returns to His Childhood Home in China." *The Alliance Witness* 121 (January 15, 1986) 4–16.

Bondfield, G. H., ed. *China Mission Year Book 1913.* Vol. 4. Shanghai: Christian Literature Society for China, 1913.

"The Boxer Rebellion." *The Christian and Missionary Alliance*, n.d. https://www.cmalliance.org/about/history/in-the-line-of-fire/boxer-rebellion.

Boynton, Charles Luther, ed. *Directory of Protestant Missions in China.* Shanghai: Christian Literature Society, 1916.

Brockey, Liam M. *Journey to the East: The Jesuit Mission to China, 1579–1724.* Cambridge: Harvard University Press, 2007.

Broomhall, Marshall, ed. *The Chinese Empire: A General & Missionary Survey.* London: Morgan & Scott, 1907.

———. *The Jubilee Story of the China Inland Mission.* Philadelphia: China Inland Mission, 1915.

Byrde, Louis. "The Aborigines of China." *The Newsletter. C.M.S. Central China Mission* 25 (February 1911) 9–10.

———. "The Evil Arrows of Famine." *The Kwangsi Hunan Newsletter* 3 (December 1904) 6–9.

―――. "Foreign Demons." *The Kwangsi Hunan Newsletter* 5 (October 1905) 38–44.

―――. "How We Escaped in 1900." *The Newsletter. C.M.S. Central China Mission and Tokyo Student Mission* 13 (February 1908) 8–14.

―――. "Kueilin Native Church Funds." *The Kwangsi Hunan Newsletter* 4 (February 1905) 18–19.

―――. "Kueilin Notes." *The Kwangsi Hunan Newsletter* 5 (October 1905) 46–47.

―――. "Little Mei." *The Kwangsi Hunan Newsletter* 8 (November 1906) 103–5.

―――. "Traveling by Land." *The Newsletter. C.M.S. Central China Mission* 24 (November 1910) 67–69.

―――. "Two Pressing Financial Needs." *The Kwangsi Hunan Newsletter* 3 (December 1904) 4–5.

Cannell, M. C. "Spirit Streams." *The Kwangsi-Hunan Diocesan Newsletter* 130 (October 1941) 7–8.

Cannell, W. R. "Kweilin." *The Newsletter of the Kwangsi Hunan Mission of the C.M.S. & C.E.Z.M.S.* 83 (August 1928) 825–29.

―――. "Kweilin Notes." *The Newsletter of the Kwangsi Hunan Mission of the C.M.S. & C.E.Z.M.S.* 78 (December 1926) 726–28.

―――. "On Sowing Seed." *The Kwangsi-Hunan Diocesan Newsletter* 97 (March 1932) 12–14.

―――. "The Revolution: An Experience." *The Kwangsi-Hunan Diocesan Newsletter* 90 (June 1930) 5–8.

Carter, R. W. "Transformations—Actual and Possible." *The Kwangsi-Hunan Diocesan Newsletter* 114 (July 1936) 18–21.

Caterer, Helen. *Foreigner in Kweilin: The Story of Rhoda Watkins, South Australian Nursing Missionary.* London: Epworth, 1966.

Chan, Albert. "Michele Ruggieri, S.J. (1543–1607) and His Chinese Poems." *Monumenta Serica* 41 (1993) 129–76.

Chao, Leo T. "A Unique Memorial." *The Alliance Weekly* 72/21 (May 22, 1937) 323–27.

Chao, Leo T., James A. Poole, and Margaret Oppelt. "South China Alliance Mission Conference." *The Alliance Weekly* 65/42 (October 18, 1930) 681–82.

Charbonnier, Jean-Pierre. *Christians in China: A.D. 600 to 2000.* Translated by Maurice Couve de Murville. San Francisco: Ignatius, 2007.

Chen, Chi-chang. "Kweilin: Its Past and Future." *The Kwangsi-Hunan Diocesan Newsletter* 97 (March 1932) 10–11.

Child, A. B. "Drops of Blessing at Kueilin." *The Newsletter. C.M.S. Central China Field* 9 (February 1907) 5–8.

―――. "Everyday Life at Kueilin." *The Kwangsi Hunan Newsletter* 5 (October 1905) 48–51.

―――. "Snap-Shots from Kweilin." *The Newsletter. C.M.S. Central China Mission and Tokyo Student Mission* 17 (February 1909) 79–81.

―――. "Some Needed Changes." *The Newsletter. C.M.S. Central China Field* 12 (November 1907) 58–59.

―――. "Sunday in Kueilin." *The Newsletter. C.M.S. Central China Field* 11 (August 1907) 42–43.

―――. "The Women of Kweilin." *The Newsletter. C.M.S. Central China Mission and Tokyo Student Mission* 14 (May 1908) 22–24.

Child, Frank. "Encouragement at Kueilin." *The Kwangsi Hunan Newsletter* 8 (November 1906) 95–97.

———. "A Journey to Yungchow." *The Kwangsi Hunan Newsletter* 2 (August 1904) 10–14.

———. "Kueilin Notes." *The Kwangsi Hunan Newsletter* 5 (October 1905) 46–47.

———. "A Trip to Hunan." *The Church Missionary Gleaner*, October 1, 1903, 146–47.

China Continuation Committee, ed. *The Christian Occupation of China: A General Survey of the Numerical Strength and Geographical Distribution of the Christian Forces in China.* Shanghai: The Committee, 1922.

———. *Directory of Protestant Missions in China.* Shanghai: Kwang Hsüeh, 1921.

China Inland Mission. *China's Millions: North American Edition.* Philadelphia: China Inland Mission, 1911.

Christian and Missionary Alliance. "The Alliance Family: With the Lord." *The Alliacs Witness* 100/7 (March 31, 1965) 16.

———. *Atlas Showing Mission Fields of the Christian and Missionary Alliance.* Rev. ed. New York: Christian and Missionary Alliance, 1924.

———. "A Bible School for China." *The Alliance Witness* 116/14 (July 8, 1981) 18–19.

———. "Blessing in South China." *The Alliance Weekly* 81/25 (June 22, 1946) 394.

———. "Carrying on in Kwangsi." *The Alliance Weekly* 75/10 (March 9, 1940) 153.

———. "Change in the Chairmanship of Our South China Field." *The Alliance Weekly* 65/47 (November 22, 1930) 758.

———. "Department of Prayer." *The Alliance Weekly* 74/52 (December 30, 1939) 824–25.

———. "Department of Prayer." *The Alliance Weekly* 76/26 (June 28, 1941) 408–10.

———. "Department of Prayer." *The Alliance Weekly* 76/39 (September 27, 1941) 617–21.

———. "Department of Prayer." *The Alliance Weekly* 78/5 (January 30, 1943) 72–80.

———. "Department of Prayer." *The Alliance Weekly* 78/13 (March 27, 1943) 200–202.

———. "Department of Prayer." *The Alliance Weekly* 78/31 (July 31, 1943) 488–90.

———. "Department of Prayer." *The Alliance Weekly* 79/9 (February 26, 1944) 136–38.

———. "Editorial." *Christian Alliance and Missionary Weekly* 10/27 (July 7, 1893) 2–5.

———. "Editorials." *The Alliance Weekly* 58/17 (June 21, 1924) 278–79.

———. "Editorials." *The Alliance Weekly* 61/20 (May 15, 1926) 323.

———. "Entering New Areas with the Gospel." *The Alliance Weekly* 72/2 (January 9, 1937) 32.

———. "From Every Tongue and Tribe." *The Alliance Weekly* 73/20 (May 14, 1938) 320.

———. "General Wong Remakes the Province of Kwangsi." *The Alliance Weekly* 63/41 (October 13, 1928) 665–72.

———. "God Moves among the Chuangs." *The Alliance Weekly* 84/31 (July 30, 1949) 489.

———. "Good News from Quangsi." *The Christian and Missionary Alliance* 18/8 (February 19, 1897).

———. "The Gospel at Work in Foreign Lands." *The Alliance Weekly* 70/34 (August 24, 1935) 552.

———. "Gospel Fruit in San Fang." *The Alliance Weekly* 84/7 (February 12, 1949) 104.

———. "The Hill Tribes." *The Alliance Weekly* 73/43 (October 22, 1938) 682.

———. "Growing Tall." *The Alliance Weekly* 81/50 (December 14, 1946) 778–79.

———. "Joseph R. Cunningham." *The Alliance Weekly* 59/14 (October 4, 1924) 223–24.

———. "Last Minute Foreign News." *The Alliance Weekly* 78/21 (May 22, 1943) 323–30.

———. "New York, October 1, 1904." *The Alliance Weekly* 33/18 (October 1, 1904).

———. "Old Missionary Mail Bag." *The Alliance Weekly* 63/7 (February 18, 1928) 107.

———. "One for Another." *The Alliance Weekly* 82/13 (March 29, 1947) 203.

———. "Other Honorees." *The Alliance Witness* 109/25 (December 4, 1974) 26.

———. "Our China Fields." *The Alliance Weekly* 69/52 (December 29, 1934) 832.

———. "Our Foreign Mail Bag." *The Alliance Weekly* 47/26 (March 31, 1917) 410–14.

———. "Our Foreign Mail Bag." *The Alliance Weekly* 60/1 (October 5, 1918) 9–11.

———. "Our Foreign Mail Bag." *The Alliance Weekly* 74/20 (May 20, 1939) 312–14.

———. "Outgoing Missionaries." *Christian Alliance and Foreign Missionary Weekly* 16/3 (January 17, 1896) 49–52.

———. "Personalia." *The Alliance Weekly* 64/30 (July 27, 1929) 489–92.

———. "The Passing of Miss Edith Dyer." *The Alliance Weekly* 47/24 (March 17, 1917) 377.

———. "Recent Cablegrams." *The Alliance Weekly* 61/26 (June 26, 1926) 422.

———. "Touring in South China." *The Alliance Weekly* 66/20 (May 16, 1931) 317–18.

———. "Transformed Lives in Far-off Fields." *The Alliance Weekly* 71/37 (September 12, 1936) 596.

———. "Tribesmen Hear and Accept the Message." *The Alliance Weekly* 76/46 (November 15, 1941) 732–40.

———. "Tribespeople Won for Christ." *The Alliance Weekly* 77/7 (February 14, 1942) 105.

———. "Work and Workers." *The Alliance Weekly* 70/31 (August 3, 1935) 501–2.

———. "Work and Workers." *The Alliance Weekly* 71/43 (October 24, 1936) 688–89.

———. "Work and Workers." *The Alliance Weekly* 80/9 (May 5, 1945) 139–40.

———. "Work and Workers." *The Alliance Weekly* 81/8 (February 23, 1946) 125.

———. "The Workings of God." *The Alliance Weekly* 79/12 (March 25, 1944) 185–92.

Christie, William. "Department of Prayer." *The Alliance Weekly* 65/43 (October 25, 1930) 699–700.

———. "Department of Prayer." *The Alliance Weekly* 67/26 (June 25, 1932) 411–14.

———. "Department of Prayer." *The Alliance Weekly* 69/17 (April 28, 1934) 264–70.

———. "Department of Prayer." *The Alliance Weekly* 70/21 (May 25, 1935) 328–31.

———. "Department of Prayer." *The Alliance Weekly* 71/39 (September 26, 1936) 620–24.

———. "Department of Prayer." *The Alliance Weekly* 73/9 (February 26, 1938) 136–38.

Church Missionary Society. "A Chinese Fire-Engine." *The Newsletter. C.M.S. Central China Mission* 24 (November 1910) 76–77.

———. *The Church Missionary Gleaner, Volume 3, 1902–1915.* Cleveland, OH: Church Missionary Society, 1915.

———. "Editorial Notes." *The Newsletter of the Kwangsi Hunan Mission of the C.M.S. & C.E.Z.M.S.* 54 (1919) 202–8.

———. "News in Brief." *The Newsletter. C.M.S. Central China Mission* 20 (December 1909) 129–30.

———. "Questions and Answers." *The Newsletter of the Kwangsi Hunan Mission of the C.M.S. & C.E.Z.M.S.* 47 (October 1916) 61–63.

———. "The Rev. J. L. Bacon." *The Newsletter of the Kwangsi Hunan Mission of the C.M.S. & C.E.Z.M.S.* 54 (1919) 204.

————. "Roderick Macdonald, M.D." *The Newsletter. C.M.S. Central China Mission and Tokyo Student Mission* 17 (February 1909) 75–76.

————. "Statistics for the Kwangsi-Hunan Mission for 1918." *The Newsletter of the Kwangsi Hunan Mission of the C.M.S. & C.E.Z.M.S.* 56 (1920) 261–62.

Clark, Anthony E. *China's Saints: Catholic Martyrdom during the Qing (1644–1911).* Bethlehem, PA: Lehigh University Press, 2011.

Clarke, Samuel R., and China Inland Mission. *Among the Tribes in South-West China.* London: Morgan & Scott, 1911.

Clemmer, Hazel Marcella, C. B. Poole, E. T. Maude, and T. P. Worsnip. "Greetings from South China." *The Alliance Weekly* 71/40 (October 3, 1936) 636–38.

Clemmer, Raymond M. "God's Advance Provision for the Miao." *The Alliance Weekly* 74/2 (January 14, 1939) 24.

Clift, Caroline Winifred Lechmere. *Very Far East.* London: Marshall Brothers, 1909.

Cochrane, Thomas. *Survey of the Missionary Occupation of China.* Shanghai: Christian Literature Society for China, 1913.

Cordier, Henri. "China." In *Catholic Encyclopedia: An International Work of Reference on the Constitution, Doctrine, Discipline, and History of the Catholic Church,* edited by Charles G. Herbermann, vol. 3. New York: Robert Appleton, 1908.

————. "The Church in China." In *Catholic Encyclopedia: An International Work of Reference on the Constitution, Doctrine, Discipline, and History of the Catholic Church,* edited by Charles G. Herbermann, vol. 3. New York: Robert Appleton, 1908.

————. "Martyrs in China." In *Catholic Encyclopedia: An International Work of Reference on the Constitution, Doctrine, Discipline, and History of the Catholic Church,* edited by Charles G. Herbermann, vol. 9. New York: Robert Appleton, 1910.

Couche, Edith. "Biblewomen." *The Kwangsi-Hunan Diocesan Newsletter* 116 (January 1937) 9–10.

————. "A Chinese Language Lesson." *The Newsletter. C.M.S. Central China Mission* 22 (May 1910) 26–27.

————. "Continued from Our Last." *The Kwangsi-Hunan Diocesan Newsletter* 102 (July 1933) 4–8.

————. "Dining Out." *The Newsletter. C.M.S. Central China Mission* 27 (August 1911) 50–52.

————. "The Rear Guard." *The Kwangsi-Hunan Diocesan Newsletter* 109 (April 1935) 17–18.

Couling, Samuel. *The Encyclopedia Sinica.* Shanghai: Kelly & Walsh, 1917.

Cuenot, Joseph C. *Kwangsi: Land of the Black Banners.* Translated by George F. Wiseman. St. Louis, MO: B. Herder, 1942.

Cunich, Peter. "Women Missionaries and Sino-British Relations." In *Bonds across Borders: Women, China, and International Relations in the Modern World,* edited by Priscilla Roberts and Peiqun He, 201–16. Newcastle, UK: Cambridge Scholars Publishing, 2007.

Cunningham, Joseph R. "The Work in Kweilin, South China." *The Alliance Weekly* 16/1 (October 4, 1913) 8–10.

Davis, Bradley Camp. *Imperial Bandits: Outlaws and Rebels in the China-Vietnam Borderlands.* Seattle: University of Washington Press, 2017.

Desterhaft, August Frederick. "God Is Still Working in China." *The Alliance Weekly* 85/37 (September 16, 1950) 587.

———. "Mr. Su of South China." *The Alliance Weekly* 79/15 (May 6, 1944) 233–34.

———. "Our Foreign Mail Bag." *The Alliance Weekly* 67/40 (October 1, 1932) 632.

———. "Our Foreign Mail Bag." *The Alliance Weekly* 74/16 (April 22, 1939) 248–50.

———. "Our Foreign Mail Bag." *The Alliance Weekly* 77/31 (August 15, 1942) 488–89.

———. "With the Tong Tribe of South China." *The Alliance Weekly* 65/46 (November 15, 1930) 748–51.

Donaldson, Clair. *The Call from the Far East: Being a Comprehensive Statement of the Facts Which Constitute the Call from the Far East to the Church of England Prepared by a Commission Appointed by the Missionary Council of the Church Assembly.* Westminster, UK: Press and Publications Board of the Church Assembly, 1926.

Erb, Paul, ed. "T'ung Tribe Christian Movement." *Gospel Herald* 51/45 (November 11, 1958) 1079.

Falkenheim, Victor, and Ping-chia Kuo. "Guangxi." *Encyclopedia Britannica*, 2014. https://www.britannica.com/place/Guangxi.

Fant, David J. "In Memoriam." *The Alliance Weekly* 65/26 (June 28, 1930) 403.

———. "Publisher's Column." *The Alliance Weekly* 71/29 (July 18, 1936) 468.

Farmer, Ada Beeson. "Immediate Evangelization of the World." *The Alliance Weekly* 26/6 (August 11, 1906) 88–89.

Farmer, William A. *Ada Beeson Farmer: A Missionary Heroine of Kuang Si South China.* Atlanta: Foote & Davies, 1912.

Field, Alvin W. "A Rice Christian?" *The Alliance Weekly* 16/9 (November 29, 1913) 137–38.

———. "The Yao Tribesmen." *The Alliance Weekly* 52/24 (September 6, 1919) 24.

Field, Alvin W., Walter Herbert Oldfield, and E. K. Marsh. "South China Conference." *The Alliance Weekly* 49/7 (November 17, 1917) 104.

Findlay, George G., and William West Holdsworth. *The History of the Wesleyan Methodist Missionary Society.* Vol. 5. London: Epworth, 1924.

Fletcher, Jesse C. *Bill Wallace of China.* Nashville, TN: Broadman, 1963.

Foreign Mission Society of America. *Maryknoll Mission Letters, China.* Vol. 1. New York: MacMillan, 1923.

Foster, Arnold. *Christian Progress in China: Gleanings from the Writings and Speeches of Many Workers.* London: Religious Tract Society, 1889.

Foust, Ethel L., Myra E. Rolie, Isabel A. MacMillan, Walter Herbert Oldfield, and William C. Newbern. "Greetings from South China." *The Alliance Weekly* 60/7 (February 14, 1925) 105–6.

Fulton, Mary H. *"Inasmuch": Extracts from Letters, Journals, Papers, Etc.* West Medford, MA: Central Committee on the United Study of Foreign Missions, 1915.

Garrison, C. M., M. E. Turley, and E. H. Carne. "The Spiritual Side at the 1917 South China Conference." *The Alliance Weekly* 48/23 (September 8, 1917) 361.

Geary, D. Norman, Ruth B. Geary, Chaoquan Ou, Yaohong Long, Daren Jiang, and Jiying Wang. *The Kam People of China: Turning Nineteen?* New York: Routledge Curzon, 2003.

Glover, Robert H. "Our Foreign Mail Bag." *The Alliance Weekly* 46/5 (April 29, 1916) 74–77.

———. "Our Foreign Mail Bag." *The Alliance Weekly* 49/10 (December 8, 1917) 154.

Goodman, E. "Returning to Kweilin." *The Kwangsi-Hunan Diocesan Newsletter* 106 (July 1934) 6–7.

Graves, Roswell Hobart. *Forty Years in China*. Baltimore, MD: R. H. Woodward, 1895.

———. "Statistics of the Southern Baptism Convention Mission." *The Chinese Recorder and Missionary Journal* 7 (June 1876) 184–85.

Gray, G. F. S. "An Athletic Festival at Kweilin." *The Kwangsi-Hunan Diocesan Newsletter* 93 (March 1931) 28–29.

———. "Kweilin Parish." *The Kwangsi-Hunan Diocesan Newsletter* 107 (October 1934) 12–14.

———. "The Parish of Kweilin." *The Kwangsi-Hunan Diocesan Newsletter* 101 (April 1933) 12–14.

———. "A Tale of Two Cities." *The Kwangsi-Hunan Diocesan Newsletter* 103 (October 1933) 14–15.

———. "With the Faithful at Ta Yong Kiang." *The Kwangsi-Hunan Diocesan Newsletter* 93 (March 1931) 38–39.

Grist, William Alexander. *Samuel Pollard: Pioneer Missionary in China*. London: H. Hooks United Methodist Pub. House, 1919.

"Guangxi." *New World Encyclopedia*, July 18, 2017. http://www.newworldencyclopedia.org/entry/Guangxi.

Guinness, M. Geraldine. *The Story of the China Inland Mission*. 2nd ed. Vol. 2. London: Morgan & Scott, 1894.

Hague, Eric. "Religion in Ruins." *The Kwangsi-Hunan Diocesan Newsletter* 132 (May 1946) 15–16.

Halsey, Abram Woodruff. *"Go and Tell John": A Sketch of the Medical and Philanthropic Work of the Board of Foreign Missions of the Presbyterian Church in the U.S.A.* New York: Board of Foreign Missions of the Presbyterian Church in the U.S.A., 1914.

Hattaway, Paul. *China's Christian Martyrs*. Oxford: Monarch, 2007.

Hefley, James C., and Marti Hefley. *By Their Blood: Christian Martyrs of the 20th Century*. Milford, MI: Mott Media, 1978. http://www.ccel.us/bytheirblood.toc.html.

Herbermann, Charles G., Edward A. Pace, Conde B. Fallen, Thomas J. Shahan, and John J. Wynne, eds. *Catholic Encyclopedia: An International Work of Reference on the Constitution, Doctrine, Discipline, and History of the Catholic Church*. New York: The Encyclopedia Press, 1913. https://en.wikisource.org/w/index.php?title=Catholic_Encyclopedia_(1913)/Prefect_Apostolic&oldid=4654616.

Hess, Isaac. "Immediate Evangelization of the World: Annual Report of South China Mission." *The Alliance Weekly* 25/20 (May 26, 1906) 320–22.

Holden, Elsie M. "Touring in the Chuanchow Parish." *The Kwangsi-Hunan Newsletter* 89 (March 1930) 8–10.

Holden, John. "A Big Dose." *The Newsletter of the Kwangsi Hunan Mission of the C.M.S. & C.E.Z.M.S.* 56 (1920) 257–59.

———. "The Bishop's Letter." *The Kwangsi-Hunan Diocesan Newsletter* 91 (September 1930) 2–5.

———. "The Bishop's Letter." *The Kwangsi-Hunan Diocesan Newsletter* 93 (March 1931) 22–25.

———. "The Bishop's Letter." *The Kwangsi-Hunan Diocesan Newsletter* 95 (October 1931) 2–5.

———. "The Bishop's Letter." *The Kwangsi-Hunan Diocesan Newsletter* 101 (April 1933) 2–4.

————. "The Bishop's Letter." *The Newsletter of the Kwangsi Hunan Mission of the C.M.S. & C.E.Z.M.S.* 69 (September 1924) 537–39.

————. "The Bishop's Letter." *The Newsletter of the Kwangsi Hunan Mission of the C.M.S. & C.E.Z.M.S.* 77 (September 1926) 698–700.

————. "The Bishop's Letter." *The Newsletter of the Kwangsi Hunan Mission of the C.M.S. & C.E.Z.M.S.* 83 (August 1928) 818–19.

————. "The Bishop's Letter." *The Newsletter of the Kwangsi Hunan Mission of the C.M.S. & C.E.Z.M.S.* 84 (November 1928) 842–44.

————. "A Door to Be Opened." *The Newsletter. C.M.S. Central China Mission* 19 (August 1909) 115–17.

————. "Editorial Notes." *The Newsletter. C.M.S. Central China Mission* 53 (November 1918) 182–86.

————. "The Ven. Archdeacon Byrde." *The Newsletter of the Kwangsi Hunan Mission of the C.M.S. & C.E.Z.M.S.* 54 (1919) 214–17.

The Hong Kong Council of the Church of Christ in China. "About Us: Historical Prospective," n.d. http://www.hkcccc.org/Eng/1main.php.

Hsu, Addison K. S. "A Chinese View of the Sixth Diocesan Synod." *The Newsletter of the Kwangsi Hunan Mission of the C.M.S. & C.E.Z.M.S.* 82 (April 1928) 806–8.

————. "My First Trip to Kweilin." *The Kwangsi-Hunan Diocesan Newsletter* 93 (March 1931) 29–31.

————. "Turn Again Our Captivity, O Lord." *The Kwangsi-Hunan Diocesan Newsletter* 132 (May 1946) 7–8.

Hutchings, Graham. "A Province at War: Guangxi during the Sino-Japanese Conflict, 1937–1945." *The China Quarterly* 108 (1986) 652–79.

Ibbotson, T. C. "Flight in Winter." *The Newsletter of the Kwangsi Hunan Mission of the C.M.S. & C.E.Z.M.S.* 79 (March 1927) 756–59.

"Inflation Calculator." *Bank of England*, n.d. https://www.bankofengland.co.uk/monetary-policy/inflation/inflation-calculator.

Irvin, Maurice R. "The Persecuted Professor's Daughter." *Alliance Life* 128/22 (December 15, 1993) 12–14.

Jaffray, Robert A. "The City of Po-She." *The Alliance Weekly* 65/18 (May 3, 1930) 273–84.

————. "A General Resume of the Stations of Kwang-Si." *The Alliance Weekly* 55/23 (May 15, 1920) 103–6.

————. "The Gospel in Foreign Lands." *The Alliance Weekly* 55/23 (August 20, 1921) 358–61.

————. "Thou Crownest the Year with Thy Goodness." *The Alliance Weekly* 57/40 (December 1, 1923) 641–63.

James, Edward T., ed. *Notable American Women, 1607–1950: A Biographical Dictionary.* Vol. 1. Cambridge: Harvard University Press, 1971.

Kaup, Katherine P. *Creating the Zhuang: Ethnic Politics in China.* Boulder, CO: Rienner, 2000.

Keen, Rosemary. "Church Missionary Society Archive: General Introduction and Guide to the Archive." *Adam Matthew Digital*, n.d. http://www.ampltd.co.uk/digital_guides/church_missionary_society_archive_general/editorial%20introduction%20by%20rosemary%20keen.aspx.

Kendall, R. Elliot. *Beyond the Clouds: The Story of Samuel Pollard of South-West China.* London: Cargate, 1954.

King, Louis L. *Missionary Atlas: A Manual of the Foreign Work of the Christian and Missionary Alliance.* Harrisburg, PA: Christian Publications, 1964.

Kowles, Al G. "Ebenezer!" *The Alliance Weekly* 75/20 (May 18, 1940) 313–14.

————. "Our Foreign Mail Bag." *The Alliance Weekly* 79/16 (May 20, 1944) 248–49.

Kowles, Raymond A. "Marketing for Souls." *The Alliance Weekly* 74/32 (August 12, 1939) 505–6.

————. "Our Foreign Mail Bag." *The Alliance Weekly* 74/44 (November 4, 1939) 697–98.

Lackey, Margaret M. *Laborers Together: A Study of Southern Baptist Missions in China.* New York: Revell, 1921.

"'Lady' Physicians in the Field: Women Doctors and Presbyterian Foreign Mission Work, 1870–1960." *The Journal of Presbyterian History (1997–)* 82/4 (2004) 271–73.

Lambert, Tony. *China's Christian Millions.* Oxford: Monarch, 2006.

Lang, H. E. "Itinerating in China." *The Alliance Weekly* 81/36 (September 7, 1946) 570.

Latourette, Kenneth S. *A History of Christian Missions in China.* New York: MacMillan, 1929.

Launay, Adrien. *Histoire Des Missions de Chine: Mission Du Kouang-Si.* Paris: Douniol, 1903.

Law, S. E. "Easter in Kwanyang." *The Kwangsi-Hunan Diocesan Newsletter* 103 (October 1933) 16–17.

————. "Impressions on Returning to China." *The Kwangsi-Hunan Diocesan Newsletter* 132 (May 1946) 14–15.

————. "An Itineration in the Chuanchow Parish." *The Kwangsi-Hunan Diocesan Newsletter* 99 (October 1932) 13–15.

Leach, Joseph. "And as He Sowed, Some Seeds Fell by the Wayside." *The Kwangsi-Hunan Diocesan Newsletter* 124 (May 1939) 13–15.

————. "On the King's Business." *The Kwangsi-Hunan Diocesan Newsletter* 134 (May 1947) 14–15.

————. "Our Autumn Offensive." *The Kwangsi-Hunan Diocesan Newsletter* 133 (December 1946) 9–10.

————. "Our Doings and Mis-Doings." *The Kwangsi-Hunan Diocesan Newsletter* 123 (March 1939) 15–17.

————. "Sowing the Seed." *The Kwangsi-Hunan Diocesan Newsletter* 117 (April 1937) 10–12.

————. "A Visit to Kweilin Parish." *The Kwangsi-Hunan Diocesan Newsletter* 122 (October 1938) 6–8.

Liu, Yu. "The True Pioneer of the Jesuit China Mission: Michele Ruggieri." *History of Religions* 50/4 (2011) 362–83. doi:10.1086/658128.

Lobenstine, E. C., ed. *China Mission Year Book 1916.* Vol. 8. Shanghai: Christian Literature Society for China, 1916.

————, ed. *China Mission Year Book 1917.* Vol. 8. Shanghai: Christian Literature Society for China, 1917.

Love, J. F. *Seventy-Fourth Annual Report of the Foreign Mission Board Southern Baptist Convention.* Richmond, VA: Southern Baptist Convention Foreign Mission Board, 1919.

———. *Seventy-Sixth Annual Report of the Foreign Mission Board Southern Baptist Convention*. Richmond, VA: Southern Baptist Convention Foreign Mission Board, 1921.

———. *Seventy-Third Annual Report of the Foreign Mission Board Southern Baptist Convention*. Richmond, VA: Southern Baptist Convention Foreign Mission Board, 1918.

Lowe, C. J. "Evangelism on the Kwei Lin Field." In *Gleanings: The Mandrin Field, Kwei Lin, Kwangsi, China*, edited by C. J. Lowe, 3–5, 1920.

———. *My Daily Prayer Book for Southwest China Baptist Mission Station*, n.d.

Lu, Zhouxiang. *Politics and Identity in Chinese Martial Arts*. New York: Routledge, 2018.

Lyall, Leslie T. *A Biography of John Sung*. London: Overseas Missionary Fellowship, 1954.

Macdonald, Margaret. *Roderick Macdonald, M.D.: A Servant of Jesus Christ*. London: Robert Culley, 1908.

MacGillivray, Donald, ed. *A Century of Protestant Missions in China (1807–1907)*. Shanghai: American Presbyterian Mission Press, 1907.

———. *The China Mission Year Book 1910*. Vol. 1. Shanghai: Christian Literature Society for China, 1910.

McCloy, Thomas. "Sketch of Eight Years' Work in the Province of Kwong-Sai." *The Chinese Recorder and Missionary Journal* 26/1 (January 1895).

Montanar, Valentine. "Kwang-Si." In *Catholic Encyclopedia: An International Work of Reference on the Constitution, Doctrine, Discipline, and History of the Catholic Church*, edited by Charles G. Herbermann, vol. 8. New York: Robert Appleton, 1910.

Morton, W. Scott, and Charlton M. Lewis. *China: Its History and Culture*. 4th ed. New York: McGraw-Hill, 2005.

Newbern, William C. "The China Bible Seminary: Sixtieth Anniversary." *The Alliance Witness* 94/22 (November 4, 1959) 12–13.

———. "Communism Returns to Poseh, South China." *The Alliance Weekly* 65/40 (October 4, 1930) 650–51.

———. "Custodians of the Unfinished Task." *The Alliance Weekly* 80/13 (June 30, 1945) 200–202.

———. "Impressions of the South China Chinese Conference." *The Alliance Weekly* 67/1 (January 2, 1932) 9–10.

———. "Our Foreign Mail Bag." *The Alliance Weekly* 69/16 (April 21, 1934) 249–50.

———. "The Regions Beyond and the 'Many Adversaries.'" *The Alliance Weekly* 66/9 (February 28, 1931) 136–37.

"A 19th-Century View of Fever." *H2g2*, June 18, 2012. https://h2g2.com/edited_entry/A87758185.

Oldfield, Mabel Dimock. *With You Alway: The Life of a South China Missionary*. Harrisburg, PA: Christian Publications, 1958.

Oldfield, Walter Herbert. "After Ten Years." *The Alliance Weekly* 63/50 (December 15, 1928) 826.

———. "Amid Falling Bombs." *The Alliance Weekly* 74/21 (May 27, 1939) 329–30.

———. "Among Kwangsi's Tribesmen." *The Alliance Weekly* 48/15 (July 13, 1917) 232–33.

———. "Atrocities in Kwangsi." *The Alliance Weekly* 18/17 (February 6, 1915) 296–98.

———. "Attacked by Chinese Robbers." *The Alliance Weekly* 67/3 (January 16, 1932) 41–42.

———. "A Baptismal Service in a Chinese University." *The Alliance Weekly* 82/16 (April 19, 1947) 330.

———. "The Bible through Chinese Eyes." *The Alliance Weekly* 54/48 (February 26, 1921) 761–62.

———. "Challenges, Opportunities, and Privileges." *The Alliance Weekly* 73/38 (September 17, 1938) 600–602.

———. "Disastrous Floods in South China." *The Alliance Weekly* 44/24 (September 11, 1915) 377–78.

———. "Fightings and Fears." *The Alliance Weekly* 75/38 (September 21, 1940) 602.

———. "Five Months in a Chinese Prison." *The Alliance Weekly* 74/31 (October 5, 1939) 488–96.

———. "From Village to Village in Kwang Si, South China." *The Alliance Weekly* 66/43 (October 24, 1931) 696.

———. "Fruit in Pan-Yang." *The Alliance Weekly* 75/22 (June 1, 1940) 344–45.

———. "A God-Prepared Messenger." *The Alliance Weekly* 73/31 (July 30, 1938) 489.

———. "God's Grace in Kwangsi." *The Alliance Weekly* 77/28 (July 11, 1942) 440–41.

———. "Golden Opportunities in Kwangsi Province." *The Alliance Weekly* 69/18 (May 5, 1934) 280–81.

———. "Immediate Evangelization of the World." *The Alliance Weekly* 26/12 (September 22, 1906) 185.

———. "Immediate Evangelization of the World." *The Alliance Weekly* 26/21 (December 1, 1906) 344.

———. "In Memoriam: Rev. Thomas P. Worsnip." *The Alliance Weekly* 82/23 (June 7, 1947) 361.

———. "In Much Tribulation." *The Alliance Weekly* 78/39 (September 25, 1943) 617.

———. "In the Hands of Chinese Robbers." *The Alliance Weekly* 61/10 (May 13, 1922) 150–51.

———. "In the Midst of Alarms." *The Alliance Weekly* 75/20 (May 18, 1940) 312–14.

———. "In the Wilds of Kwangsi, South China." *The Alliance Weekly* 47/19 (February 10, 1917) 298.

———. *Kidnapped by Chinese Bandits*. Harrisburg, PA: Christian Alliance, 1930.

———. "Last Minute Foreign News." *The Alliance Weekly* 77/13 (March 28, 1942) 195.

———. "National Christian Service for Wounded Soldiers." *The Alliance Weekly* 76/23 (June 7, 1941) 360–61.

———. "A Night in Chwang Village." *The Alliance Weekly* 44/23 (September 4, 1915) 361.

———. "A Notable Gathering of Chinese Workers." *The Alliance Weekly* 66/47 (November 11, 1931) 764–65.

———. "O'er Mountain Trails to Many Tribes." *The Alliance Weekly* 74/15 (April 15, 1939) 232–33.

———. "Official's Friendliness Draws Large Crowds." *The Alliance Weekly* 67/35 (August 27, 1932) 552–53.

———. "Our Foreign Mail Bag." *The Alliance Weekly* 66/24 (June 13, 1931) 380–83.

———. "Our Foreign Mail Bag." *The Alliance Weekly* 77/17 (April 25, 1942) 265.

———. "Our Foreign Mail Bag." *The Alliance Weekly* 78/4 (January 23, 1943) 57.

———. "Our Foreign Mail Bag." *The Alliance Weekly* 78/21 (May 22, 1943) 329–30.

——. "Pioneer Evangelism in the Chinese Church." *The Alliance Weekly* 68/18 (May 6, 1933) 280–86.

——. "Pioneering in Kwang Si's Neglected Territory." *The Alliance Weekly* 63/31 (August 4, 1928) 505–9.

——. "Pioneering in Kwang Si's Neglected Territory." *The Alliance Weekly* 63/34 (August 25, 1928) 554–55.

——. *Pioneering in Kwangsi: The Story of Alliance Missions in South China.* Harrisburg, PA: Christian Publications, 1936.

——. "Pioneering in Western Kwangsi." *The Alliance Weekly* 49/20 (February 16, 1918) 312–13.

——. "Preaching amid Persecution." *The Alliance Weekly* 71/24 (June 13, 1936) 380–96.

——. "Seed Sowing in War Time." *The Alliance Weekly* 75/27 (July 6, 1940) 424–26.

——. "A Smallpox Epidemic in Linchow Fu." *The Alliance Weekly* 49/26 (March 30, 1918) 410.

——. "South China under Air Attack." *The Alliance Weekly* 78/27 (July 23, 1943) 424–25.

——. "Touring among the Tribesmen of Kwangsi, South China." *The Alliance Weekly* 66/49 (December 5, 1931) 797–98.

——. "Tragedy on the West River." *The Alliance Weekly* 69/5 (February 3, 1934) 73–74.

——. "The Tribespeople of South China." *The Alliance Weekly* 73/43 (October 22, 1938) 680–82.

——. "Uncle Eight." *The Alliance Weekly* 71/21 (May 23, 1936) 331–33.

——. "Widespread Witnessing in Kwangsi." *The Alliance Weekly* 77/33 (August 15, 1942) 520–21.

——. "A Word of Cheer from China." *The Alliance Weekly* 55/42 (December 31, 1921) 659.

——. "A Year of Blessing." *The Alliance Weekly* 69/32 (August 11, 1934) 504–6.

Papi, Hector. "Prefect Apostolic." In *Catholic Encyclopedia: An International Work of Reference on the Constitution, Doctrine, Discipline, and History of the Catholic Church*, edited by Charles G. Herbermann, vol. 12. New York: Robert Appleton, 1911.

Parker, James. "Kweilin Notes." *The Newsletter of the C.M.S. Kwangsi Hunan Mission* 36 (November 1913) 72–74.

Pim, Mary B. "In Touch with China's Young People." *The Kwangsi-Hunan Diocesan Newsletter* 109 (April 4, 1935) 11–12.

——. "One by One." *The Kwangsi-Hunan Diocesan Newsletter* 106 (July 1934) 16–17.

——. "Quiet Roads." *The Kwangsi-Hunan Diocesan Newsletter* 89 (March 1930) 13–16.

——. "Yellow Ox Market." *The Kwangsi-Hunan Diocesan Newsletter* 96 (December 12, 1931) 13–15.

Planchet, Jean-Marie. *Les Missions de Chine et Du Japon, 1917: Deuxième Année.* Beijing: Impr. des Lazaristes, 1917.

Pletcher, Kenneth. "Opium Wars." *Encyclopedia Britannica*, March 9, 2017. https://www.britannica.com/topic/Opium-Wars.

Poole, James A. "Chinese Tribal Chief Accepts Christ: The Gospel Penetrates the Yao Mountaineers." *The Alliance Weekly* 58/12 (May 17, 1924) 203.

———. "The Cross Bearers." *The Alliance Weekly* 69/26 (June 30, 1934) 409.

———. "A Motor Cycle Trip in Northwestern Kwangsi." *The Alliance Weekly* 64/39 (September 28, 1929) 632–33.

———. "The South China Evangelistic Band at Work." *The Alliance Weekly* 67/50 (December 10, 1932) 796–98.

Poston, Larry. "Jaffray, Robert (1873–1945)." In *The Encyclopedia of Christian Civilization*, edited by George Thomas Kurian. Blackwell, 2011. doi:10.1002/9780470670606. wbecco717.

Prentice, Edith M. "Refugees." *The Kwangsi-Hunan Diocesan Newsletter* 125 (September 1939) 7–9.

Pritchard, John. *Methodists and Their Missionary Societies: 1760–1900*. Burlington, VT: Ashgate, 2013.

Quick, L. B. "An Incident in Quangsi." *Christian Alliance and Foreign Missionary Weekly* 17/5 (July 31, 1896) 97–99.

Ray, Rex. *Cowboy Missionary in Kwangsi*. Nashville, TN: Broadman, 1964.

Ray, T. Bronson. *Southern Baptists in China*. Richmond, VA: Foreign Mission Board Southern Baptist Convention, 1924.

Reeves, C. H. "Missionary Letters." *The Christian Alliance and Missionary Weekly* 11/13 (September 29, 1893) 206.

Reinsch, Paul Samuel. *World Politics at the End of the Nineteenth Century*. New York: Macmillan, 1900.

Rogers, Freda J. "An Open Door." *The Kwangsi-Hunan Diocesan Newsletter* 135 (September 1947) 9–10.

———. "Resurrection." *The Kwangsi-Hunan Diocesan Newsletter* 134 (May 1947) 13–14.

Ryan, Joseph P. "American Contributions to the Catholic Missionary Effort in China in the Twentieth Century." *The Catholic Historical Review* 31/2 (1945) 171–80.

Santler, Grace. "A Great Need." *The Kwangsi-Hunan Diocesan Newsletter* 86 (June 1929) 13–14.

Shortt, Melva. "Oddments." *The Kwangsi-Hunan Diocesan Newsletter* 116 (January 1937) 7–8.

Simpson, A. B. "Annual Survey." *The Alliance Weekly* 44/11 (June 12, 1915) 168–72.

"Sino-French War." *Encyclopedia Britannica*, April 17, 2015. https://www.britannica.com/event/Sino-French-War.

Sisters Marianites of Holy Cross. *The Ave Maria*. Notre Dame, IN: Congregation of Holy Cross, 1902.

Smylie, James. "Notable Presbyterian Women." *Journal of Presbyterian History (1962–1985)* 52/2 (1974) 99–121.

Snead, A. C. "Advancing into New Fields." *The Alliance Weekly* 67/44 (October 29, 1932) 701–2.

———. "Causes for Thanksgiving." *The Alliance Weekly* 67/29 (July 16, 1932) 456–58.

———. *Missionary Atlas: A Manual of the Foreign Work of the Christian and Missionary Alliance*. Harrisburg, PA: Christian Publications, 1936.

———. *Missionary Atlas: A Manual of the Foreign Work of the Christian and Missionary Alliance*. Harrisburg, PA: Christian Publications, 1950.

———. "A People for His Name." *The Alliance Weekly* 68/27 (July 8, 1933) 424–26.

———. "Rev. A. F. Desterhaft." *The Alliance Weekly* 87/5 (January 30, 1952) 76.

———. "Walter H. Oldfield: Modern Pioneer." *The Alliance Witness* 93/24 (November 19, 1958) 15.

———. "War, the Work, and the Word." *The Alliance Weekly* 77/15 (March 28, 1942) 265.

Society for the Propagation of the Faith. *Annals of the Propagation of the Faith*. London: Burnes & Oates, 1850.

Southern Baptist Convention. *Annual of the Southern Baptist Convention, 1940*. Nashville, TN: The Executive Committee, 1940.

———. *Annual of the Southern Baptist Convention, 1950*. Nashville: The Executive Committee, 1950.

———. *Annual of the Southern Baptist Convention, 1952*. Nashville: The Executive Committee, 1952.

———. *Annual of the Southern Baptist Convention, 1954*. Nashville: The Executive Committee, 1954.

———. *Annual of the Southern Baptist Convention, 1955*. Nashville: The Executive Committee, 1955.

Stanford, Edward. *Atlas of the Chinese Empire*. London: Morgan & Scott, 1908.

Staunton, George Thomas. *Miscellaneous Notices Relating to China and Our Commercial Intercourse with That Country: Including a Few Translations from the Chinese Language*. London: Murray, 1822.

Stevens, Percy. "Archdeacon Louis Byrde." *The Newsletter of the Kwangsi Hunan Mission of the C.M.S. & C.E.Z.M.S.* 52 (1918) 153–72.

———. "Bishop's Foreword." *The Kwangsi-Hunan Diocesan Newsletter* 106 (July 1934) 2–4.

———. "Bishop's Foreword." *The Kwangsi-Hunan Diocesan Newsletter* 116 (January 1937) 2–5.

———. "Bishop's Foreword." *The Kwangsi-Hunan Diocesan Newsletter* 122 (October 1938) 2–4.

———. "Bishop's Foreword." *The Kwangsi-Hunan Diocesan Newsletter* 125 (September 1939) 2–6.

———. "Bishop's Foreword." *The Kwangsi-Hunan Diocesan Newsletter* 126 (March 1940) 2–8.

———. "Bishop's Foreword." *The Kwangsi-Hunan Diocesan Newsletter* 127 (September 1940) 2–5.

———. "Bishop's Foreword." *The Kwangsi-Hunan Diocesan Newsletter* 128 (May 1941) 2–4.

———. "Bishop's Foreword." *The Kwangsi-Hunan Diocesan Newsletter* 131 (July 1945) 2–4.

———. "Bishop's Foreword." *The Kwangsi-Hunan Diocesan Newsletter* 133 (December 1946) 3–5.

———. "Bishop's Foreword." *The Kwangsi-Hunan Diocesan Newsletter* 140 (April 1950) 3–6.

———. "Notes of the Bishop's Address at the Opening of Synod, February, 1948." *The Kwangsi-Hunan Diocesan Newsletter* 137 (August 1948) 4–5.

———. "Outline of Events since Early in 1941." *The Kwangsi-Hunan Diocesan Newsletter* 131 (July 1945) 8–14.

———. "Peeps into the Past." *The Kwangsi-Hunan Diocesan Newsletter* 141 (January 1951) 11–20.

Stock, Eugene. *The History of the Church Missionary Society*. London: Church Missionary Society, 1916.

Strand, David. *Rickshaw Beijing: City People and Politics in the 1920s*. Los Angeles: University of California Press, 1989.

"Taiping Rebellion." *Encyclopedia Britannica*, July 25, 2017. https://www.britannica.com/event/Taiping-Rebellion.

Tatchell, W. Arthur. *Medical Missions in China: In Connexion with the Wesleyan Methodist Church*. London: Culley, 1909.

Taylor, James Hudson, ed. *China's Millions, 1880*. London: Morgan & Scott, 1881.

———, ed. *China's Millions, 1883*. London: Morgan & Scott, 1883.

———. *China's Spiritual Needs and Claims*. London: Morgan & Scott, 1887.

———. *Three Decades of the China Inland Mission*. Toronto: China Inland Mission, 1895.

Tiedemann, R. Gary. *Handbook of Christianity in China*. Leiden, Netherlands: Brill NV, 2010.

———. *Reference Guide to Christian Missionary Societies in China: From the Sixteenth to the Twentieth Century*. New York: Routledge, 2015.

Tindall, T. P. "In Journeyings Often." *The Newsletter of the Kwangsi Hunan Mission of the C.M.S. & C.E.Z.M.S.* 83 (August 1928) 834–38.

Tobin, B. K. L. "Child-Refugees." *The Kwangsi-Hunan Diocesan Newsletter* 123 (March 1939) 13–15.

———. "The End of a Chapter." *The Kwangsi-Hunan Diocesan Newsletter* 111 (October 1935) 9.

———. "Evangelism in Kwanyang County." *The Kwangsi-Hunan Diocesan Newsletter* 113 (May 1936) 4–5.

———. "An Unfinished Story." *The Kwangsi-Hunan Diocesan Newsletter* 106 (July 1934) 13–14.

———. "A Visit to Hingan Parish." *The Kwangsi-Hunan Diocesan Newsletter* 100 (December 1932) 15–17.

Tobin, Blanche, and W. R. Cannell. "Student Work in Kweilin." *The Kwangsi-Hunan Diocesan Newsletter* 86 (June 1929) 9–13.

Tomatala, Yakob Yonas. "The Dynamic Missionary Leadership of Robert Alexander Jaffray." D.Miss., Fuller Theological Seminary, School of World Mission, 1990. http://search.proquest.com/pqdtglobal/docview/303912902/abstract/4BBA7B091DBF4EB3PQ/1.

"Top Ten Pirate Weapons." *Pirate Attack*. Accessed July 12, 2018. http://pirateattack.co.uk/top-ten-pirate-weapons.

Tozer, A. W. *Let My People Go: The Life of Robert A. Jaffray*. Kindle Edition. Camp Hill, PA: WingSpread, 2010.

Tubbs, George W. "In Needy Kwangsi." *The Alliance Weekly* 83/29 (July 17, 1948) 458.

———. "To Earth's Remotest People." *The Alliance Witness* 106/21 (October 13, 1971) 5–6.

Tucker, Ruth. "The Role of Bible Women in World Evangelism." *Missiology* 13/2 (1985) 133–46.

Turley, Maude E., Thomas P. Worsnip, and Pauline Woerner. "The South China Conference." *The Alliance Weekly* 70/42 (October 19, 1935) 673–74.

Ure, Gavin. *Governors, Politics and the Colonial Office: Public Policy in Hong Kong, 1918–58*. Hong Kong: Hong Kong University Press, 2012.

Verbyla, Bernice A. *Aunt Mae's China: This Is the Story of Beatrice Mae Tonkin 1886–1957*. Xulon, 2010.

Wakeman, Frederic. *The Great Enterprise: The Manchu Reconstruction of Imperial Order in Seventeenth-Century China*. Berkeley: University of California Press, 1985.

Walsh, James Edward. "From Our Latest Center in China." In *The Field Afar*, 87–92, 1921.

Wang, Xiuhua. "Explaining Christianity in China: Why a Foreign Religion Has Taken Root in Unfertile Ground." MA thesis, Baylor University, 2015.

Waterson, M. Florence. "Joy at Hingan." *The Kwangsi-Hunan Diocesan Newsletter* 130 (October 1941) 9–10.

Watkins, R. E. L. "Changes." *The Kwangsi-Hunan Diocesan Newsletter* 114 (July 1936) 12–13.

———. "Hospital Stories." *The Kwangsi-Hunan Diocesan Newsletter* 91 (September 1930) 11–12.

———. "In Peril of Robbers." *The Newsletter of the Kwangsi Hunan Mission of the C.M.S. & C.E.Z.M.S.* 84 (November 1928) 845–47.

———. "Kweilin Hospital." *The Kwangsi-Hunan Diocesan Newsletter* 98 (July 1932) 12–13.

Wells, H. R. "Bible-Selling in Kwong Sai." *Bible Society Record* 33/10 (October 18, 1888) 148–49.

———. "Mr. Wells' Report." In *Seventy-Third Annual Report of the American Bible Society*, 144–45. New York: American Bible Society, 1889.

Wiest, Jean-Paul. "Catholic Mission Theory and Practice: Lessons from the Work of the Paris Foreign Mission Society and Maryknoll in Guangdong and Guangxi Provinces." *Missiology: An International Review* 10/2 (1982) 171–84.

———. *Maryknoll in China: A History, 1918–1955*. Armonk, NY: Sharpe, 1988.

Williams, J. T. "A Trip to Kwei Lin." In *Gleanings: The Mandarin Field, Kwei Lin, Kwangsi, China*, edited by C. J. Lowe, 12–16, 1920.

Wilson, J. R. "Fellowship in the Gospel." *The Kwangsi-Hunan Diocesan Newsletter* 113 (May 1936) 12–15.

———. "Kwangsi Life." *The Kwangsi-Hunan Diocesan Newsletter* 108 (January 1935) 9–11.

———. "Schoolboys." *The Kwangsi-Hunan Diocesan Newsletter* 93 (March 1931) 35–36.

———. "When the Mists Have Rolled Away." *The Kwangsi-Hunan Diocesan Newsletter* 114 (July 1936) 6–8.

———. "When Troubles Come." *The Newsletter of the Kwangsi Hunan Mission of the C.M.S. & C.E.Z.M.S.* 55 (1919) 237.

Wilson, L. M. "A City of Rubbish-Heaps." *The Newsletter of the Kwangsi Hunan Mission of the C.M.S. & C.E.Z.M.S.* 65 (June 1923) 431–32.

Woerner, Gustave. "An Angel Guard in South China." *The Alliance Weekly* 66/48 (November 28, 1931) 781–86.

———. "Impressions of the South China Conference." *The Alliance Weekly* 67/1 (January 2, 1932) 9–10.

———. "Present Evangelistic Opportunities in Kwangsi." *The Alliance Weekly* 64/43 (October 26, 1929) 697–98.

Wolferstan, Bertram. *The Catholic Church in China from 1860 to 1907*. St. Louis: Herder, 1909.

Yan, Xiaohua 颜小华. *Guangxi Jiduzongjiao Lishi Yu Xiankuang Yanjiu* 广西基督宗教 历史与现状研究 [Studies in the History and Current Situation of Christianity in Guangxi]. Beijing: Social Sciences Academic Press, 2014.

Yang, Tongyin. "Aspects of the Kam Language, as Revealed in Its Narrative Discourse." PhD diss., University of Texas at Arlington, 2004.

Index